Common Ground

Edited by
Elizabeth G. Peck and JoAnna Stephens Mink

Common Ground
Feminist Collaboration in the Academy

STATE UNIVERSITY OF NEW YORK PRESS

Photo of Elizabeth G. Peck was taken by Kathryn N. Benzel.
Photo of JoAnna Stephens Mink was taken by Suzanne Bunkers.

Production by Ruth Fisher
Marketing by Fran Keneston

Published by
State University of New York Press, Albany

© 1998 State University of New York

All rights reserved

Printed in the United States of America

No part of this book may be used or reproduced in any manner whatsoever without written permission. No part of this book may be stored in a retrieval system or transmitted in any form or by any means including electronic, electrostatic, magnetic tape, mechanical, photocopying, recording, or otherwise without the prior permission in writing of the publisher.

For information, address the State University of New York Press, State University Plaza, Albany, NY 12246

Library of Congress Cataloging-in-Publication Data

Common ground : feminist collaboration in the academy / edited by
  Elizabeth G. Peck and JoAnna Stephens Mink.
      p.   cm.
  Includes bibliographical references (p.   ) and index.
  ISBN 0-7914-3511-3 (hardcover :alk. paper). — ISBN 0-7914-3512-1
(pbk. : alk. paper)
  1. Feminism and education. 2. Group work in education.
3. Rhetoric. 4. Authorship—Collaboration. I. Peck, Elizabeth
1945–[Date]. II. Mink, JoAnna Stephens.
LC197.C65 1998
370'.82—dc21   96-54244
                                                              CIP

10 9 8 7 6 5 4 3 2 1

For Dee-Dee, riding the peace train,
For Ali, reading the stars,
and
For Janet, in friendship

Contents

Acknowledgments	ix
Introduction • *Elizabeth G. Peck and JoAnna Stephens Mink*	1
1. "Educate, Organize, and Agitate": A Historical Overview of Feminist Collaboration in Great Britain and America, 1640–1930 • *Melodie Andrews*	11
2. Beyond Feminism: An Intercultural Challenge for Transforming the Academy • *Paula D. Nesbitt and Linda E. Thomas*	31
3. Writing against the Romantic Grain • *Carol Shiner Wilson and Joel Haefner*	51
4. In League with Each Other: The Theory and Practice of Feminist Collaboration • *Carol J. Singley and Susan Elizabeth Sweeney*	63
5. What's Feminist about It? Reflections on Collaboration in Editing and Writing • *Helen Cafferty and Jeanette Clausen*	81
6. Self-Connection Shared: Integrating Collaborative and Autonomous Impulses within Feminist Projects • *Kimberly A. McCarthy and Sandra A. Steingraber*	99
7. The Role of Talk in the Writing Process of Intimate Collaboration" • *Mary Alm*	123

8. Merge/Emerge: Collaboration in Graduate School
   • *Constance L. Russell, Rachel Plotkin, and
   Anne C. Bell*   141

9. Lesbian Collaboration and the Choreography of
   Desire • *Angela M. Estes and Kathleen Margaret Lant*   155

10. Common Ground, Difficult Terrain: Confronting
    Difference through Feminist Collaboration
    • *Mary Ann Leiby and Leslie J. Henson*   173

11. Collaborative Leadership: Feminist Possibility, Feminist
    Oxymoron • *Diane Lichtenstein and Virginia Powell*   193

12. Reflections on Scholarly Collaboration • *Anne O'Meara
    and Nancy R. MacKenzie*   209

13. Going against Nature? Women's Resistance to
    Collaborative Learning • *Sally Barr Ebest*   227

14. Revisioning Space: From Territoriality to Collaboration
    • *Elaine Allen Karls and Roslyn Z. Weedman*   249

15. Feminist Theory and Practice and the Pedantic I/Eye
    • *Jamie Barlowe and Ruth Hottell*   269

Biographical Notes   283

Index   289

Acknowledgments

Two Faculty Research grants and one Arts and Humanities Research grant from Mankato State University provided us with financial support for travel, postage, and photocopying. A grant from the Research Services Council of the University of Nebraska at Kearney provided us with financial support for assistance in proofreading and indexing. We thank the Departments of English at University of Nebraska at Kearney and at Mankato State University for providing photocopying, postage and clerical support.

JoAnna S. Mink thanks Elizabeth G. Peck and Susan Koppelman for including her and Janet Doubler Ward, with whom she co-edited three anthologies, on their panel on feminist collaboration at the 1991 Midwest Modern Language Association Conference. It was as a result of this participation that the idea for this project began.

For help with computer-related problems, we thank Barbara Amundson, Steve Amundson, Kelley Brigman, Gwen Griffin, Daryl Kelley, and Roland Nord. For office and clerical assistance, we thank Karla Murphy. For assistance in proofreading and indexing we thank Darcy R. Schultz.

For serving as outside reviewer of a chapter, we thank Jeff Green. For distributing calls for abstracts at professional conferences, we thank Kathryn N. Benzel, Kathy Hurley, Nancy MacKenzie, Anne O'Meara, and Richard Robbins.

We are also grateful to the following people at SUNY Press who assisted us throughout the publication process: Christine Worden, Jenny Doling, Zina Lawrence, Ruth Fisher, Kay Bolton, and Fran Keneston.

Constance L. Russell, Rachel Plotkin, and Anne C. Bell wish to thank professors Leesa Fawcett, David Selby, and Roger Simon for their support of their desire to collaborate and to acknowledge the editorial suggestions of John Ankenman.

In addition to the scholars whose work comprises the following chapters, we thank the many who responded to our calls for papers, who sent manuscripts for our consideration, and who otherwise indicated an interest in this work.

Most of all, we thank the contributors to this anthology—without whose ideas, energy, cooperation, and inspiration our task would have been insurmountable.

E.G.P. and J.S.M.

Elizabeth G. Peck and JoAnna Stephens Mink

Introduction

Because we have participated in feminist scholarship and collaborative activities for many years, we were drawn to the idea of pursuing collaboration as a subject of discussion and research. Our experiences previous to the development of this anthology were dissimilar, yet taken together, they cover much of the spectrum of collaborative activities within academe. As a graduate student, Liz team taught courses and in the professorial track, she has codirected conferences with colleagues at her institution and in another state and coplanned activities with community members as well. This is the fourth published collection of essays JoAnna has coedited; she has also team taught courses and coauthored an article and a conference presentation.

When we began to share our own experiences, as women and as academics, we realized how complex and intricate the collaborative process actually is. In fact, as we surveyed our various endeavors and accomplishments, we discovered that we were raising more questions about collaboration than we could answer. Individually, we had worked with both women and men, but our experiences suggested that successful collaboration was not necessarily guaranteed by the collaborative partner's being either a female or a male. As we analyzed more carefully the activities which had come, more or less, naturally to us in our professional careers, we became more aware that an anthology on this topic was pertinent and necessary.

Consequently, one of our first questions as we began to discuss working together on an anthology about feminist collaboration was, Is collaboration between women the same or different from collaboration between men, or collaboration between women and men?

Other important questions were, How and why do collaborative projects get under way? How do collaborators "find" each other, and once the partnership is established, what accounts for the particular dynamics of their relationship? What processes, if any, do all collaborative projects have in common? We turned to our own experiences for possible answers.

Liz has codirected Women's Studies conferences, cochaired conference sessions, and, during her two-year term as Director of Women's Studies, coordinated the activities of the Women's Studies Advisory Council, which includes faculty representatives from all four colleges on her campus. In order to ensure inclusiveness in these activities, she encouraged the participation of students, faculty, and administrators at all levels of planning. In the case of JoAnna's two coauthored pieces, one was literally a cut-and-paste blending of two separate manuscripts written by herself and by a colleague with whom she had never before collaborated and hasn't since this temporary partnership; the other, a conference presentation, was written from beginning brainstorming ideas to the final copy during long-distance telephone calls with her long-time friend and coeditor of three anthologies. Additionally, JoAnna has team taught with three other professors—two men in her field of specialization and a woman from a related discipline.

Of course, not all of our separate professional accomplishments have been collaborative endeavors. But certainly, the reception on the part of university administrators who evaluate for promotion and tenure decisions was a factor when we made individual decisions about when and how to invest our academic energies. We were acutely aware of the tradition of rewarding individual scholarship and knew that collaboration was risky business, indeed. Such risk taking is inherent in our decisions and, as our contributors attest, to theirs. Thus, we identified other questions: What benefits and risks do such projects pose to professional advancement? How do they enhance personal and social relationships? Why is collaboration often viewed suspiciously by members of the academy, particularly by colleagues and administrators in the humanities?

Not all of these questions were fully articulated at the outset of our project, nor, in its initial stages, could we have been able to explain why we immediately felt that we could congenially work together. We met for the first time at the 1991 Midwest Modern

Language Association conference, where JoAnna and her coeditor Janet Doubler Ward were members of the session on collaboration cochaired by Liz and Susan Koppelman. Our prior professional contact, conducted solely by correspondence, had been relatively brief and limited to the details of our panel discussion. The day following the conference session, we got to know each other somewhat better over a chance meeting in the hotel coffee shop, but this occasion was coincidental rather than planned and no project was in the offing at the moment. Nonetheless, we began to develop a sense of the one ingredient upon which collaboration depends: mutual trust. Consequently, when JoAnna wrote about a month later to suggest working together on an anthology on feminist collaboration, Liz responded without hesitation.

What followed were an exchange of ideas for a call for abstracts and advertisements of the call, frequent correspondence between us and with our respondents, and a series of telephone meetings during which the project was more fully outlined, deadlines were set, and the criteria for selecting essays were developed. We increasingly strengthened our trust in each other's judgments and, about two years into the project, without any dissention, we regretfully decided that we had to extend our project. While some of the essays received in response to our "first round" were excellent, we simply did not have enough for what we considered to be a full discussion of the topic of feminist collaboration. Thus, this project was delayed by over a year. A second call for abstracts, another round of selections, a steady stream of correspondence (this time, much facilitated by e-mail) and additional telephone meetings followed. As we learned— and as many of our contributors point out—collaboration is time consuming. Moreover, collaborators' schedules often have to be reconciled with other academic, scholarly, and family responsibilities, as well as different academic calendars.

We always remained goal oriented and faithful to our deadlines, but we never approached our work as though it were a "fight to the finish." Indeed, our lack of competition with each other was apparent in our individual first drafts of the call for abstracts. Although we had not discussed name placement, we each put the other's name first. While this occasioned much laughter when we discovered what the other had done, a more important hypothesis was considered: Is this the way in which two women, with different backgrounds in collaboration but who both subscribe to feminist principles of cooperation, work together? Similarly, in our selection of abstracts and essays, rather than engaging in arguments and negotiations, we found our ratings and our selections seldom varied. Even more uncanny was the fact that the comments we wrote on our criteria sheets—while we were hundreds of miles apart—were often comparable, even to identical word choice.

We hasten to point out that our collaboration was not a "perfect two-step." On a few occasions, we quibbled about a word choice, we assured the other that she was not "sloughing off," we listened politely to the other's description of ever-higher piles of ungraded student papers and ever-increasing demands of academic committees. But, these occasions were very few indeed. That we complemented each other so well was a fortuitous happenstance in that we "found" each other at the hotel coffee shop. From our coeditorship has developed a firm friendship. While this relationship has been a gift, it is not unique; many of the contributors to *Common Ground* provide similar testimonials.

Might we assume, then, that collaboration is a magical merging of hearts and minds? And that women, because of their other-directed socialization, are likely to be able to work together without conflict? We think not. Instead, we recall the time and effort we devoted to listening to each other, discussing the problems and complications we envisioned, describing our hopes and expectations of the project, and admitting our possible shortfalls. All of this communication—whether by letter, phone and e-mail, or occasionally in person—constituted an ongoing dialogue that created consensus and often resolved potential disputes before they arose. In short, our verbal interactions weren't "just talk"; they were idea exchanges through which we discovered our shared identities as coeditors and collaborators.

Why—given the difficulties of coordination, especially over long distances—would academic professionals choose to collaborate? In addition to the cliched response of two heads are better than one, the reasons are probably best summed up in the complex dynamic of the shared responsibilities, respect, and reciprocal enjoyment that grows out of the relationship itself. For the compensations of such a relationship extend well beyond the objective goal of creating a finished "product." Our prior collaborative activities may have shaped our expectations of each other and recognition that in order to be successful, this relationship needed to be a complementary one. The coediting of this anthology was still a unique enterprise in our individual professional lives. We began as collaborators; now we are friends as well. But, as the following chapters discuss, in many ways our experiences reflect the broad range of experiences and feelings which many collaborators share.

This collection begins with a historical overview of women's collaborative efforts. Melodie Andrews locates "nascent feminism" in the seventeenth and eighteenth centuries and shows how early feminist activities prepared the way for women's collaborative participation in nineteenth- and twentieth-century political activism and social reform. Building on Gerda Lerner's analysis of feminism, Andrews demonstrates that women's challenges to patriarchal authority depended upon their passage through successive stages of feminist consciousness. Though feminist collaboration has at times suffered setbacks and never fully resolved problems of race and class, early feminists created models for education, organization, and agitation that continue to serve as common ground for feminists today. Paula D. Nesbitt and Linda E. Thomas address many of the unresolved problems of race and marginalization as they argue for collaboration that produces *solid scholarship* that is thoroughly pluralistic. They point out that undertaking such research requires risk taking because it has the revolutionary potential of upsetting traditional academic norms; nonetheless, those who engage in authentic collaboration provide the hope and direction for a paradigm shift in which mutually negotiated differences will be valued, resulting in a creative opportunity to explore our shared human reality.

Carol Shiner Wilson and Joel Haefner return to a historical viewpoint insofar as their chapter was inspired by the canonical exclusion of women, which led them to question traditional assumptions about solitary male genius and Romantic ideas of singular authorship, or the "writer-writes-alone," as Linda Brodkey calls it. Their chapter reveals how, by working together on *Re-Visioning Romanticism: British Women Writers, 1776–1837*, they directly addressed questions of gender within the collaborative writing and editing project, particularly those raised by Lisa Ede and Andrea Lundsford in *Singular Texts/Plural Authors*. Carol J. Singley and Susan Elizabeth Sweeney also challenge traditional notions of single authorship and beliefs about knowledge as individually acquired and owned. By bringing together the insights of composition theory, literary theory, liberation politics, and feminist theory, they argue for the interdisciplinary nature of collaboration and for collaboration as a means of building women's confidence and enhancing their performance in the competitive academic environment.

Collaborative editing and writing is further explored in Helen Cafferty and Jeanette Clausen's description of their three-year tenure as coeditors of the *Women in German Yearbook,* as well as in their discussion of how their experience led to the formulation of a working definition of feminist collaboration. By examining the relationship between product and process, they reveal that feminist politics of egalitarianism, inclusion, power sharing, and consensus provide a "dialogic" space in which *process* is privileged to the extent that it may become as important as *goal.* A dialogue of creative processes also frames Kimberly A. McCarthy and Sandra Steingraber's chapter, which exemplifies the possibilities inherent in the merger of content and form by juxtaposing the traditional, linear presentation of shared ideas with dual, parallel columns or "duologues." This bivocal text allows the reader to experience the simultaneous presentation of multiple ideas in both form and content. Moreover, the description of the performance in which McCarthy's music was merged with Steingraber's poetry serves as an example of the multilayered processes of collaboration that occur among performers, composers and audience members.

Multiple layers of collaboration and the importance of process over product are also evident in Mary Alm's chapter. Alm's interviews with women engaged in the process of intimate collaboration reveal that their talk enables them to create and test ideas, judge the effectiveness of their written presentations, and nurture intellectual and social friendships that support them as scholars in often hostile academic environments. Mutual support and empowerment are also key issues in Constance L. Russell, Rachel Plotkin, and Anne C. Bell's "Merge/Emerge: Collaboration in Graduate School." As women and fledgling scholars engaged in "negotiating the patriarchal terrain of graduate school," this trio of ecofeminists credits collaboration with broadening their learning opportunities, increasing their willingness to support unpopular positions, and helping to affirm their "commitment to honouring a multiplicity of voices."

"Lesbian Collaboration and the Choreography of Desire" offers yet another perspective on the emotional benefits and liberatory value of transcending boundaries through collaboration. In this chapter Angela M. Estes and Kathleen Margaret Lant describe how their collaborative efforts (publishing critical articles, writing a book, teaching classes, and giving conference papers together) have been made possible and have been enriched by their former relationship as lovers. Their present relationship is based upon a powerful bond, strengthened by the fact that their same-sex interaction is not compromised by the resentments and competition of the heterosexist culture in which women must compete for men and for heterosexual privilege.

Problems of identity, issues of classism, heterosexism and homophobia, ableism, anti-Semitism, and other forms of oppression are at the forefront of Mary Ann Leiby and Leslie J. Henson's theoretical/practical model for recognizing and resolving differences through collaboration. "Common Ground, Difficult Terrain" reveals how Leiby and Henson's own struggles with complex political and cultural determinants of "subjectivity" taught them to encourage students to engage with one another collaboratively, in hopes of creating what Kenneth Bruffee calls an "unending conversation." Rather than downplaying the significance of difference, Henson and Leiby argue for the "head-on collisions" that Cherrie Maraga claims are necessary for building coalition.

Consensus and coalition building are approached from a different perspective in Diane Lichtenstein and Virginia Powell's chapter on their collaborative administration of the Women's Studies Program at Beloit College. While conceding that their inclusive strategies at times became tedious and frustrating, they also find that small bureaucratic decisions sparked important debates about the nature of their collective identity and group work. Their analysis clarifies the distinction between managing a program and providing it with leadership.

Anne O'Meara and Nancy MacKenzie likewise delve into the tensions and rewards of arriving at consensus, in this case, the consensus a single text requires. Using their own experience to expand upon the insights of other researchers, O'Meara and MacKenzie address five central concerns: (1) the influence of context on collaborative processes, (2) the benefits of maintaining dual perspectives,

(3) the importance of collaborative talking, (4) the insights to be gained by examining what distinguishes collaborative invention and research, and (5) drafting procedures particularly suited to collaborative writing. Their analysis of collaborative processes highlights the importance "of studying collaboration in a variety of contexts."

Context is similarly important to Sally Barr Ebest who challenges assumptions about solitary male writers and collaborative female writers by moving questions about gender and writing into the classroom to examine the effects of collaborative learning on female graduate students. From her observations of these students' interactions in group discussions and close analysis of their writing, she concludes that collaboration may not come naturally to all women. She posits that rather than delineating the differences between male and female behaviors and learning styles, one must look at their similarities in order to promote collaboration in the classroom.

Assumptions about male and female behaviors are further investigated by Elaine Allen Karls and Roslyn Z. Weedman as they humorously record the choice they faced as new, nontenured hires forced to share an office "smaller than most federal prison cells." Rather than resorting to the masculine mode of staking out their own private territory, they responded by reimagining the space as the nexus of a symbiotic, synergistic partnership that galvanized their creativity. During two years, this collaborative space yielded numerous joint projects. The most intriguing of these—their first learning community on Race, Class, and Gender in Popular Culture—is detailed to show how noncompetitive space can create a positive environment for learning, critical thinking, and intellectual enrichment. As feminist teachers and scholars, Jamie Barlowe and Ruth Hottell also view the classroom as "a collaborative community." By foregrounding multiple perspectives on feminism, they disrupt the polarity of subject/object dyads and create a space in which students and teachers collaborate with each other recursively. This environment is not entirely free of "all pedantic authoritarianism," but it is a space that encourages the development of critical consciousness and a form of learning designed to foster the creation of "other inclusive environments."

In many ways, all of these chapters reinforce the ideas presented in our first in that they extend the discussion of the ways in which feminist collaborators have continued to work together. In addition, they echo our hope that members of the academy eventually will value collaborative accomplishments as much as individual ones. As we have tried to indicate briefly here, the experiences of our contributors provide a continuing dialogue about the importance of collaboration and ensuing professional and personal benefits. Regardless of the mode of the collaborative activity, certain principles remain constant. This common ground opens vistas for revision and reevaluation of the importance of feminist collaborative activities in the academy.

Melodie Andrews

1

"Educate, Organize, and Agitate"

A Historical Overview of Feminist Collaboration in Great Britain and America, 1640–1930

"Educate, Organize and Agitate, must be the watchwords for all women," Lady Henry Somerset wired the National Prohibition Convention meeting at Newcastle, England, in 1897 (qtd. in Shinman 204). By the late nineteenth century, as a result of the collaborative efforts of several generations of feminists, women in Great Britain and the United States were becoming educated on the "woman question," organizing their movement, and agitating for a host of reforms. Because suffrage was the most radical and politically contentious aspect of the "woman question," it has been closely linked with the emergence of feminism. In fact, until recently suffragists were often the only women that historians designated as feminists before the twentieth century (Black 15). In *The Grounding of Modern Feminism,* Nancy Cott suggests an even narrower definition, arguing that the term *feminist* is anachronistic if it is applied to those who lived or worked before the word was introduced into the language (4). According to the 1933 *Supplement* to the *Oxford English Dictionary* (OED), the first recorded use of the term *feminism* in English was derived from the French word *feminisme* in 1894. However, the word did not enter into common usage in Europe and America until the years immediately before World War I. By 1933 the term had assumed the definition that is most widely accepted today: "Advocacy of the rights of women (based on the theory of the equality of the sexes)" (Black 19).

In the twentieth century the concept of feminism has become an essential tool for intellectual analysis, assuming many nuances of meaning in the process. As a result, contemporary scholars apply the term *feminist* to women—or men—in previous centuries in a variety of different, even contradictory ways. For some, like Moira Ferguson, any articulate and active women, and particularly those who wrote about themselves or their lives, can be seen as feminists. For others, the designation entails particular beliefs or activities, although there is no agreement as to exactly what these are or how they changed over time (Offen 119–21; Delmar 9–14). In her influential study of the American woman suffrage movement, Aileen Kraditor suggests that the standard definition of feminism focusing on inequality between men and women is inadequate. What women wanted was "autonomy" and that, she asserts, was the essential core of feminism (8). Gerda Lerner sees both concerns encompassed under the umbrella of feminism, differentiating the campaigns for civil and political equality as "woman's rights" movements and the struggle for autonomy and self-determination as "woman's emancipation" movements. The distinction is an important one because scholars have traditionally seen the first emergence of feminism manifested through the political women's rights movement of the nineteenth century. In recent years, however, some historians have traced a much earlier development of feminism in the emancipatory ideas evident in the work of seventeenth-century writers such as Mary Astell and Aphra Behn and the fifteenth-century author Christine de Pizan (Ferguson; Smith; Kelly).

This essay will build upon Lerner's analysis to suggest that feminism began to develop much earlier than the nineteenth century. By focusing on the period from 1640 to 1930, it is evident that the quest for personal autonomy became the chief manifestation of feminism until the closing years of the eighteenth century, when demands for civil and political equality also began to be heard, culminating in the suffrage campaigns. To encompass the activities of women over such a broad sweep of time, the term *feminist* will be used as Jane Rendall has defined it, to describe women who "claimed for themselves the right to define their own place in society," as well as the "few men who sympathized with that claim" (1). Because these women and men did not necessarily believe in a total equality of the roles played by each sex within society, many of them interpreted the word *equality* very differently than it is understood today. They spoke primarily in terms of moral and rational worth, thereby avoiding the difficult and contentious issues of political and economic equality. Others asserted an equality based upon complementary differences between men and women, which could also be put to feminist purposes. A belief in the latent moral superiority of women, for example, led many nineteenth-century feminists to new expressions of confidence, energy, and autonomy, which did not, however, challenge the economic and political hegemony of men.

Expressions of feminist aspirations are evident as early as the seventeenth century—perhaps even earlier—but the "modern" campaigns of the nineteenth century, as Rendall styles them, have received the most attention from historians of women. Scholars have tended to concentrate on the lives and writings of individual feminists or on the organizations that they founded. In addition, there is now a wealth of scholarship available on nineteenth- and twentieth-century women's friendships, work, wit, art, professions, social work, suffrage, abolition, and other reform efforts. Far less work has been done on the actual interaction of these feminists—on the ways that they worked together through education, organization, and agitation to assert in their lives and in their actions the values of self-determination and autonomy. This essay endeavors to address this oversight by providing a selective historical overview of some of the objectives and manifestations of feminist collaboration in Great Britain and America from the seventeenth century to the culmination of the woman suffrage campaigns in the early decades of the twentieth century.

Feminism appears, according to Sally Alexander, when women "distinguish themselves and their needs, from those of their male kin within families, communities and class" (31). Feminism transforms the discontents of women into a self-conscious female identity. It also constructs the demands and aspirations necessary to transform the social relations in which women and men live. The dissatisfactions experienced by women have sprung from a variety of concerns since the seventeenth century, including lack of education, men's property rights over women in marriage, "domestic drudgery," prohibitions on female labor, the double standard of sexual morality, the evils of alcohol abuse, and exclusion from the franchise. Gerda Lerner calls the understanding of female identity born out of such concerns "feminist consciousness." To Nancy Cott this consciousness is evident in women's willingness or reluctance to say *we* (9). Lerner suggests that feminist consciousness develops in distinct stages marked by (1) the awareness of women that they belong to a subordinate group; (2) the awareness that women have suffered wrongs as a group; (3) the awareness that the subordination of women is not natural, but societally determined; (4) the awareness that women must develop a sense of sisterhood and join with other women to remedy these wrongs; (5) the autonomous definition by women of their goals and strategies for changing their condition; and (6) the development of an alternate vision of societal organization in which women as well as men will enjoy autonomy and self-determination *(Creation of Feminist* 14). An examination of almost three centuries of cooperative endeavors by women suggests that *feminist* collaboration has become possible only after the first four stages of consciousness have been reached, and that these efforts have been directed historically toward actualizing change.

Nascent feminism is evident by the 1640s in Great Britain, although it has been argued that women in seventeenth-century Great Britain were not sufficiently conscious of themselves to ever write or speak for themselves as women, much less engage in collaboration (Vann 210). For example, women were participating in public political activity by this period. Patricia Crawford points out that on several occasions during the 1640s and 1650s women joined together to present petitions to Parliament in support of jailed Puritans and other religious dissenters (223). In doing so, they were forced to argue that women possessed political rights. In a petition presented in February 1642, for example, although the signatories disclaimed any desire for equality with men, they did offer "several Reasons why their sex ought thus to petition as well as the men." Political activity was, they said, part of "that duty we owe to God, and the cause of the Church" (223). Although these women grounded their claims in Scripture, they were developing a doctrine of political rights with potentially radical consequences, as evident in another petition presented in May 1649:

> That since we are assured of our Creation in the image of God, and of an interest in Christ, equal unto men, as also of a proportionable share in the Freedoms of this Commonwealth, we

cannot but wonder and grieve that we should appear so despicable in your eyes, as to be thought unworthy to Petition or represent our Grievances to this Honourable House. . . . Let it be accounted folly, presumption, madness, or whatsoever in us, whilst we have life and breath, we will never leave them. (qtd. in Crawford 224)

Four years later, Katherine Chidley led a group of women presenting to Parliament a petition reportedly signed by six thousand women (Crawford 224). Until women acquired the vote, petitioning was the only mechanism they had to exert their influence on politics. Disenfranchised men also made effective use of petitioning. Through this collaborative activity, some seventeenth-century women gained a way of conceptualizing political rights and learned how conservative ideas could be used to argue for an autonomous voice in public affairs. This lesson would not be lost on their nineteenth-century sisters in America or Great Britain. Petitioning campaigns became the most massive acts of collaboration ever engaged in by feminists.

The quest for autonomy is also evident in the writings of women published during this period. Few women wrote for publication before 1640. According to Lerner, patriarchal culture kept many women from creative thinking by the lack of education, the lack of contact with a group of educated people, and by the lack of private time *(Creation of Patriarchy* 223). Those relatively few women who took up the pen knew that they were invading masculine territory. As Katherine Rogers notes, "for women who wished to study and to write, there has always been an uncomfortable sense of going against the grain of their societies' attitudes, and of lacking a supportive structure which would give them authority to write" (1). But a number of women did become authors in the seventeenth century, compelled by the knowledge that their experiences as women were fundamentally different from those of men (Crawford 212). Hilda Smith has identified twelve of these writers, including Mary Astell, Margaret Cavendish—the Duchess of Newcastle, Sarah Egerton, and Hannah Woolley, as feminists. Her study suggests that these women clearly experienced the first four stages of feminist consciousness by becoming aware of their societally created subordinate position and the wrongs it engendered, and developing a sense of sisterhood. Mary Astell, generally regarded the first systematic feminist in England, spoke of herself as being a "lover of my sex," while Sarah Egerton wrote of "being too much a woman" to ignore the plight or wishes of other members of her sex (qtd. in Smith 8).

It was at Lerner's fifth and sixth stages of consciousness, the development of autonomous goals and an alternative vision, that the perspectives of seventeenth- and most eighteenth-century feminist writers were unavoidably incomplete. They did have autonomous goals centered primarily around better opportunities for education, the eradication of domestic subordination, and a more equal partnership with men in social and intellectual life. Their writings also attempted to change the attitudes of society by advocating the cause of women, but these women lacked a comprehension of the political and legal changes that would eventually be necessary in order to achieve their goals. Mary Astell, for example, advocated total mental independence for women but did not suggest extending this independence into the economic and political spheres (Rogers 79).

Although there is no evidence of direct collaboration among these feminists, the women knew of each other's work. In addition, their individual efforts built a foundation for future cooperative efforts aimed at establishing an autonomous place for women in literary culture by creating a growing awareness that women could write for publication. Sandra M. Gilbert and Susan Gubar point out that women writers often began the creative process by seeking "a *female precursor*" who demonstrated by her example that a revolt against "patriarchal literary authority" was possible (49). In the 1670s Aphra Behn became the first professional woman author in England. By the middle of that same decade, the female author of a book of medical advice for women could observe, "it is little of Novelty to see a Woman in print" (Crawford 231). Women also gained a sense that they were developing their own literary tradition when women authors recommended other writings by women to their readers (231).

In the last half of the eighteenth century, a small group of learned women created the supportive structure they needed to pursue their intellectual interests in an atmosphere of educational exclusion by establishing the "bluestocking circle." Up until this time there had been no organized way for women to meet others who shared their love of learning. This informal group of men and women, including Elizabeth Montagu, Elizabeth Carter, Catherine

Talbot, Elizabeth Vesey, and their London friends, hosted social gatherings at which women associated with men as intellectual equals. They also drew public attention to the idea that respectable women could study, write, and publish. The Bluestocking hostesses published relatively little themselves, but helped many professional women writers through direct patronage and by introducing them into society, thereby preventing the social marginalization experienced by many earlier feminist writers (Rogers 32).

While the majority of women writing in the eighteenth century published novels, some of the Bluestockings took advantage of their unique access to a classical man's education provided by sympathetic fathers or husbands, and developed an intellectual community that nurtured more scholarly work as well. Their efforts resulted in the publication by women of translations from the Greek, history, literary criticism, as well as imaginative literature—in an age when some people still believed that this kind of writing required a degree of learning beyond women's intellectual grasp (Rogers 22). Although the Bluestockings never questioned that women belonged in private life or should abstain from politics, they nonetheless challenged patriarchal assumptions and laid the groundwork for women's claims to equal treatment by insisting on a single human standard of mind and character (Rogers 71). Building on this presumption a century later, Emmeline Pankurst would organize an effective political movement based on "the fact—a very simple fact—that women are human beings" (qtd. in Smith 202).

According to Susan Yadlon, the Bluestockings also used their writings to create what Michael Foucault refers to as a "reverse discourse" (114). Employing the rhetoric and ideology of domesticity, these women began to speak on their own behalf and to demand an intellectual legitimacy that exceeded the domestic sphere. Through their writings the Bluestockings created a "discourse that simultaneously perpetuates and resists dominant ideology" (Yadlon 115). By insisting on class privilege, for example, the Bluestockings were unable to create a broad feminist politics that transcended class to address the needs of all women. However, they did manipulate both Enlightenment and domestic ideology to invoke some change in the eighteenth-century construction of feminity (Yadlon 130).

The limited aspirations of seventeenth- and eighteenth-century feminists are also explained, in part, by the fact that the only model available to women to state their demands for autonomy was the political language of men. Seventeenth- and eighteenth-century conceptions had to be transformed toward an idea of inalienable rights, especially by the American and French Revolutions, before feminists could come together and employ this ideology to demand equal rights for women. The relatively stable political situation in Britain provided few opportunities to raise in public debate the question of women's political rights or to suggest legislative changes which might improve their situation, such as divorce or the revision of married women's property rights (Rendall 55). Beginning in the 1790s, however, political transformation in France inspired a significant increase in feminist thinking and writing about women's condition. Wielding rhetoric derived from the republican notion of the domestic power of motherhood and from the feminized language of evangelicalism, a small group of feminists on both sides of the Atlantic embarked upon a diverse range of collaborative activities, which culminated in the second decade of the twentieth century in the crowning achievement of "first-wave" feminism—women's suffrage.

What were the factors that came together in the nineteenth and early twentieth centuries to produce such an unprecedented flowering of collaborative activity by women directed toward self-determination and autonomy? What was it that enabled women, in the words of Martha Vicinus, "to attack male domination in every area of society, and to fight for legal, educational, political and social reforms with an effectiveness that we have yet to match" (qtd. in Levine 21). Steven Buechler has analyzed the circumstances that facilitated the development of feminist movements in America. His comparative sociological analysis of the woman suffrage movement and the modern women's movement offers a useful theoretical framework for understanding the historical origins of feminist collaboration.

Buechler argues that strong connections had to be established between women as a unified group before cooperation could take place. The establishment of these connections, as well as the development of feminist consciousness, was complicated in the nineteenth century, as it is today, by the differences among women created by class interests and racial identity. Women who confronted multiple forms of oppression, based on class, race, and gender, were less likely to initiate or participate in women's movements, according to

Buechler. As a consequence, feminist collaboration tended to be most manifest among white, middle-class women, who were not preoccupied with the daily struggle to survive, had more access to relevant resources, and identified gender inequality as their most pressing grievance. But the connections between women—Lerner's "sisterhood"—did not coalesce into organized collaboration until the women were politicized (Buechler 10–12).

Historians have identified a number of background factors, as well as more immediate causes, that acted as catalysts for feminist mobilization in the nineteenth century. Capitalist industrialization separated work from home, consigned each to a separate sphere, and removed many white, middle-class women from a directly productive role in the economy at the same time that they were experiencing a significant decline in their reproductive role as well. But within the home women gained an enhanced position designed to complement the masculine role of economic provider (Buechler 12–13). Respectable feminity was now codified by what Barbara Welter has called the "cult of true womanhood" in America and what Catherine Hall describes as the "domestic ideology" of nineteenth-century England. Isolated in private, conjugal families, and imbued with a romanticized, "essentialist conception of feminity," middle-class women created homosocial worlds of female friendship, which promoted some of the collective identity and gender solidarity imperative for subsequent collaborative endeavors (Buechler 14). As Carroll Smith-Rosenberg has noted, "women, who had little status or power in the larger world of male concerns, possessed status and power in the lives and worlds of other women" (4).

Two institutional forces also encouraged what Keith Melder calls "the beginnings of sisterhood"—organized religion and formal education. Some of the most visible and successful examples of feminist collaboration in the nineteenth century are found in the profusion of women's voluntary associations that sprang up in America in the wake of the New England Great Awakening between 1798 and 1826, and in England several decades later with the renewal of religious enthusiasm provoked by "the second evangelical awakening" (Rendall 79; Shinman 99). The associations born out of the revivalist movement brought likeminded women together and offered opportunities for action that were socially approved. A complex network of women's organizations evolved in both countries with far-reaching, unforeseen consequences. Within this network women learned how to conduct business, carry on meetings, speak in public, and manage money. In their own associations "women learned to be professionals before the traditional professions were open to them," Ann Scott notes, "and developed a recognizable female style of professional behavior that relied heavily on cooperation" (3). These experiences prepared women for politics and foreshadowed a collapse of the distinction between the public and private spheres.

However, most of the women active in voluntary associations, far from rejecting domestic ideology, embraced and manipulated it. Feminists made one of the ideology's fundamental values—the moral superiority of women—their most effective weapon against the unjust disabilities they opposed. Ultimately, according to Levine, it was the "conscious woman-centeredness" of these associations—"a strength and pride in their shared femaleness"—that made them intrinsically feminist and led to the emergence of more radical women's movements (14–23).

In both Great Britain and the United States, expanded access to higher education for women also helped create the essential preconditions for feminist collaboration in the nineteenth century. Although female academies were established to legitimize domestic ideology and prepare young women for their "appropriate sphere" as wives, mothers, moral guardians, household managers, and teachers, these endeavors produced a host of unforeseen consequences as well. American schools like Mount Holyoke and Rockford Seminary and British institutions like Queen's College and Bedford College demonstrated that women possessed the mental capacity for serious discipline, abstract thinking, and problem solving. They also encouraged self-confidence and intellectual curiosity as they nurtured friendships and gender solidarity. Through the leadership and example of vigorous advocates on both sides of the Atlantic like Mary Lyon, Catharine Beecher, and Elizabeth Reid, students learned that women could act and succeed in advancing their own interests. But by providing an education separate from and unequal to that of men, these schools also created grievances, including a double standard of learning, limited opportunities for women to use their new skills and intellectual abilities, and unequal pay for the same work as performed by men (Melder 23–29). Advanced education widened the gap between women's rising aspirations and the ability to achieve them within the limitations of sphere. This incongruity, most keenly perceived by middle-class women, produced an anxiety and frustration many historians link to status deprivation (Buechler 37; Melder 156–57). Access to higher education also served to further separate the lives and experiences of middle- and upper-class women from those of the working class, leaving their disenfranchisement as the most glaring handicap all women continued to share.

Academy students like Lucy Stone and Elizabeth Stanton, as well as their British counterparts like Barbara Leigh Smith, graduated with a heightened awareness of wrongs and an emerging sense of sisterhood. They also came away with many of the skills necessary to develop autonomous goals and an alternative vision of the future. Teachers were semipublic figures with considerable autonomy in their classrooms and authority over students of both sexes, Melder notes (29). Through teaching, women learned to lecture, speak in public, and focus their exertions. Thus educational changes, in conjunction with the emergence of voluntary associations, helped to create a nascent feminist consciousness in middle-class women and moved some of them to reform activity. It is hardly a coincidence that many of the nineteenth century's leading feminists had advanced educations and worked as teachers. In order for this rising consciousness to coalesce into an organized collaborative effort on behalf of women, however, it had to be politicized. In America, it was the abolitionist movement that created the impetus necessary to transform grievances and sisterhood into concerted action.

Opposition to slavery began in the eighteenth century but first burgeoned into a large-scale movement in the 1830s in Great Britain, where women played an active role in the cause. In 1833 they submitted an antislavery petition to Parliament signed by 800,000 women (Melder 57). Later the same year, Parliament outlawed slavery throughout the British Empire. William Lloyd Garrison lauded the abolitionist activities of British women in his antislavery newspaper, the Boston *Liberator,* and called upon his female readers to join the crusade: "The ladies of Great Britain are moving the sympathies of the whole nation, in behalf of the perishing slaves in the British Colonies. We cannot believe that our ladies are less philanthropic or less influential. In their hands is the destiny of the slaves" (qtd. in Melder 57). Inspired by the example set by their British sisters and inflamed by the vivid depictions of slavery's assault on womanhood and the family presented in the torrent of abolitionist literature produced between 1830 and 1860, thousands of American women joined antislavery societies and began massive petitioning campaigns of their own. As slavery came increasingly to dominate American politics, the highly visible participation of women in "so public a cause" raised objections which provoked a spirited response from a prominent Ohio abolitionist: "'In Christ there is neither male nor female.' That is, in moral enterprises, moral worth and intellect are the standard. A mind whether deposited in a male or female body is equally valuable for all moral and intellectual purposes. Indeed there is no station in life but what may be filled as ably and as beneficially by woman as by man. The difference is made principally by education" (qtd. in Melder 60).

This man's views were echoed by the most controversial female abolitionists of the period, Sarah and Angelina Grimke, who defied the limitations of sphere and conventions of acceptable womanly behavior in the 1830s by speaking before "promiscuous" audiences, comprised of both sexes. Soon they were spending more time defending their right to speak than their abolitionist beliefs. As other women followed the Grimkes onto the podium, their actions helped spark the "woman question," a strident controversy over the right of women to engage in antislavery agitation. This issue divided abolitionists and laid the philosophical foundation for the woman's rights movement. In 1840 the "woman question" made its way across the Atlantic and disrupted the World Antislavery Convention meeting in London. Elizabeth Cady Stanton, the young bride of an American delegate to the convention, later dated the movement for women's suffrage in both England and America from this convention. While in London, Stanton made a new friend, Lucretia Mott, and the two women initiated the discussions that culminated in the first woman's rights convention at Seneca Falls, New York, eight years later.

The angry opposition American women faced by publicly participating in the abolitionist movement had a radicalizing effect, and helped some of them to recognize that women had common goals requiring collective action to be achieved. As the abolitionist Abbey Kelley observed, "We had good cause to be grateful to the slave. In striving to strike his irons off, we found most surely, that we were manacled ourselves" (qtd. in Woloch 185). Militant feminists like

Margaret Fuller, Lucretia Mott, and Elizabeth Cady Stanton now argued for human rights, or justice, not only for slaves but for women as well. According to Kraditor, they also advocated autonomy—the prerogative of women "to be recognized, in the economic, political, and/or social realms, as individuals in their own right" (qtd. in Melder 156).

In the middle of the nineteenth century, women in Britain also began to acknowledge that they had autonomous concerns separate from those of men. Previously, women and men of similar rank had generally shared the same interests and perspectives, with social status assuming more importance than gender. The emergence of the "woman question" sparked an awareness that men and women could have distinct economic, political, and social interests and that the dependence of women on men could be disadvantageous if the two interests came to diverge. For many women the process of awareness began with marital legislation and was heightened by the Contagious Diseases Acts of 1864 and 1866 (Shinman 122–24). This legislation politicized many British reformers and helped activate a true feminist movement among them. The question of the property of married women, perhaps more obviously than any other issue, revealed to British women the friction between the public and private spheres. According to Levine, "many women cut their feminist teeth within this area of protest and through addressing the problems of property within marriage came to a clearer understanding of other aspects of female subjugation" (140). One of the best known of these women was Barbara Smith (later Bodichon). In 1855 she brought together a small group of women to promote passage of a married women's property law. Although their initial efforts failed, the continued association of these women evolved into the Langham Place Circle, the country's first organized group of self-consciously feminist women (Rendall 228).

Two decades earlier, when the Reform Act extended the franchise to upper- and middle-class males, British women had lacked the organization and lobbying skills needed to pressure the government for voting rights. The anti-Contagious Diseases Acts campaign, under the leadership of Josephine Butler, played a crucial role in developing these skills. It created the first truly national women's organization in nineteenth-century Britain and helped draw women into other issues constituting the "woman question" (Shinman 202).

Although Butler did not see herself as a feminist, she helped to promote women's rights by indicating how they were being eroded by pressure from the masculine church, military, and medical establishments. Her campaign had the same politicizing effect on many British women that abolitionism produced in their American sisters.

By focusing women's attention on the political process, the Contagious Diseases Acts controversy also gave impetus to the emerging belief that the only avenue to power and protection for women was the franchise. In 1867 Barbara Smith and the Langham Circle established the first suffrage society for women, the Kensington Society, and John Stuart Mill presented a woman's suffrage petition to Parliament. Across the Atlantic, passage of the Fifteenth Amendment, which prohibited black male disfranchisement, spurred American women to organize their own suffrage movement the next year. Although the franchise eventually came to be accepted as the key to all reform for women, it was just one of the many issues that made up the woman's rights movement and inspired feminist collaboration in the last decades of the nineteenth century (Shinman 123).

Once women had identified positively with one another in a context of political struggle, their collaborative efforts took them in many directions at once. The anonymous author of an outline of women's grievances which appeared in the British journal *Metropolitan Magazine* in 1838 foresaw "associations of determined and enlightened women springing up in every town and village" (qtd. in Rendall 130). In the second half of the nineteenth century, this prediction was realized as interconnecting networks of women's organizations flourished in both America and Britain. Although these associations dealt with a variety of individual issues ranging from temperance and moral reform to economic, educational, and political inequalities, they frequently drew on the same core of women, who viewed their individual campaigns as part of the larger war against female subjugation. The women's movement coalesced, as Eugenia Palmegiana has suggested, with "no acknowledged leader, no powerful organization, [and] no official propaganda" (qtd. in Levine 20). Within their networks, feminists rejected the hierarchies of male political organization with their internecine power struggles in favor of what Levine has termed an "alternative politics," characterized by diffused leadership and a close-knit sense of female community (20). Many feminists did adhere to political beliefs which undoubtedly influenced their feminist tendencies, but in their collaborative endeavors they tended to distance themselves from mainstream politics. Within their own associations, women of different political persuasions worked harmoniously together to build a close-knit sense of community.

An important tool used by feminists to create community and facilitate collaboration was the official journal. In 1858 Barbara Smith and some of her associates established the *English Woman's Journal,* the century's first feminist periodical (Levine 15). Employees of the *Journal* also organized their own printing firm, the Victoria Press, run by women (Shinman 87). By the last quarter of the nineteenth century, most major women's organizations had established a journal for their membership. In America, the weekly *Advocate of Moral Reform* lived up to its name, while *Revolution* and the *Woman's Journal* represented the two wings of the suffrage movement. In Britain, *The Shield* articulated opposition to the Contagious Diseases Acts and the British Women's Temperance Association published its *Journal.* These publications educated their readers in organizational matters and, equally important, gave members a sense of being part of a larger group. Women's journals raised feminist consciousness by publicizing issues affecting women and providing women's perspectives on their resolution. They also showed that women had the ability to organize, run, and write for their own papers (Shinman 125).

The affirmative sense of community that nurtured feminist collaboration in the nineteenth and early twentieth centuries derived much of its strength from social homogeneity, as well as a shared recognition of the common disabilities women struggled against. Although the women's rights movement in both Britain and America was dominated by leisure-class women, many feminists saw their principles and campaigns as a way of winning a voice for working-class women as well as themselves, and bridging the chasm of class. The English journal *Work and Leisure,* edited by Louisa Hubbard, and Emily Faithfull's *Women and Work* focused on the problems of single women in search of employment. They published advice, articles on specific trades, job advertisements, and cogent critiques of male employment practices. Because working women seldom found endorsement in mainstream literature, these journals provided sorely needed comfort through their positive stance on women's usefulness. They also presented "an alternative interpretation to that of the destitute and sad governess who graced the pages of popular literature" (Levine 92). In America, the Women's Trade Union League was established in 1903 by upper-class feminists and a few women unionists to facilitate the organization of working women (Woloch 206). But for American feminists, the issue of race proved far more problematic than class.

In *The Majority Finds Its Past,* Gerda Lerner suggests that black and white American women have a history of "ambivalent interdependence" (95). When the women's movement drew its moral tone and political impetus from the abolitionist movement, racial and gender issues conjoined. As Bettina Aptheker writes, "The female presence helped to shape the revolutionary character of abolitionism, and practical engagement in the struggle against slavery impelled a consciousness of a distinctly feminist vision" (qtd. in Caraway 134). But most abolitionists attacked slavery, not racism, and black women found themselves unwelcome in most white women's antislavery groups. When passage of the Fifteenth Amendment gave birth to the suffrage movement, Elizabeth Stanton and Susan B. Anthony adopted a strategy of "opposing feminism to Black suffrage" (Caraway 141). They constructed a hierarchy of rights and embraced a reactionary politics which American feminism "is still struggling to live down" (145). In the last two decades of the nineteenth century, feminists acquiesced to what historians have labeled "strategies of expediency" and continued to exclude Black women from suffrage activities through the final push for the Nineteenth Amendment in 1920 (Lerner, *Majority* 104). Black feminists collaborated on a variety of reform activities during these years, most notably the antilynching crusade, which made rape a political issue, but they generally did so within separate organizations. Within American feminism, sisterhood was segregated.

The early twentieth century saw some decisive shifts in the women's movement and strategies of feminist collaboration. In 1911 Ethel Snowden called Britain "the present stormcentre of the world's feminist movement" (qtd. in Levine 156). Suffragette activity assumed a more militant character, climaxing in physical struggle as feminists endured arrests, prison ordeals, and hunger strikes. The sacrifices of the suffragettes tended to overshadow the vast range of other collaborative activities taking place, prompting a feminist to complain in 1914, "One hears people talk sometimes as if the suffrage movement *were* the women's movement, and as if when the vote shall be won, there will be no more women's movement. . . . Shall the vote be at once the record of the progress of women and its grave?" (qtd. in Levine 156).

Many of the other issues that feminists had wrestled with in the nineteenth century remained at least partially unresolved, like equal pay, equal rights to divorce, and access to many professions including the law. And yet, by 1928, when British women finally won the right to vote, public feminism and much of the vibrant collaboration it nurtured was in decline. In the next several decades it appeared to many that the vote indeed marked the grave of the women's movement. What caused the apparent disintegration of the common ground feminists had labored so hard to create?

Feminism flourished in the nineteenth and early twentieth centuries because it was rooted in a self-consciously female community that helped sustain women's participation in both social reform and political activism. Feminists rejected the partisan character of existing politics and promoted an autonomous, collective identity based on gender. Through their networks, feminists collaborated to created a separate, public sphere that mobilized women and gained them political leverage in the larger society. Estelle Freedman argues that the achievements of early feminism came "less through gaining access to the male domains of politics and the professions than in the tangible form of building separate female institutions" (10). Female community began to disintegrate in the 1920s just as "new women" were attempting to assimilate into male-dominated institutions. As a result, feminists were unable to create a strong women's political block that might have protected and expanded the gains made by the earlier women's movement.

Between 1640 and 1930 feminist collaboration focused on the creation of separate female organizations, prompted by discrimination in the public, male sphere and the positive attraction of the female world of close, personal relationships and domestic institutional structures. The rhetoric of equality that became popular after passage of female suffrage subverted the women's movement, in Freedman's view, by denying the need for continued feminist organization (19). When women tried to assimilate into male-dominated institutions without securing feminist social, economic, or political bases, they lost the momentum and the networks which had made the women's rights movement possible. In the 1960s a new generation of middle-class, college-educated American women were politicized by the civil rights movement. Through education, organization, and agitation, they created a new women's rights movement and rediscovered their common ground. Through collaboration today's feminists strive to preserve and expand it.

REFERENCES

Alexander, Sally. "Women, Class and Sexual Differences." *British Thought, A Reader.* Ed. Terry Lovell. Oxford: Basil Blackwell, 1990.

Black, Naomi. *Social Feminism.* Ithaca, NY: Cornell University Press, 1989.

Buechler, Steven M. *Women's Movements in the United States.* New Brunswick, NJ: Rutgers University Press, 1990.

Caraway, Nancie. *Segregated Sisterhood, Racism and the Politics of American Feminism.* Knoxville: University of Tennessee Press, 1991.

Cott, Nancy. *The Grounding of Modern Feminism.* New Haven, CT: Yale University Press, 1987.

Crawford, Patricia. "Women's Published Writings 1600–1700." *Women in English Society.* Ed. B. Prior. London: Methusen, 1985.

Delmar, Rosalind. "What Is Feminism?" *What Is Feminism.* Ed. Juliet Mitchell and Ann Oakley. Oxford: Oxford University Press, 1986.

Ferguson, Moira. *First Feminists: British Women Writers, 1578–1799.* Bloomington: Indiana University Press, 1975.

Freedman, Estelle. "Separatism as Strategy: Female Institution Building and American Feminism, 1870–1930." *Women and Power in American History.* Ed. Kathryn Kish Sklar and Thomas Dublin. Englewood Cliffs, NJ: Prentice Hall, 1991.

Gilbert, Sandra M., and Susan Gubar. *The Madwoman in the Attic: The Woman Writer and the Nineteenth-Century Literary Imagination.* New Haven, CT: Yale University Press, 1979.

Kelly, Joan. "Early Feminist Theory and the *Querelle des Femmes.*" *Women, History and Theory.* Ed. J. Kelly. Chicago: University of Chicago Press, 1984.

Kraditor, Aileen. *The Ideas of the Woman Suffrage Movement.* New York: Columbia University Press, 1965.

Lerner, Gerda. *The Creation of Feminist Consciousness.* New York: Oxford University Press, 1993.

_____.*The Creation of Patriarchy*. New York: Oxford University Press, 1987.

_____. *The Majority Finds Its Past*. New York: Oxford University Press, 1979.

Levine, Phillipa. *Victorian Feminism 1850–1900*. Tallahassee: Florida State University Press, 1987.

Melder, Keith. *Beginnings of Sisterhood, The American Woman's Rights Movement 1800–1850*. New York: Scheken, 1977.

Offen, Karen. "Defining Feminism: A Comparative Historical Approach." *Signs* 14 (1988): 119–57.

Rendall, Jane. *The Origins of Modern Feminism: Women in Britain, France and the United States, 1780–1860*. London: Macmillan, 1985.

Rogers, Katherine. *Feminism in Eighteenth-Century England*. Urbana: University of Illinois Press, 1982.

Scott, Anne Firor. *Natural Allies: Women's Associations in American History*. Urbana: University of Illinois Press, 1991.

Shinman, Lilian Lewis. *Women and Leadership in Nineteenth-Century England*. New York: St. Martin's, 1992.

Smith, Hilda L. *Reason's Disciples, Seventeenth-Century English Feminists*. Urbana: University of Illinois Press, 1982.

Smith-Rosenberg, Carroll. "The Female World of Love and Ritual: Relations between Women in Nineteenth-Century America." *Signs* 1 (1975): 1–29.

Vann, Richard. "Towards a New Life Style: Women in Pre-Industrial Capitalism." *Becoming Visible: Women in European History*. Ed. R. Bridenthal and C. Koonz. Boston: Houghton Mifflin, 1977.

Woloch, Nancy. *Women and the American Experience*. New York: Knopf, 1984.

Yadlon, Susan M. "The Bluestocking Circle: The Negotiation of 'Reasonable' Women." *Communication and Women's Friendships: Parallels and Intersections in Literature and Life*. Ed. Janet Doubler Ward and JoAnna Stephens Mink. Bowling Green, OH: Bowling Green State University Popular Press, 1993. 113–31.

Paula D. Nesbitt and Linda E. Thomas

2

Beyond Feminism

An Intercultural Challenge for Transforming the Academy

> then i awoke and dug
> that if i dreamed natural
> dreams of being a natural
> woman doing what a woman
> does when she's natural
> i would have a revolution.
>
> **Nikki Giovanni, from "Revolutionary Dreams"**[1]

Giovanni's "Revolutionary Dreams," in its entirety, illustrates the complexity of race and gender as categories used to produce relations of dominance and marginality for the structure and maintenance of knowledge as a justification for particular social arrangements. The poet's awakening reflects the realization that replacing one set of categories with another, constructed by the dominant knowledge system, was not the revolutionary step. Transformative power, rather, lies in working beneath and across categories, in ways that are not responses to the control of a prevailing discourse. Transformation of the academy, which since Platonic times has perceived itself as the "philosopher king" of what is ideal as well as normative in the discernment of knowledge, must come from creative and collaborative ways of showing how various constituencies on the margin intellectually relate.

Where scholarly productivity is the basis for professional standing in the academy and members are assessed according to their output of prestigious research grant awards, refereed publication in distinguished journals, or by the most selective publishers, truly collaborative research can be costly. But transformative breakthroughs, both in scholarship and in how knowledge is constructed and organized, depends upon the efforts of researchers who bring highly differing perspectives to their shared investigation and are willing to take risks. We are convinced of this. For women scholars, racial differences represent the most radically disjunctive social locations from which such collaboration can begin, since the dominant discourse in most disciplines has rested upon European American assumptions, subject matter, and articulation.

What is true collaborative research? "Research" includes the range of activity from scientific investigation and scholarly writing to communicating ideas through teaching and other forms of education. Research constructs and shapes what becomes regarded as knowledge. The purpose of collaborative research is to reconstruct the basis of what is considered authoritative knowledge so as to more accurately correspond to the human diversity that constitutes our social reality. Efforts by a dominant scholar, or undertaken in a singular scholarly mode of discourse, with consideration and, perhaps, input added from others in different social locations, is not collaboration. Neither is research that is structurally but not functionally pluralist, that which strategically gives "equal time" to varied perspectives but makes no attempt to listen and comprehend the disparate voices. Nor is research that "plays to the market" of dominant scholarly interests or efforts that do not transcend a dominant paradigm of thought or discourse. Authentic collaborative research is the conception, investigation, and nurturance of ideas through a naturalness of interaction that underlies any concurrent attention to power disparities resulting from the researchers' particular social locations. Authentic collaboration can occur only when the mutual respect and trust—between those from the dominant paradigm and those who have had to work from the margins—is sufficient to produce interaction that is naturally egalitarian, rather than mediated by vigilant awareness of status difference. In Giovanni's words, it is "woman doing what a woman/does when she's natural" (Giovanni, 1979, p. 452). Because the academy is biased toward the dominant perspective, those who work within its boundaries must regard the prospect of collaborative research as a process to work toward. The very impossibility, for instance, of listing our two names as authors concurrently, while knowing the disproportionate weight the academy places on the lead author's name, makes authentic collaboration impossible.

The risks inherent in working toward authentic collaboration also signify its revolutionary potential in upsetting academic norms. Most tenure decisions are based on an assessment of one's potential scholarship; and such evaluations are typically based on individual research and publication. Besides a "who gets the credit" dilemma, collaborative research poses other risks for scholars facing the tenure clock. One problem is time. Individual research can be more efficient, if not as effective. Authentic collaboration is "chronologically messy"; mutual respect and trust must develop before the fruits of collaboration can be harvested for publication. Requisite openness by the partner with a greater stake in the dominant paradigm is needed for her to radically question how she constructs her assumptions and conclusions. While transformative, this can wreak havoc on a tight research schedule.

Then there are structural problems. If funding is sought, collaborative womanist/feminist researchers face pursuing topics which are of noninterest to foundations, as Geis and Fuller found when approaching the European American, male-dominant paradigm operating in potential funding sources for their project, "The Effects of New-Born Skin Color and Changes in Skin Color on Maternal Bonding." As they point out, the European American and African American researchers were not only given different responses to their funding inquiries, but they were urged to refocus from a soft, qualitative emphasis on maternal bonding to a hard quantitative accent on optical physics of pigmentation more acceptable to those in charge of decision making (Geis and Fuller, 1990). These researchers, having found a paucity of literature and an insensitivity toward their project, concluded that their experience illustrated a presumption of value-free assessment that was in fact laden with value assumptions of the socially dominant frame of reference.

Problems in finding publication opportunities in prestigious journals can be even more intense. Then come the subjective evaluations by scholars whose reputations in a discipline are respected for setting normative trends. For those fixedly invested in European American understandings of a particular discipline, topics of collaborative research can be perceived as outside the main discourse of a discipline and they may challenge head-on its key assumptions.

These are heavy risks for the career development of junior scholars seeking to work toward a transformative collaborative paradigm. As Whicker, Kronenfeld and Strickland (1993) advise, "... tenure is more likely if you do not appear to threaten the general status quo of power relationships within your department" (pp. 26–27). So why are we junior scholars willing to take such risks? We believe that developing authentic collaborative research models is integral to the direction that the academy must take. If it is to survive as a nexus where scholars seek truths in diverse forms, what is deemed to be "solid scholarship" will necessarily become more multicultural. This involves not only making womanist/feminist scholarship central to its endeavors, but also scholarship from all marginalized constituencies, particularly those from different racial and cultural perspectives. As Kuhn (1962) has pointed out, the increase in various articulations of a theory is symptomatic of a paradigmatic crisis and results in a blurring of the rules, or norms, for research. The transition to a new paradigm does not come from improvisation or extension of the old model but from "a reconstruction that changes some of the field's most elementary theoretical generalizations as well as many of its paradigm methods and applications. . . . When the transition is complete, the profession will have changed its view of the field, its methods, and its goals" (Kuhn, 1962, pp. 84–85).

The direction and hope for a paradigm shift that constitutes legitimate academic knowledge and how its quality is assessed lie in the movement toward authentic collaborative research, where *academic common ground* is mutually negotiated and differences valued as a creative opportunity to explore shared human reality. From the perspective of our social locations, we now elaborate on why such collaboration is critically important.

Collaborative Research: A Womanist Perspective

The title of this chapter signifies an extremely important point of departure for me as a woman of color teaching in a predominately white institution of higher education. First, it signifies that feminist is but one expression of a woman's liberationist perspective. Second, the title offers me, a black woman, the space to assert that feminism as a category does not capture the context and complexities of my existence. It does not deal with the realities, concerns, or values that are important to me and my community. I identify as a "womanist," that is, as a black woman who takes seriously my womanhood and who is committed to the welfare of African Americans and other marginalized communities, and who critically engages the social construction of race, gender, and class and the impact these categories have in culture particularly as they affect communities of color.[2] Third, "beyond feminism" means there are lessons for feminists to learn from womanists and other women of color with liberationist perspectives, particularly related to the academy. Hence, our subtitle, "an inter-cultural challenge for transforming the academy," means that there are a variety of cultural perspectives that merit discussion within the women's community and within the academy generally. Women of color in higher education bring together two issues the academy has struggled with for decades: race and gender. Women of color must negotiate many issues as they enter institutions with white, male, hierarchical norms. Many white males feel under seige as an emergent discourse on multiculturalism prevails. This means that women of color are targets and will likely have to deal with the latent anger of backlash. White women can choose to blend in with the expectations of white cultural norms and benefit from white male structures by being "good women," by not advocating concerns about women and issues of women of color and others who are marginalized. Carter, Pearson, and Shavlik (1988) describe the double jeopardy of women of color in higher education:

> At the intersection of race and gender stand women of color, torn by the lines of bias that currently divide white from nonwhite in our society, and male from female. The worlds these women negotiate demand different and often wrenching allegiances. . . . In their professional roles, women of color are expected to meet performance standards set for the most part by white males. Yet their personal lives extract a loyalty to their culture that is central to acceptance by family and friends. At the same time, they must struggle with their own identity as women in a society where "thinking like a woman"

is still considered a questionable activity. At times, they can even experience pressure to choose between their racial identity and their womanhood. (p. 98)

The climate for black women at white colleges and universities, as well as at historically black institutions, is chilly (see Moses, 1989). Administrators of white institutions aggressively disseminate information that shows that there is "a" woman of color on its faculty, while she experiences affirmation from some colleagues and backlash from others, who believe she was hired not because of her intellectual acumen but because the institution got credit for hiring a black and a woman in "one specimen." The "token" syndrome is a real dilemma for women of color who teach in white institutions. As Yolanda Moses suggests, the cultural group that has the largest number of representatives controls the norms and worldview of the institution. This means that the dominant group views the group with fewer numbers as tokens and as spokespersons for the group they represent (Moses, 1989, p. 15). These tokens are drafted to serve on committees to articulate the point of view that would otherwise be absent. A dilemma arises for the woman of color because the absence of her point of view may lessen the possibility of movement toward diversification of the faculty. On the other hand, serving on committees does not enhance one's publication record. Moreover, if a woman of color serves on policy committees and is outvoted on key issues, then she is seen as colluding with maintaining the status quo. After all, committee decisions are usually presented without an indication of how people voted. Should the woman of color insist on bringing a "minority" report to the decision-making body, then she risks losing the support of persons she may need help from in the future. This is an untenable position, particularly for junior faculty.

Collaborative research between those who are structurally dominant and those who have been historically marginalized is an important way to transform the academy. Assuming that those who have been structurally marginalized claim their history and insert its centrality in scholarly work and assuming that the structurally dominant person is teachable and open to shifting dominant paradigms, then the final product is bound to result in an original and distinctive contribution to the academy. It is essential for pioneers of collaborative research across race lines to be dedicated to understand the context from which the research is originating, appreciate the perspectives that each collaborator brings to the research, be able to be comfortable and uncomfortable in a variety of cultural contexts, be able to move between individualistic and group cultures, and consider process openly and accept unpredictability as normal.[3]

Doing collaborative research is likely to be more costly to the woman of color than the white woman.[4] But, the woman of color has the advantage of knowing subjectively and emotively about categories of knowledge and meaning from her experience of being marginalized. This is critical information for those interested in transforming the academy but is seldom valued. Thus, the intellectual ability to integrate subjective awareness and objective knowledge is the talent that women of color intellectuals bring to the academy.

Often women of color in the academy find themselves and their communities trivialized by the dominant discourse in the name of objective research. The cognitive dissonance that results from attempts by women of color to participate in so-called objective "truth" sessions is illustrated in an experience shared by a womanist scholar.

> At a lecture offered by an eminent scholar on the history of slavery in the United States, the lecturer, a young white male, deeply detached from his subject matter talked about the economic merits of slavery and the good business it generated for those power brokers who participated in it. I tried to be objective, but I could not be. I thought to myself, this man is talking about the destruction of my relatives being good business for white people. Thousands of black people died; others continue to suffer the economic and emotional scars of those who not only thought that slavery was economically advantageous for the state and themselves, but perpetuated a brutal form of human suffering.

The marginalized do not dwell on past sufferings to induce feelings of guilt in white people. Rather, marginalized intellectuals who are carriers of a distinct history of the construction of race in the U.S. are strengthened by the very experiences that were life threatening in the past. We are also aware that this same history continues to entrap many in destructive systems. Collaborative research that incorporates a womanist perspective brings together intellectuals who acknowledge the strengths and suffering of people on the margins (see Townes, 1993). If this paradigm becomes central to collaborative research, the academy will never be the same.

Collaborative Research: A Feminist Perspective

As a European American, I've identified with the emergent feminist tradition shaped by women in social locations similar to my own. Admittedly, feminism has focused on gender as the critical variable, too often trivializing or ignoring race. I claim my feminist self-understanding as a legacy of my social location, and seek to bring to it an interactive richness that interracial and multicultural critique can offer. My feminist awakening came as a growing awareness of how my ideas, values, and very identity had been shaped by a European American, male-defined paradigm of what was "feminine" and socioculturally normative, which women conformed to or deviated from with rewards and punishments meted accordingly. At the core of my conscious rejection of such norms as male defined, with men's self-interests at stake, was a liminal awareness that I had the choice to repent of my feminist leanings and conform like a "good white girl" to a system that would offer me protection and privilege in return for my loyalty. As I developed greater racial consciousness, of what it means to be European American in a society where the dominant cultural discourse and powerful, racist interests strive to maintain an institutional and social structure that protects that dominance, I became acutely aware that my sisters of other racial backgrounds did not have choices that would grant them privilege despite the costs. Feminism for me, then, became a moral choice. Retreat to the comfort of those male-dominant paradigms would represent blatantly unethical behavior.

My self-identification as a feminist scholar has become a racial acknowledgment as well, partly as the result of collaborative dialogue with women colleagues of other racial backgrounds. Specifically, "feminist" is a response from a particular constituency signified by a European American, male-constructed definition of what constitutes the "feminine," a definition meant to apply to

European American women as a means to control and trivialize them and to conspicuously marginalize women of color.[5] Consequently, a feminist response in the academy is not only always a European American response, but it is incomplete unless expressed in collaborative relationship with counterpart responses from women of other racial locations.

Part of any collaboration involves doing one's own work. In my case and in that of my European American colleagues, it involves doing my "white" work. Naming this represents an embarrassment, a recognition that what I've perceived as scholarship in general is in fact a very particular perspective through the lens of racial dominance. Thus, the core of feminist collaborative work must involve an awareness of feminism as a fragment among the many—a fragment that locks uncomfortably easily into European American dominance, power, and privilege within the academy. To go against such a lockstep can be considered treasonous to those who seek to offer European American feminists a certain amount of scholarly security in return for their loyalty.

The moral commitment to collaborative models must be underscored. If, as European American feminists, we know that our knowledge system is partial, to use Minnich's (1990) terminology, and we deliberately choose to do nothing to expand our inquiry or admit the particularity of our research, then our scholarly works become little more than professional products—products with alarming similarities to advertising jingles where persuasion, deception, and fraud are matters of degree rather than of fundamental difference. Products, however, have a limited marketing lifespan. As academic boards of trustees increasingly seek to shape academia in the mold of "smart business," as pressure is put on academic departments to be held accountable to a management-by-objectives, profit-center approach where grants, publications, and student—writ "consumer"—popularity have tangible bottom-line value, the academy as a forum for the exploration of truths will survive only if it rejects those influences that play to the socioeconomically and politically dominant at the expense of the margin. And ethically, the academy can survive only if it comes to consciously reject adherence to what Minnich calls "partial knowledge" and "faulty generalization" once it knows that European American normative standards for scholarship are incomplete and their continued generalization as the universal standard of authoritative discourse does injustice to those seeking deeper and broader truths.

Collaborative Research: An Interactive Perspective

Thomas: If white scholars and scholars of color do not engage in collaborative research, there is little possibility for white culture to be critically involved in holistic research. Scholarship solely from a European American focus cannot be transformative without the experiences of scholars of color. This is so even with the pluralism within the European and European American community, because dominant knowledge structures universalize the experiences of a few. Writing from a singular perspective or European American point of view is similar to males being the sole writers of history. Women were marginalized and essential perspectives were lost. Hence, transformation can best be augmented through collaborative research between scholars of color and white scholars. If such an approach is utilized, we can move from "thinking" about transformation to "doing" transformation. While in several liberal institutions where people "talked" about transformation, I had the impression that they were willing to talk, but rarely put their ideas into action. I wonder if some scholars feel that they have to give up too much.

Transformation means changing the dominant paradigm on many levels. One essential way is through personnel. White institutions must create ways for scholars of color, who identify with their particular communities, to be hired in positions that are central to the curriculum. My ideas are not radical; they are essential for transformation. As a womanist scholar, I live with the complexities of life in the African American community. For instance, I am concerned that African American males constantly struggle to have a meaningful life in the United States. This is not an abstract idea, but a fact supported by hard data. My scholarship must deal with theoretical and empirical issues. I hope that these issues can be approached collaboratively.

Nesbitt: I do too. But one of the challenges has to do with authority. Ideas are important, but when it comes to discerning quality, oftentimes those decisions regress to the paradigm that currently has academic authority. Everything else is seen as variant or deviant. That's where I see a great split in values. The liberal side of academia is willing conceptually to step forth, but it has not been willing to struggle with how we move to a new understanding of what is authoritative. In truly collaborative research, how do we distinguish what has qualitative merit from what may not? Does "anything go"? Or do you see some criteria as particularly important?

Thomas: It is important to understand what the dominant system establishes as authoritative. As a black woman living in the United States, I must understand the structures of the dominant culture and decide what expectations I will fulfill and which ones I will not. These choices are calculated and decisive. There are times when I must take my own authority and move out into the deep. I want to proceed confidently with my ideas, believing that they are good and of use to the academy. If I am stopped by dominant structures, then I have to organize some alternative approach. This is time consuming and draining, but many have blazed the trail for me. I think about the collaborative work that the womanist movement has produced in the American Academy of Religion (AAR). I can turn to many women of color scholars for mentoring and support for publishing, which is one of the deeply embedded authoritative determinants of the academy.

I want to note some practical things about collaborative research. First, a fairly high degree of trust must be established between those engaged in it. The persons involved must be able to indicate what is comfortable and uncomfortable about the process and the product. Collaborative work requires an extraordinary amount of time. Those involved will often wonder if the benefits merit the commitment. I believe that the benefits are great.

Nesbitt: Another variable that needs to be looked at, in terms of collaborative work, is how student evaluations are weighted. In my experience, whenever I team teach with a white male, a certain number of student evaluations come back that are extremely negative in a way that has to do with my femaleness. I also suspect that they are coming from women. As long as we are individually evaluated, team teaching works against collaborative styles. Whether you cross gender or racial boundaries there is going to be an interaction that invests a disproportionate amount of authority in those students who haven't necessarily worked through their own issues. This can boomerang on the faculty member less identified with the dominant system whether by race, gender, or both. The criteria for quality need to be set forth before teaching or collaborative research can be undertaken; work can't truly be collaborative if people are going to be evaluated differentially. Other women scholars have had similar problems when team teaching with men—very liberal, European American men. A few angry student evaluations are disproportionately weighted in the women's teaching evaluations.

Thomas: My immediate response is, "Is it in my best interest to teach with white men when more than likely those whom I am teaching may be more comfortable with a white male professor than a black female professor?" Common sense says I cannot do anything to disadvantage myself because the system already favors dominants. I do not like to say that the system works against me, because I do not like to do system blaming, but I am aware that the system favors people who make up the majority, because it was set up by them. That's not so much a complaint as a statement of reality. Persons with power set up systems to benefit themselves; others have to adjust to the system.

The AAR womanist group spent time in a session talking about black women students. Across the country, a few unexpected and negative episodes are happening between black women students and black women faculty. For example, in one predominately white institution, a black woman student, upon learning that a new black woman faculty had been hired, announced that she would "cut the new black woman faculty down to size." Many of us have to deal with women who have not dealt with their own issues. For black women, issues are particularly complicated because of internalized racism. Some black women internalize the negative images that the dominant culture emits about black people. This self-loathing often results in horizontal violence. Marginalized people attack each other rather than confront the system that causes them to dislike the self-image they see in each other. In other words, the marginalized may not deal with the unconscious internalization of self-hatred systematically encouraged by the larger system. It is anguishing when the interaction between two black women in white institutions is not positive. I am pleased that the womanist community is talking about this conflict openly because growing numbers of black women professors and black women students are in institutions of higher education. The womanist community has given notice that a few students are targeting the most vulnerable people in institutions, women of color faculty. This is not ethical behavior. Women of color faculty have enough to deal with, without getting the "Anita Hill/Clarence Thomas syndrome" going between two women of color in white institutions.

It takes so much energy to think about this, and ultimately our goal is to help women of color get their degrees. However, I will not tolerate abusive behavior from any person. Being a womanist means being concerned about the community. We want the very best scholars to be in our communities and in the academy. We are not just turning out cars on an assembly line. We want quality people out there.

Nesbitt: To some degree I hear an internal script among European American women faculty and students saying, "Get your own house in shape." I also hear you saying that, from your perspective. This signifies to me that we are operating on the margin, that we still feel adjunct. It is important for us to discern what about the institution is giving us this perception so that once we name it, we then can be empowered to talk—to share our experiences—and then to do something about it.

Thomas: I have a question for you. What does it take for a feminist to decide that she is going to live on the margin? White women can make a choice about where they stand on gender, race, and other issues that affect the marginalized. Does it take an experience of being radically marginalized?

Collaborative research that is intercultural requires that white people try to at least be "bicultural." My experience as an African American woman in North America, within a dominant white culture, means that I understand how white culture works. I can operate in it as well as in my culture of origin. It is rare for me to find white women who are willing to be "bicultural." White women have to make a moral choice, because there are no material benefits for those who consciously live with the concerns of those who are marginalized. As we talk about collaborative research, I think that it would benefit white feminists to hear you articulate what it has meant for you to intentionally upset the dominant paradigm. I am not sure there are very many other women with whom I would venture down this road.

Nesbitt: Once I realize that I have a choice, once I know what, ethically, I ought to do, if I refuse to do it I know that I am behaving unethically. Ethics is not just a matter of "doing the right thing." I need to do it because I truly believe what is right is also good and just. That is the basis of my commitment. Opting for money and privilege but despising what I am doing to gain it is a choice that I've rejected twice in my life. That is at the heart of why I want to take whatever risks necessary to help transform the academy. For me, what is right and just and good are all interwoven.

Thomas: So it really is an individual choice that you made.

Nesbitt: It always has to be. For every white woman who comes to a feminist awareness that she has a choice to make, it becomes a moral choice. It's a choice that never goes away as long as the European American culture is dominant, because she is constantly having to choose to forsake what would give her privilege in return for her loyalty. On the other hand, as a person involved in both the social science and religion academies, I make an affirmation of that choice each morning when I wake up, as a form of prayer.

I also cannot say that I am bicultural, because I have no indepth cultural experience other than my Northern European American background. I try to open my process of growth to learn and appreciate truths of people from other cultures, and to listen to their wisdom in an authoritative way. For me, authority comes down to Giovanni's image of "natural truths." A natural truth cuts across different academic perspectives and is intercultural and interracial. Real authority is about those wisdoms, those truths we can share from diverse cultures and constituencies.

Do you have advice for other women of color who might be interested, or might be approached about the possibility of collaborative research?

Thomas: When the woman of color is involved in collaborative research, it means that she is probably teaching the person with whom she is working about issues peculiar to marginalized people, unless the person with whom she is collaborating has worked at understanding what it means to be white and privileged, whether male or female. The woman of color takes risks constantly; thus, it is best to have an informal contractual agreement between intercultural collaborative researchers. The informal contract should make clear that the woman of color does not have an obligation to teach the person with whom she is working. The burden of self-education rests upon the dominant who needs to understand that she is unaware of what it means to be a person of color in white culture. For instance, as a heterosexually identified woman, I am in a position of dominance. If a lesbian and I are doing collaborative research, I have an obligation to educate myself on the central issues that lesbians define as important. I hope that my willingness to educate myself is rigorous enough that my collaborator assists me. I understand that I am making work for her because I'm playing catch-up and she has no obligation to teach me anything. It is my work.

If a woman of color chooses to live in North America, then she chooses to be engaged in issues of racism, sexism, heterosexism, and elitism. If we work at predominantly white institutions, we will spend time helping people who are willing learners and fighting systems that are destructive. It means that we must have a net of support for ourselves. We cannot do this without getting emotionally tired, because we are dealing with some of our deepest core values in institutions that may be hostile to what we think is important. To sing our song in a strange land there need to be sources for grounding. In my case, I have a Sojourner Truth meditation room in my home. I also have a fitness program. I believe illness is a function of the environment we work and live in. Environmental toxicities can be destructive on our bodies. My blood pressure can shoot up just from the stress of being in a meeting. I have to do a lot of self care and also say no even to people in authority. When people ask me to be on a committee, I say, "Let me think about it." I try not to feel trapped, but to have a proactive vision of what I want to do. I also have a personal board of visioners similar to an institutional board of directors or trustees. I call them this because from time to time I need to ask people, "Can you help me to do some visioning?" These are people that I can call any time, any place, and who will listen to me and have my interests at heart.

What would you say to white women who want to understand race and diversity? I notice that white women are shocked and put off when a person of color calls them racist.

Nesbitt: This is characteristic of white women who see themselves as liberal and feminist, when being called "racist" does not match their self-image. My advice to such a person would be to write her defensive response in a journal but to keep her mouth shut. She should ask herself, "Why would that person say this? Why would it even come up?" She should also ask others outside her sphere of influence, particularly across racial lines. The danger is that if there is no trust, they aren't going to be candid. In short, her response should be to do ten times more listening and questioning than talking.

Why would a person of color be interested in doing collaborative research, particularly with a European American who is part of the dominant academic culture?

Thomas: I am going to speak only for myself. I am selective with whom I do collaborative research. There are benefits for me. It is rare to find a white person who really wants to do intercultural collaborative research. You and I are creating something new. We are moving toward what it means to authentically live in a multiculturally transformed society. This is ultimately my life goal. This work is satisfying, exciting, and meaningful. Moreover, it is important to write about this work so that others have something from which to draw. It inspires me when I read about black women who lived in the nineteenth century, like Sojourner Truth, Ida B. Wells, and Anna Julia Haywood Cooper, who left their mark and tried to create a transformed world. These black women were instrumental in confronting the adversities black people lived with in U.S. culture. There have been improvements, but as our society has become increasingly complex, so have issues about diversity. When intercultural scholars work together to do collaborative research then we move toward the possibility of creative solutions. This is what I like to contribute.

Conclusion

How do we move beyond feminism to collaborative models of research that transform the academy? This is the central question for scholars who want to change firmly embedded knowledge systems whose singular focus suppresses the creative intelligence other perspectives can bring to the academy. If collaborative research is to be one of the core methods for moving toward transforming the academy, how do institutions utilize it as a model? What must institutions do to be committed to collaborative research?

First, the creative potential of the faculty must be assessed. One might call this an audit of the scholarly interests of those who teach. Faculty need to make honest self-assessments of where their research is going and how it will be expanded through collaborative research. In North America race is a category that scholars must make central to their work. White scholars must deal with the category of "whiteness" (Frankenberg, 1993) and try to build relationships with scholars of color who most radically challenge their thinking in these areas. Second, faculties ought to consider consulting with experts in diversity. An institution cannot always have all the answers. In transformation, even the most creative people need support in ways that will help strengthen their research and allow it to move into new areas. This creates a win/win situation for all involved. Third, there needs to be interest, commitment, and leadership from the faculty that diversity is important and that transformation is desirable for the institution. If leadership is lacking in this area, the institution may become polarized to a point of stagnation. Leadership can help faculty think about these issues, strategize, and borrow ideas from other institutions which have been successful in moving toward transformation and multiculturalism.

Elitism is a characteristic of higher education institutions. What would it mean for an institution to focus less on being "the biggest and the best" and instead develop leadership that would reconfigure the paradigms that until now have universalized the experiences of a few? How could an institution organize its resources so that the ideas of others—particularly those who have been historically marginalized—have a place to be heard, in a manner that illustrates steadfast commitment to the common integrity of all humanity? If institutions have a will to do this, then they must do so deliberately and without hesitation. Having institutional goals that signal a commitment to transformation will attract some of the finest, most creative minds in the world. Such a community of scholars would be diverse racially and culturally.

Institutions involved in changing paradigms ought to be prepared to bring together individuals who are willing to risk marginalization within their disciplines. Authentic transformation can occur if people are not personally invested in having the most esteemed reputation or being highly regarded by those who thrive on European American competitive individualism. Scholars who identify with a more conservative European American, male-dominant paradigm will consider such people eccentric and may trivialize their work. Individuals who choose to travel this road need to be bold. If they are not willing to take risks, then they will foul the work for others. Finally, institutions that are willing to take action to move to collaborative and multicultural paradigms also need to be willing to negotiate new forms of authority and criteria for what is held as authoritative—forms and criteria that have to be multiculturally and collaboratively determined.

NOTES

1. Nikki Giovanni, "Revolutionary Dreams," in Edward Field (ed.) *A Geography of Poets* (New York: Bantam, 1979), p. 452. Used with permission.

2. Walker defines "womanist" as a black feminist or feminist of color who is strongwilled, decisive, loving, and "committed to survival and wholeness of entire people, male and female" (Walker, 1983), pp. xi–xii.

3. For a graphic depiction of new paradigms for collaborative work across race lines, see Thomas and Pierce (1988).

4. Geis and Fuller (1990) report that dominant research structures gave Geis more access to data than it did Fuller. In this case, Geis's access to information was pivotal for getting funding (see p. 212).

5. I recommend especially to other European American women, Collins (1990, chap. 4); also Spelman (1988).

REFERENCES

Carter, D., Pearson, C., and Shavlik, D. (1987/1988, Fall/Winter). Double jeopardy: Women of Color in higher education. *Educational Record* 68, 69.

Collins, P. H. (1990). *Black feminist thought*. New York: Routledge.

Frankenberg, R. (1993). *White women, race matters: The social construction of whiteness*. Minneapolis: University of Minnesota Press.

Geis, S. B., and Fuller, R. L. (1990, Fall). Inadvertent discrimination in medical research. *Journal of Religion and Health* 29(3), 207–17.

Giovanni, N. (1979). Revolutionary dreams. In Edward Field (ed.) *A geography of poets* (p. 452). New York: Bantam.

Kuhn, T. (1962). *The structure of scientific revolutions*. Chicago: University of Chicago Press.

Minnich, E. K. (1990). *Transforming knowledge*. Philadelphia: Temple University Press.

Moses, Y. T. (1989, August). *Black women in academe: Issues and strategies*. Project on the Status and Education of Women, Association of American Colleges.

Spelman, E. V. (1988). *Inessential woman: Problems of exclusion in feminist thought*. Boston: Beacon.

Thomas, L., and Pierce, C. (1988). *A Black/White continuum in White culture*. Laconia, NH: New Dynamics.

Townes, E. M. (ed.). (1993). *A troubling in my soul: Womanist perspectives on evil and suffering*. Maryknoll, NY: Orbis.

Walker, A. (1983). *In search of our Mother's gardens*. New York: Harcourt Brace Jovanovich.

Whicker, M. L., Kronenfeld, J. J., and Strickland, R. A. (1993). *Getting tenure*. Newbury Park, CA: Sage.

Carol Shiner Wilson and Joel Haefner

3

Writing against the Romantic Grain

As we write this chapter, we are in the final stages of our collaboration on a collection of critical essays, *Re-Visioning Romanticism: British Women Writers, 1776–1837,* for publication with the University of Pennsylvania Press. Collaborating on this chapter gives us the opportunity to reflect upon four years of mutual respect and affection, empathy, frustration (never with one another), appreciation of our mentor, Romanticist Stuart Curran, and appreciation of newly forged links of friendship that we have developed, not just with one another but with one another's families. It also gives us an opportunity to examine our collection of essays, as well as the nature of our collaboration, in conversation, as it were, with Lisa Ede and Andrea Lunsford in *Singular Texts/Plural Authors* (1990), Joan DeJean in *Fictions of Sappho, 1546–1937,* and Carey Kaplan and Ellen Cronan Rose in "Strange Bedfellows: Feminist Collaboration" (1993). We also find ourselves in conversation with the spirit of Barbara McClintock who noted that, above all, "a feeling for the organism" is necessary to see deeply into the life of one's subject of research.

Our volume of critical essays grew out of an NEH Summer Seminar, "Women and Men Poets of British Romanticism," led by Stuart Curran at the University of Pennsylvania in the summer of 1990. Ten women and three men participated in the seminar; five of these seminarians contributed essays to our volume. Curran had set the tone for the seminar in his influential article, "Romantic Poetry: The 'I' Altered," in *Romanticism and Feminism,* a 1987 volume edited by Anne K. Mellor. In that piece, Curran argued that "true" Romantic literature as the exclusive domain of six male solitary geniuses—Blake, Wordsworth, Coleridge, Byron, Keats, and Shelley—was a myth. Women were writing outstanding literature in the period and were celebrated for their work. Yet, their works had come to be overlooked as male canon fashioners in the Victorian period and twentieth-century critics privileged male writers. As Curran claimed, these vast—and vastly ignored—writings by women are a "terra incognita beneath our very feet." He went on to argue that examining these texts would alter our conventional notions of Romanticism: specifically, quotidian values and ways of seeing of an Anna Barbauld would modify the valorization of grand vision of a Wordsworth or Shelley and "the portrayal of an alienated sensibility" of a Charlotte Smith would displace the integration of self and world of a Coleridge. With this background, we expected to be engaged in a radical act of discovery and of reinvention.

But none of us was really prepared for either the immensity of this "terra incognita" or the profundity of this challenge to our thinking about Romanticism. The reading list was staggering, not only because of its length, but also because we "experts" didn't recognize all the names. Anna Barbauld, Hannah More, Helen Maria Williams, Anna Batten Cristall, Mary Robinson, Anna Seward, Charlotte Smith, Amelia Opie, Felicia Hemans, Mary Mitford, Sydney Owenson, Letitia Landon (L.E.L.), Constance Garnett—most, very familiar to us now—were then unknown to us. A few we recognized dimly, like Felicia Hemans, as names dismissed in a footnote of an authoritative anthology as "minor" or in a canonical author's journal as an object of ambivalence (derivative, Byron claims in one entry and awfully good in another). We had never heard Wordsworth's praise of Smith's innovative work with the English sonnet or knew that he had been so moved by Barbauld's meditation on death that he memorized it upon first hearing it. We were awed, too, by the brilliance of some of the verse, by the portentous cultural and aesthetic issues the texts raised. It is fair to say that all of us in the seminar went from feeling overwhelmed and ignorant, to enthusiastic and ebullient, to disbelieving and even angry, feeling betrayed over the material we had never studied in undergraduate or graduate courses on British Romanticism. We would never be able to look in the same innocent way at our previous syllabi, constructed on the model of prevailing male-dominated scholarship, and vowed to include in meaningful ways the works of Smith, Barbauld, Robinson, and others. We have met that vow.

About halfway through the seminar, as we were reading in particular Charlotte Smith, Mary Robinson, and Felicia Hemans, a proselytizing spirit began to infect our group. Some of the participants began to discuss ways in which this "new" material could be incorporated into survey courses like British Literature II and Romanticism. Others began to discuss how to get and reproduce texts for classroom and research uses. And some of us began to think about a volume of critical essays that would seriously study these writers and spread the word about the quality and breadth of women's writing during the period.

So the collaboration started with a mixture of anger, enthusiasm, even missionary zeal; and those elements persisted throughout the entire project, with, of course, despair, disgust, and ennui prevailing at certain points. We felt intellectually and personally compatible early on. Joel knew from the start that he would really want to work with Carol. Her comments during our sessions seemed smart, insightful, well-grounded in a broad reading in the period. Carol had been impressed by Joel's obvious delight and unaffected sophistication in discussing the texts and theoretical issues surrounding them, and by his accessible manner. We seemed to share the same feelings about the material and the way it had been buried by the Romanticism critical industry throughout our undergraduate and graduate educations. And of course there was the intangible: chemistry. We both seemed to know, "Here is someone I can work with." Perhaps it was the similarity of our backgrounds: Midwesterners, same age, Big Ten grads, marginalized adjuncts with spouses in tenure-line jobs, uninterested in the pretentiousness that can inform academe. One day, we held preliminary discussions with a half dozen seminarians at Le Bus, a delicatessen near Penn. And toward the end of the seminar, the two of us met over breakfast at the White Dog Cafe to seal the deal.

"Stars," the pragmatic Carol had insisted from the beginning. We need to get fine scholars who are committed to this enterprise and willing to contribute—for the quality of the contributions and so that the academic community will take the work seriously. We invited submissions as well as solicited them, and received an impressive number of proposals. Indeed, as it turned out, the exhilaration of the enterprise outstripped the concern over market value as we explored new literary terrain with contributors, both new and established voices, including Jane Aaron, Catherine Burroughs,

Stuart Curran, Julie Ellison, Susan Allen Ford, Jerome J. McGann, Judith Pascoe, Katharine Rogers, Marlon Ross, and Susan Wolfson. We also discovered a network of colleagues willing to give advice and to read proposals and essays. Curran continued to provide moral support, labor, and good advice, but scholars like Mary Lynn Johnson of the University of Iowa, Steve Behrendt of the University of Nebraska, Susan Wolfson of Princeton University, and June Schlueter of Lafayette College also proved helpful in responding to the scholarly content of the volume and in suggesting strategies for putting together a collection. Publishers also provided us with ideas about which angles to pursue, how to make the collection hang together, which areas in the field were fresh and ready for exploration. We also found, in an age of shrinking purchases of books and increasing production costs, that producing a safely saleable book was a concern of all publishers.

Both of us found friends to give us direction, and in that sense the volume is very much a broad collaboration: a collaboration in drafting, editing, and revising, of course, with composing by the contributors and editorial comments from both of us, outside readers, and press readers, but also a collaboration in the prewriting stage when our planning and brainstorming took place.

From the start we were naturally aware that gender would be the locus of our collaboration, in many senses. First, it was clear that the texts to be examined would have to be read in different ways than those male texts tagged as *the* Romantic canon. Romantic women writers' experiences were substantially different than those of men, and their poetry and prose reflected those experiential differences. Curran had already suggested two major differences—concepts of vision and the alienated sensibility—but we both knew that there were many more issues that would be shaped by the dynamics of gender.

Second, the history of Romantic criticism, and the reception of the book, was and would be deeply entwined in gender issues. Marlon Ross's (1989) *The Contours of Masculine Desire: Romanticism and the Rise of Women's Poetry,* a book that had come up repeatedly during the seminar, skillfully outlines the ways, often ambivalent, in which writers like Hazlitt, Byron, De Quincey, and others had denigrated women's writing. In relatively new territory, we thought we might experience some of the same hostility or defensive dismissiveness from readers and critics, but we also knew that this project had to be pursued. We found ourselves passionately committed to having these women writers heard after years of silencing by the male critical establishment. As adjuncts marginalized in numerous ways in the academy, we no doubt identified with our writers' marginalized status in the critical world. Our desire to have them heard has been no doubt in part our desire to be heard.

About six presses were very interested and asked to see a full-blown proposal. There were glitches along the way, of course. One press had our proposal for six months—adrift in a sea of paper and misplaced during an office move. But the university presses we approached seemed to sense that the field of Romanticism was on the verge of major changes, altered by cultural materialism and feminism, and that our volume would be a valuable contribution to that change. The outside readers at three presses confirmed the timeliness and value of the project.

Third, we knew that, in ways we couldn't foresee and see now only with difficulty, gender would shape the nature of our collaboration, our editorial tasks, and our writing itself. The difficulty with which, even as the project moves toward completion, we "read" the impact of gender on our work signifies the cultural imperative of the "invisibility" of gender and the extent to which we interiorize that invisibility. In other words, it was easier to analyze the dimensions of gender in the texts we were studying than our own texts.

We are still working out ways in which gender influenced our choice of essay topics. Carol's essay was "Lost Needles, Tangled Threads: Stitchery, Domesticity, and the Artistic Enterprise in Barbauld, Edgeworth, Taylor and Lamb," appearing in the section on Gender and the Cultural Matrix. Joel's essay was "The Romantic Scene(s) of Writing" and appeared in the section on revisioning Romantic aesthetics. Carol explored the complex textual and cultural manifestations of needlework, the overlooked female quotidian in children's literature, and the poems and letters of four women writers. She claims, characteristically, that this essay and her larger book project on needlework as lived reality and literary figure help her work out her "needle envy." She sews miserably. Joel took up a topic he had started during the NEH Seminar: the paradigms of space in Romantic poetry. In some ways this was a "safe" topic (the literary representation of space had been a valid critical subject since Joseph Frank's 1949 article) but Joel posited a "solitary," Bardic, masculine writing space against the salon—largely female, collaborative, process directed. In doing so, of course, he ran into the problematics of binarism and essentialism.

As we worked with the material and one another, we were keenly aware of another way in which we were working against the Romantic grain: the emphasis in female traditions of Romantic writing on conversation. While male writers promulgated the idea of the singular author, the "writer-writes-alone," as Linda Brodkey calls it (396), women emphasized the social and especially the conversational qualities of "composing" in the broadest, most collective sense. The fabric of the NEH seminar itself had already suggested this conversational dimension to writing; and our reading of Hannah More's poem "Bas Bleu" had underlined the importance of talk for the Bluestockings, a group made up of women where men like Samuel Johnson were welcome. Moreover, Carol had enjoyed six years of invigorating academic conversation and warm friendship with her own bluestocking friends, the Feminist Research Group. Made up of over a dozen academics from a variety of disciplines, members of that group had critiqued her essays on Louisa May Alcott, Alice Walker, Jane Barker, and the essay for the *Re-Visioning Romanticism* collection. In fact, this chapter was critiqued by the Feminist Research Group who suggested, based on the passion Carol and Joel felt for the recovery of women writers, that a strong tie to the career of Barbara McClintock, pioneer in DNA studies, should be made. As Evelyn Fox Keller notes, McClintock's motivating force for endless hours of work, often unrelieved by professional support, was her "feeling for the organism" to which she devoted her life of study (198).

We shared our commitment to the project in writing—through letters, the collaboratively written introduction, our own essays, via e-mail and fax—and orally—at conferences and over the telephone. As we did so we were aware that we were negotiating the misleading "solitary genius" hegemony that has dominated critical discourse and composition pedagogy, the shibboleths that Christine Battersby anatomizes in *Gender and Genius*. As Kaplan and Rose note in "Strange Bedfellows," third-person pronouns metamorphose into "'we,' hypothetical, invisible, yet nonetheless articulate. 'We' merges from the space between our individual, different voices, its meaning elusive, dispersed, always deferred, never unitary" (549). Unlike Kaplan and Rose, we never wrangled "over some cherished perception or notion" (553). We saw nothing as contested ground.

As we worked together on the introduction to the volume, we were sensitive to questions of stylistic differences. We wanted the introduction to read smoothly, not to show the seams where one writer's text ended and the other writer's began. Joel seemed to feel there were different styles; Carol felt the piece was fairly smooth. But we continue to have different views of what happened as we revised and coordinated our text scraps. We are certain, however, of a shared goal: prose that was clear and lucid, material that would be helpful to our readers.

In retrospect, we met that goal, both in the introduction to the collection and, we feel, in this chapter. The revision process has blurred the "lines of ownership," the sentences and paragraphs that each wrote and that became woven into the final text. It might be that Joel's initial hunch—that there were stylistic differences, and that (to his dismay) he was writing in a Hazlittian "familiar style"— had some truth to it, but that those differences dissolved during revision. On the other hand, Carol's perspective—that there were virtually no stylistic differences to begin with—could well be true, too, which would explain why revision went relatively smoothly. The fact that we explored the question of stylistic differences proved more interesting than hunting for differences in our prose: it indicated the extent to which one brings ideology, concepts, and expectations into the composing process and how a changing context can alter the production of a text and what we make of it.

Another factor that shaped the structure of the collection, the essays we selected, and our own writing was the dangers of binarism—"binary logic," as Mary Poovey calls it in *Uneven Developments*. The strategy soon became to define and resist a female/male dichotomy. While we knew it was important to explore a women's tradition during the Romantic period, we also knew it was vital to articulate those texts with the male canon and with the androcentric aesthetics conveyed to all of us in graduate seminars in the last half of this century. This was hardly novel; Lillian Robinson had already indicated this direction in "Treason Our Text": "while not abandoning our newfound female tradition, we have to return to confrontation with 'the' canon, examining it as a source of ideas, themes, motifs, and myths about the two sexes" (118).

As a result of our awareness of both the need to affirm the female tradition and to articulate it in a meaningful and challenging way with the male aesthetic/critical tradition, we aimed at both breadth and balance in the collection itself. We were conscious of the need to include both female and male Romanticists; we were looking, as we chose essays, for direct critiques of and challenges to the traditional canon and its aesthetic assumptions as writers discussed texts by women. We also wanted to cover genres not generally privileged in the traditional scheme of the Romantic period: the essay, the long war epic, plays, memoirs, children's stories. And for both practical and political reasons we wanted a spread across the period, pushing our beginning and closing dates to 1776 and 1837, respectively. We somewhat arbitrarily chose those dates—the beginning of the American Revolution and the ascension of Queen Victoria—because we wanted to undermine the common parameters, the publication of *Lyrical Ballads* (1798) and the death of Coleridge (1834), both events from the male tradition. But we also wanted to include the writings of Bluestockings like Hannah More and Anna Barbauld and those of the late Romantic poetesses like Felicia Hemans and Letitia Landon. Most of all, we encouraged a variety of voices that spoke elegantly, passionately, discreetly, even haltingly but always sincerely and intelligently, and with commitment to the enterprise.

So *balance* was a term that came up often during our afternoon and evening telephone conversations. It came up too in readers' reactions to the essays we selected and in our own evaluations and recommendations to the writers. *Balance* is a troublesome word and it reflects a troublesome situation: the need to assert a distinct and separate tradition (which seems clearly to exist) and the need to bring such a tradition into the mainstream in an important and revisionistic way.

One of the balances or polarities that seemed to emerge naturally from the friction between these two traditions was the Sapphic and the Miltonian/Wordsworthian vision of the writer. Curran had already pointed this out, and it seemed appropriate to keep this in mind as we worked together on our project. Joan DeJean's 1989 study, *Fictions of Sappho, 1546–1937*, details how convoluted was the development of the myth of Sappho and how Sappho was known as "the female counterpart, and presumably the equal, of 'the poet,' Homer" (1). Sappho—and Madame de Staël's fictionalization of the poet, Corinne—represents an alternative creative mode to the model represented by the High Romantics. Sapphic creativity included an emphasis on spontaneity; a theory firmly rooted in invention; an aesthetics which is obviously expressive but is also clearly audience centered; a sense of the poet speaking for her audience, becoming almost a collective speaker, like a Greek chorus; an emphasis on the emotional and sympathetic dimension of discourse; and a belief in the importance of conversation and dialogue in the creative process.

The Sappho/Corinne myth was frequently celebrated by Romantic women poets, and indeed they adopted this fiction of the writer as their own, becoming, in a sense, Corinne themselves. As early as 1796 Mary Robinson published her sonnet sequence *Sappho and Phaon*. Constance Grace Garnett published a play entitled *Sappho: A Dramatic Sketch* in 1824, celebrating the martyrdom of the poetess to hopeless love. L.E.L. (Letitia Elizabeth Landon) penned several versions of the Sappho myth, including "The Improvisatrice," "A History of the Lyre," and "Sappho"; Felicia Hemans also wrote variations on the theme, including "The Dying Improvisator," "The Last Song of Sappho," and "Corinne at the Capitol" (the title of the second book of de Staël's novel). All these texts inscribe the fiction of Sappho's unrequited heterosexual love and her suicide, but they also inscribe an impromptu, collaborative, conversational, and audience-centered vision of writing.

We would not want to claim all these features for our own collaboration, but certainly the texture of the NEH seminar and our own partnership veered more toward the Sapphic tradition than the "singular" tradition (Ede and Lunsford's term) exemplified by Homer, Milton, and Wordsworth. Seminar participants, ourselves included, had developed a shared camaraderie, a sense of leading the charge, that energized our discussions and made sharing ideas and strategies easier. But our collaboration proceeded without being unduly stalled by agonizing over the dichotomy between traditional Romantic and Sapphic visions of the composing process. Ede and Lunsford argue that within collaborative writing itself there is a hierarchical form—appropriative, "self-centered," and authority driven—and a dialogic form—communal, process oriented, and egalitarian. Though they disavow the validity of "binary opposition" even as they describe it, Ede and Lunsford suggest that the two modes of collaboration may be gendered as well. The hierarchical mode "is carefully, and often rigidly, structured, driven by highly specific goals, and carried out by people playing clearly defined and delimited roles." Furthermore, it is "typically conservative, and most often . . . a masculine mode of discourse." By contrast, the dialogic mode "is loosely structured and the roles enacted within it are fluid. . . . the process of articulating goals is often as important as the goals themselves"; it is "multivoiced" and "multivalent," and, implicitly, female (133).

Our own collaboration probably falls between these two extremes, though we suspect, and perhaps Ede and Lunsford would agree, that such oppositions are conceptual constructs and can't really be found in the actual world. We did take on different tasks: writing or telephoning contributors or presses, writing sections of the prospectus and introduction, breaking up work on the bibliography or editing tasks, dividing the work load between contributors and reviewers, finding and arranging permissions for cover art, sending out copyedited manuscripts, having one contributor proof galleys and the other do the index. But we usually either volunteered for certain tasks or did it on a barter system. These tasks were driven partly by our own schedules, partly by our sense of keeping on track, partly by a sense of urgency about our project, partly by suggestions from our editor at Penn, and very much by our consideration of one another's demanding personal and professional responsibilities. No one consistently assumed a task-assigning authority over the process, and we always respected—even anticipated—one another's busy lives. Again, it may be that the marginalization of adjuncts who teach heavy loads, engage in scholarly work, and take responsibility for families and households has taken us out of the competitive loop that can harm collaboration. For many reasons, then, our collaboration is feminist.

While our goal was "highly specific"—to publish a collection of essays—our roles were not "clearly defined and delimited." On the other hand, we could not claim that our collaboration was loosely structured or fluid, or that it was not very product centered. We would, however, maintain that it was multivalent: the writing itself was indeed a shared experience, with each writer contributing a section that the other writer revised, expanded, cut, and otherwise polished. We also felt it was multivalent in two other senses: that we were speaking for Romanticists who valued the contributions of women writers but whose voices are only beginning to be heard in mainstream academic discourse, and for these women writers and their texts, excommunicated from Romantic studies in the twentieth century.

The intellectual enterprise, as exciting as it has been, would have been less rich had the Haefner/Huffs and the Shiner Wilson/Wilsons not discovered dimensions of friendship. This is surely not so different from the Bluestockings. Carol met Joel, Cynthia, and their children at conferences, enjoyed talking with Cynthia at other conferences and over the phone, cared about her academic work and personal concerns, and considers Cynthia a sympathetic traveler in Women's Studies. Daniel and Carol visited the Haefner/Huffs on a midwestern trek to see Carol's brother, whom Joel now also knows. Joel and Cynthia learned more about Carol and Daniel, including Daniel's polio research and attempts to housebreak a puppy during incessant winter storms. Cynthia and Carol shared their frustrations and successes in the politics and pedagogy of Women's Studies. One scene stands out: Carol and Cynthia sitting on a hotel bed at a conference, Joel on the floor, talking about the Romanticism project, about Cynthia's projects, about the conference papers, about Women's Studies, as the two kids interrupted, ate Ritz crackers, threw stacking cups around the room, and wondered what we were talking about. It was a quotidian moment *in extremis,* but it reflected the casual and complicated texture of our partnership. In many ways, very real to us, our collaboration stitched our two lives together, and our scene of writing has stretched out across the heartland, across several years, but always crowded with ourselves and others.

REFERENCES

Battersby, Christine. *Gender and Genius: Towards a Feminist Aesthetics.* Bloomington: Indiana University Press, 1989.

Brodkey, Linda. "Modernism and the Scene(s) of Writing." *College English* 49 (1987): 396–418.

Curran, Stuart. "Romantic Poetry: The 'I' Altered." *Romanticism and Feminism.* Ed. Anne K. Mellor. Bloomington: Indiana University Press, 1987. 185–207.

DeJean, Joan. *Fictions of Sappho, 1546–1937.* Chicago: University of Chicago Press, 1989.

Ede, Lisa, and Andrea Lunsford. *Singular Texts/Plural Authors: Perspectives on Collaborative Writing.* Carbondale: Southern Illinois University Press, 1990.

Kaplan, Carey, and Ellen Cronan Rose, "Strange Bedfellows: Feminist Collaboration." *Signs* 18 (1993): 547–61.

Keller, Evelyn Fox. *A Feeling for the Organism: The Life and Work of Barbara McClintock.* New York: W. H. Freeman, 1983.

Poovey, Mary. *Uneven Developments: The Ideological Work of Gender in Mid-Victorian England.* Chicago: University of Chicago Press, 1988.

Robinson, Lillian S. "Treason Our Text: Feminist Challenges to the Literary Canon." *The New Feminist Criticism: Essays on Women, Literature, and Theory.* Ed. Elaine Showalter. New York: Pantheon, 1985. 105–21.

Carol J. Singley and Susan Elizabeth Sweeney

4

In League with Each Other

The Theory and Practice of Feminist Collaboration

Over the past seven years, we have worked together to author essays, chair sessions at conferences, review publications, and edit a book; and we are planning still other projects. The process by which we produce this scholarship sustains and delights us. We believe that such collaboration is a particularly feminist way of developing, testing, and disseminating knowledge. It has played an integral role in the history of American feminism, from Susan B. Anthony and Elizabeth Cady Stanton's work together on the Seneca Falls Declaration (1848)—Anthony even took care of Stanton's children, so that she would be free to think and write—to the consciousness-raising sessions of the 1970s, when the sharing of women's individual stories led to collective political analysis and action. Many feminists have pooled their energies for a common purpose, and several have commented on their work together; and yet, despite its significance, feminist collaboration has received little theoretical scrutiny. Indeed, collaborative work between women has received less attention than that between men or that between men and women (see, for example, Delbanco, Koestenbaum, Seymour, and Stillinger).

In order to talk about how women collaborate, we need to explore the meaning of the word itself. To collaborate means "to work jointly with others, especially in an intellectual endeavor, to cooperate with or willingly assist an enemy of one's country and especially an occupying force." Like "fraternize," "collaborate" suggests harmonious sharing as well as competition, betrayal, and violence. "Collaboration" thus connotes both an outward connection to others and an internal struggle against a foreign, harmful force that threatens one's autonomy. Women, in particular, may feel precisely such ambivalence about affiliation with another. Because women are often defined by their relationships, they may feel unable to achieve a separate or authentic identity in collaboration. And because female identity traditionally relies on connections forged with or through men, affiliation with other women may seem odd and unfamiliar. This tension between cooperation and competition is an important feminist issue that has yet to be fully addressed.

Feminist collaboration, then, raises more questions than it answers. We are especially interested in how women write together. Does their historical exclusion from written language make them more likely than men to participate in collaborative work, or to do so differently? Do they try to avoid competition with each other? If collaboration is a feminist act, then what role does conflict play?

In this essay, we explore collaboration as both a feminist principle and a feminist practice. It empowers women who might otherwise remain isolated, silent, and fearful. In a social system that encourages female passivity, it brings women together to change the circumstances of their lives. And yet, although collaboration facilitates women's resistance, it also reflects their socialization as people whose identities depend on relations to others. In order to convey the complex nature of feminist collaboration, we draw upon theories from a range of disciplines, explaining how and why writers work together. We also explore our own experiences as collaborators and describe how they have transformed the way we think, write, and teach—both together and apart.

Meetings

Our own collaboration began in the most ordinary way. At Brown University, where we were graduate students in English in the mid-1980s, we came to exchange ideas, encourage each other, and share our anxieties about writing projects. We used to meet over lunch or late afternoon coffee at the appropriately named Meeting Street Cafe in Providence, where we commiserated, reassured each other, and applauded our individual achievements. We also worked together on a scholarly journal published at Brown. These two collegial interactions—first, reading and responding to each other's work; second, carrying out discrete but complementary editorial tasks related to literary criticism and theory—helped to lay the groundwork for our future partnership. Many such shared enterprises begin in graduate school. Carol Christ and Judith Plaskow, for example, also started collaborating as graduate students, meeting at "a local hangout" near Yale. These friendly exchanges later led to their two coedited books on feminist theology. They write of that important, early mutual encouragement: "when no one else supported us, we supported each other" (*Womanspirit* x). At a 1991 Modern Language Association panel on "Feminist Collaboration," a group of Ph.D. students from the University of California, Davis, discussed the ways they helped each other survive graduate school. Indeed, women may become interested in collaboration at this stage in their careers because they find that the academy discourages feminist perspectives.

As our own sessions at the Meeting Street Cafe became a regular habit, we grew more familiar with one another's research and more eager to share our ideas. Conversations about Edith Wharton (one of Carol's interests) and narrative theory (one of Beth's) led us to coauthor an essay on one of Wharton's ghost stories. Although we were only vaguely aware of it at the time, by agreeing to write that essay together, we made an important transition from independent, sympathetic readers to writers who are mutually and equally involved in the creative process. Our essay led us to cochair a special session at the 1989 Modern Language Association Convention and later to coedit a book of essays entitled *Anxious Power: Reading, Writing, and Ambivalence in Narrative by Women*.

Our argument in that first essay became the basis for our subsequent work. Wharton's story "Pomegranate Seed" is about a woman who gradually gains the courage to appropriate a letter addressed to her husband. (The letter, it turns out, is written by the ghost of his first wife.) Our analysis of Wharton's story led us to theorize about women's relationship to the power of language. We coined the term *anxious power* to describe both the heroine's desire to read the letter and her fear of the consequences of appropriating it—and to illuminate women's ambivalent relationship to language in general.

Reading Wharton's story helped us to acknowledge the anxieties that we brought to our individual writing tasks and to share them with each other. The notion of anxious power thus was inspired by our own writing experiences, making our subject both personally and professionally meaningful. Indeed, this dual relevance may be the mark of feminist enterprise. The concept of anxious power, which we developed in our book of essays, eventually led to our theory of feminist collaboration.

Anxious Power

The term *anxious power* describes both the ambivalence women feel about claiming their rights to language and the ways in which they express this ambivalence through their work. Language empowers; indeed, mere public identification as a writer confers status and advantage. (It is no accident, after all, that the words *author* and *authority* share a common root.) However, throughout history, women have been discouraged from expressing themselves in written discourse. When a woman does dare to "pluck for herself the strange bright fruits of art and knowledge," in Virginia Woolf's phrase (204), she may be reviled by others or judge herself as either coldly masculine or uncontrollably hysterical. For many women, then, writing and reading are anxious as well as empowering acts.

In *Anxious Power,* we explore the narrative strategies that female writers employ to express their ambivalence toward language. Such strategies include disguised narrative authority, what our contributor Christine Laennec calls "writing-without-having written" (35); and dialogic or interrupted narration, what Patricia Hannon calls "writing by addition" (74). Female authors also tend to use mixed genres and modes of discourse; narrative codes, secrets, and subtexts; and ambiguous, multivalent endings. They often include self-reflexive accounts of composing, publishing, reading, or dismembering a feminine text—especially embedded texts that are both legible and illegible, such as the "yellow wallpaper" in Charlotte Perkins Gilman's story. Our book traces these narrative strategies in order to define a distinctly female narrative tradition—from Christine de Pizan in the fourteenth century and Mary Sidney in the sixteenth, to Margaret Atwood, Toni Morrison, Maxine Hong Kingston, and Sandra Cisneros today. This tradition shows that women have consistently used multiple voices and choices to resolve their anxiety about writing.

Anxious Power focuses on the solutions that women writing alone devise to circumvent their anxiety about language. As we worked together on the book, however, we realized that we were resolving our own anxiety about reading and writing in a slightly different way: through our collaboration. Like the female writers we examined, we found multiplicity, dialogue, and doubleness to be successful strategies. But instead of one writer speaking in multiple voices, we were two writers integrating our different voices into one. Even as we completed *Anxious Power*, then, our own collaborative writing practice forced us to think again about how women relate to language.

Theories

We began searching for a theory that would make sense of our experiences working together. In particular, we sought a theoretical model of collaboration that challenges traditional notions of learning as individually acquired or owned and that offers alternatives to hierarchical figurations of knowledge. We did not discover one specific theory that explains the nature of feminist scholarly collaboration. Instead, we found a range of theories from different disciplines that helped us to integrate our analysis of anxious power with our collaborative practice. Our theory of collaboration develops from several fields: from rhetoric and composition (especially theories of the writing process and audience); from poststructuralist and narrative theory (especially theories of authorship and voice); from feminist theory (especially studies of epistemology, or "women's ways of knowing," to quote Mary Belenky and her collaborators); and from our own research on women's relationship to language. Appropriately, then, our theory of collaboration is itself drawn from a wide range of disciplines.

Recent research in rhetoric and composition has radically altered how scholars understand the writing process. The traditional image of the writer is a lonely, alienated—even mad—individual, who toils away in an isolated garret with pen in hand or fingers poised over a keyboard. That labor mysteriously, even magically, produces a finished, definitive document. Our own experiences with collaboration lead us to question the concepts both of the solitary writer and of writing as a discrete task aimed only at a final product. Patricia Sullivan identifies these concepts with the Western "myth of the independent scholar . . . which, from the time of the Enlightenment, has located knowledge in the individual" and identified intellectual activity as masculine (12). In contrast to these Enlightenment and Romantic notions, we agree with composition theorists that writing is a process—a function and outgrowth of learning itself. In particular, we follow Kenneth Bruffee's and Linda Brodkey's idea that writing is a social act. Writers learn in relation and conversation with themselves and others. They *need* others' feedback to clarify, test, validate, and extend their ideas. Indeed, it is difficult to write at all without a clear sense of audience.

Poststructuralist theory also provides us with an important theoretical base because it challenges traditional constructions of knowledge and language. We have found Mikhail Bakhtin's theory of dialogics useful for understanding our own nonhierarchical relationship to writing. Bakhtin writes cogently about multivalent voices in literary texts, particularly novels. He calls these interacting voices "play," emphasizing that textual authority is shared rather than centralized. According to Bakhtin, ideas are not universal truths but mental constructs, figments of the conceptual realm. Language is related to its surroundings rather than distinct from them. Bakhtin encourages us, then, to view language not as a universal window on fixed reality, but as a partial and relative system in relation with other languages. This linguistic multiplicity—what Bakhtin calls "heteroglossia"—complicates our notion of individual identity (263). If one's voice exists only in dialogue with other voices, then it is impossible to conceive of the self except in relation to others. And yet, at the same time, these multiple discourses paradoxically preserve the notion of distinct perspectives. Bakhtin's ideas, disconcerting if we consider writing a solitary activity, provide an ideal basis for describing collaborative authorship.

Feminist theorists working in a variety of fields—education, history, radical feminism, psychology, literature—have independently developed a theory of epistemology that resembles both Bruffee's and Brodkey's theory of learning as a social act and Bakhtin's notion of dialogics. A group of educators (Mary Belenky, Blithe Clinchy, Nancy Goldberger, and Jill Tarule) argue in their own collaborative work that "women's ways of knowing" stress relational thinking, socially constructed knowledge, and shared stories and experiences.

Other feminist thinkers explain the close connections among women that may lead to collaborative thinking and writing. Historian Carroll Smith-Rosenberg traces the importance of intimate friendships among women—what she calls "the female world of love and ritual"—in nineteenth-century America. Poet and critic Adrienne Rich discusses the "lesbian continuum" of women's relationships with each other ("Compulsory"). Several psychologists, such as Jean Baker Miller and Nancy Chodorow, explain that female identity is usually based on affiliation with others. Carol Gilligan suggests, more specifically, that women develop an "ethics of care" as opposed to a male "ethics of justice." Women's moral decisions, Gilligan says, always occur in a social context and stress the effect of these decisions on others.

Inevitably, these female "ways of knowing" affect the way women write. Many feminist literary theorists, such as Helene Cixous and Luce Irigaray, argue that women's writing tends to be fluid, shape shifting, multivalent, and polyphonal, emphasizing the parts in relation to the whole. In "When Our Lips Speak Together," for example, Irigaray writes: "It's our good fortune that your language isn't formed of a single thread, a single strand or period. It comes from everywhere at once. You touch me all over at the same time. In all senses. Why only one song, one speech, one text at a time?" (209). Irigaray's description of *ecriture feminine* suggests a collaborative writing practice. Indeed, even as Irigaray makes this argument, she invites the reader—addressed in the second person—to collaborate with her.

Cixous's and Irigaray's accounts of *ecriture feminine* accord with our own analysis of female narrative strategies in *Anxious Power*. Along with the assertions that learning occurs in a social context and that texts comprise many voices, these theories of women's ways of knowing—and writing—demonstrate why feminist collaboration is a logical and productive solution to women's anxiety about authorship.

Practices

We have often been asked what it is like to collaborate with each other. We have been barraged with questions such as, "Who *really* wrote this?" At least one of our readers has gone away puzzled because she could not decipher which of us had written which parts of an essay. (In fact, we revise together so extensively that we can't tell either.) Other colleagues have asked incredulously, "Don't you disagree?" or "Isn't it frustrating to have everything you do checked by another person? (Yes, and no.) Some of these queries are merely curious; others are skeptical—as if there is something suspicious, even traitorous, in our collaboration. In trying to answer such questions, we have come to realize that our work together is a process that we ourselves understand well but cannot easily articulate to others. Although theoretical accounts from various disciplines have helped us to explain our practice, none has addressed the delicate negotiations that feminist collaboration demands, or captured its profound, subtle delights.

Collaboration allows us to elaborate our ideas, liberate ourselves, and turn our labor into pleasure. It integrates the intellectual, emotional, and social aspects of our lives. The work seems to get done easily when we think of it as "I have to do my Beth stuff now" or "I need to make a Carol call." At times it seems to complete itself, as if by magic—like the fairy tale about the shoemaker who wakes, each morning, to find that two elves have stitched together the separate parts of shoes that he laid out the night before. How can we convey the excitement of a shared idea that one person originates but that, once developed, belongs to both? Or the moment when our interaction generates an energy that neither of us provides alone? Or the almost guilty feeling that we are accomplishing so much while having so much fun?

The closest we can come to describing the tenor, technique, and style of our work together is "conversation"—derived from "converse," which means "to talk," "to associate with," and "to change position." Conversation, then, suggests a "turning together." (Since we wrote this essay, other collaborators—Joyce Elbrecht and Lydia Fakundiny [247] and Susan Leonardi and Rebecca Pope [262]—have also used this metaphor to describe their partnership.) A true dialogue, as Brazilian educator and theorist Paulo Freire points out, is "an act of creation" in which neither party is "reduced" or oppressed by the other (70). As writers collaborating through conversation, we seek agreement on every point. Instead of a relationship in which one dominates and the other yields, we seek what Jessica Benjamin calls the paradoxical "mutual recognition" of subjects (12).

Conversation figures in collaboration in two ways: as dialogue leading to writing and as writing itself. Because talking together is so important to coauthorship—especially when it is long distance—we need to clarify how we orally communicate in order to analyze how we write together. We find that we often wait for and ask for the other's response; repeat what the other just said so that she can further develop her thinking; interrupt each other with humorous asides and words of encouragement; and finish each other's sentences. Our collaboration often occurs on the telephone, in half-hour sessions stolen from other responsibilities. We might talk during Beth's office hours or right before Carol's yoga class. In a typical phone call, we might discuss the strides Carol's toddler is making, the papers each of us is preparing for an upcoming conference, Beth's grieving process as she mourns her mother's death, and a good strategy for teaching *The House of Mirth*—as well as our current project.

As we reflect on these effortlessly productive telephone calls, we find that our practice resembles both female conversational strategies and conversational modes characteristic of the collaborative writing process. Jennifer Coates argues, for example, that women's speech is based on cooperation and men's on competition. Although such cooperation often connotes tentativeness or powerlessness, Coates points out that specific features of women's interactions promote dialogue and friendship. Women develop topics gradually and progressively, building on one another's contributions; they use more minimal responses than men do, in order to indicate active attention toward the speaker; they speak simultaneously more than men do, as a way "to produce shared meanings"; and they use epistemic modal forms (such as "perhaps," "I think," or "probably") to encourage mutual participation and negotiate sensitive topics (119–20). Our conversation produces not only shared meanings but jointly authored texts. William Van Pelt and Alice Gillam identify four kinds of conversation in collaborative composition: procedural talk, substantive talk, talk about the writing process, and social talk. We find that we engage in all four modes, shifting easily and instinctively from one to the other. We now conceive of the writer not as an isolated figure in a garret but as two people—each holding a telephone receiver to her ear.

Conversation is also a useful analogy for the actual writing that some collaborators produce. Lisa Ede and Andrea Lunsford distinguish between hierarchical and dialogic collaborative discourse; Laura Brady adds to these contrasting modes the "conversational" one. The hierarchical mode is "linearly structured, driven by highly specific goals, and carried out by people who play clearly assigned roles" (Ede and Lunsford 133). In this mode, differences in voice and authorship are problems to be solved. The dialogic mode is more flexible and fluid; individuals shift roles as the project progresses but still maintain distinct voices. In the conversational mode, on the other hand, authors discuss and reach consensus on every point, and their distinct voices merge seamlessly into one. Michael Dorris and Louise Erdrich's 1991 novel, *The Crown of Columbus*—which is itself a story about shared intellectual discovery—is a good example. So is Sandra Gilbert and Susan Gubar's critical study, *The Madwoman in the Attic.* Such collaboration, as Linda Hutcheon says of her work with her husband Michael Hutcheon, is "polyphonic" and interdisciplinary but leads to a "monovocal synthesis."

The essays, talks, and reviews that we write together are also in the conversational mode, with a shared authority and single voice. We are aware, however, that achieving such consensus through conversation—and in the conversational mode—requires a series of small, delicate, mutually satisfactory negotiations. For example, when we first started working on this chapter, we took turns articulating our ideas. At that early point, each of us thought of her ideas as her own, and we each felt anxious that they would be included. But as soon as one of us responded to the other, her idea—now enhanced, critiqued, and clarified—became *our* idea.

The issues we find ourselves negotiating most frequently are our diverse senses of organization, our distinct prose styles, and our contrary tastes in punctuation. We often approach a given writing task differently. To prepare a conference presentation, for example, Beth outlined the entire talk and Carol wrote the entire text for half of it. We turned the potential awkwardness of our different strategies into complementarity: we retained Beth's outline and integrated Carol's material into it. We also have to negotiate specific points of style. Beth tends to revise at the sentence level, Carol at the level of logic and paragraphing. Beth tends to use lots of commas, dashes, and complicated sentences involving "which." Carol prefers fewer commas, more direct sentences, and participial phrases. Although we once spent valuable telephone time arguing over where commas belong, we now routinely take turns having our own way in individual cases. We are not alone with our differences. Gilbert and Gubar have "horrible" disputes about the use of "moreover" and "however." Gubar remarks, "One person very much likes to sprinkle transitionary words, and the other person likes to take them out. There are a lot of disagreements, but usually we feel that they go somewhere, they make the prose more interesting" (Interview 60).

Composing so intimately with another person has taught each of us a great deal about the writing process. Negotiating our disagreements has made our prose "more interesting," too, and more flexible—so much so that in our individual writing projects, Carol now sometimes composes a "Beth sentence" and Beth may use participial phrases a la Carol. We have also internalized this negotiation to such an extent that we switch back and forth easily between the roles of dictator and recorder. When one of us comes up with a good idea or an effectively worded phrase, the other instinctively writes it down. We discover or invent meaning in the process of negotiating.

Divergences

So far we have described the collaborative process as if it involves relatively little conflict. That is not the case. Indeed, conflict is an important, volatile, but often ignored issue in feminist interaction in general. Collaborators must face differences in moods, methods, schedules, and energies. They must struggle to withstand cultural biases against shared labor. In the academy, for example, they may find that chairs, deans, and tenure committees look askance at collaboration, assuming an unequal division of labor, and that grants are difficult to obtain for joint writing projects.

Collaborators may also find that assumptions about women and competition—which many women internalize—make feminist collaboration even more difficult. As Adrienne Rich puts it:

> "Women have always lied to each other."
> "Women have always been in secret collusion."
> Both of these axioms are true. ("Women" 189)

One viewpoint holds that women cannot work together because they will bicker and betray each other; another assumes that they always agree. (A cultural feminist version of this prejudice is that women are naturally cooperative and should seek harmony at all costs.) And yet both of these essentialist notions—that women cannot get along and that they remain in solidarity—belie the fact that many women have worked together throughout history. These prejudices ignore women's actual differences as well as their ability to overcome them. Indeed, they say more about a hostile patriarchal climate than about women.

Such a climate persists despite everything that feminism has achieved to this point. Carey Kaplan and Ellen Cronan Rose, who trace the impetus for their work together to their participation in second-wave feminism, wonder how younger women can collaborate "in a professional environment where competition with women seems inevitable." They speculate that now that more women have entered the academy, "sisterhood gives way to sibling rivalry" (554–55). Similarly, Florence Howe cautions women against claiming to be the only true feminists and allowing competition for male approval to divide them. Certainly many feminists not only acknowledge differences among women in the academy but suggest that perhaps they cannot be resolved. Helena Michie, for example, coins the term *sororophobia* to describe the ambivalence, even hostility, that women may feel toward their literal and figurative sisters.

Although competition and conflict are a part of any collaborative interaction, in our own work together we see differences as complementary rather than divisive. This is partly because collaborating in the conversational mode itself mediates difference. But it is also because, like other feminist collaborators, we choose to emphasize our common interests as a deliberate feminist strategy. Kaplan and Rose, who learned feminism in consciousness-raising groups in the 1970s, still believe that "sisterhood is powerful, the personal is political, women do not trash women. . . . There are between us tensions, bifurcations, complexities, and ambivalences that we choose to ignore or elide for the purposes of our work and because of our profound, admittedly idealistic, personally transformative political beliefs" (552–53). And Christ and Plaskow write in the preface to their first anthology that "we have been able to move in different directions in our current thinking, while maintaining respect for each other's work" (*Womanspirit* xi). Ten years later, in their second preface, they report marked "differences" in their interests that "tested our abilities to communicate with and hear each other"; they also affirm, however, that these struggles with anger, jealousy, and rivalry strengthened their friendship and their commitment to feminism and taught them the importance of their differences (*Weaving* v). While women's socialization may be conducive to collaboration, it is important for feminists to acknowledge women's various experiences and to respect the divergent feelings and opinions they produce.

Partners

Because feminist collaboration seeks to mediate difference, it is tempting to assume that any pair of feminists would be good collaborators. But mere identification as a feminist, or sympathy with feminist causes, does not alone make for a compatible partner. We have not always found it easy to duplicate our collaboration in projects with other colleagues (editing, writing, or team teaching), or within the classroom (group discussions or collaborative writing assignments). We have both had experiences in which another party failed to meet deadlines, did not do her share of the work, insisted on her own approach, did not know how to negotiate—or was not pleasurable to work with even though the work did get done. Indeed, the sense of shared enterprise, almost by definition, cannot be easily extended to others.

For this reason, it is difficult adequately to describe our collaborative process to anyone else. Other collaborators, facing this same dilemma, have proposed various models to describe the elusive process of coauthorship. Kaplan and Rose, for example, describe their work in terms of lesbian erotics or jazz improvisation (550); Elbrecht and Fakundiny characterize their collaboration as an *extension* of oneself to the other, the forming of a "fictive self... that is neither one of us" (249, 254); and Leonardi and Pope engage a variety of metaphors for their joint authorship: "mosaic," "quilt," "part-singing," "stew," and erotic "'intercourse'" (262, 266, 269, 267).

Our own collaboration is a bond that resembles simultaneously a romance, a sibling relationship, and a business partnership. It is a marriage of true minds that not only admits impediments but is created in the process of resolving them. Rather than losing our distinctive voices, denying our selves, or "giving in," we have found that collaboration strengthens our sense of identity as individuals—and as partners. Our collaboration is an alternative to the solitary female writer's anxious struggle over language, and a strategy that helps us succeed in a competitive environment. In an academy plagued by extraordinary pressures to publish, such feminist collaboration helps women who are anxious about claiming authority to achieve it.

Like many of our feminist sisters, we combine our energies to accomplish common goals and are transformed in the process. Each of us becomes part of a "we" that cannot exist outside ourselves. Indeed, we were amused when a would-be contributor to our book, unconsciously acknowledging our interrelation, sent us a letter addressed to "Professor Swingley." This sense of intimacy, complicity, even exclusivity, is the real secret of our feminist collaboration. We are colleagues, we are in league with each other, and we are in a league of our own—all at once.

REFERENCES

Bakhtin, Mikhail M. *The Dialogic Imagination: Four Essays*. Trans. Caryl Emerson and Michael Holquist. Ed. Michael Holquist. Austin: University of Texas Press, 1981.

Belenky, Mary Field, et al. *Women's Ways of Knowing: The Development of Self, Voice, and Mind*. New York: Basic, 1986.

Benjamin, Jessica. *The Bonds of Love: Psychoanalysis, Feminism, and the Problem of Domination*. New York: Pantheon, 1988.

Brady, Laura. "Cases of Literary Collaboration." Midwest Modern Language Association Convention. Chicago. November 1991.

Brodkey, Linda. *Academic Writing as Social Practice*. Philadelphia: Temple University Press, 1987.

Bruffee, Kenneth A. "The Brooklyn Plan: Attaining Intellectual Growth through Peer-Group Tutoring." *Liberal Education* 64 (Dec. 1978): 447–69.

———. "Collaborative Learning and the 'Conversation of Mankind.'" *College English* 46 (1984): 635–52.

———. "Social Construction, Language, and the Authority of Knowledge: A Bibliographical Essay." *College English* 48 (1986): 773–90.

Chodorow, Nancy. *The Reproduction of Mothering: Psychoanalysis and the Sociology of Gender.* Berkeley: University of California Press, 1978.

Christ, Carol P., and Judith Plaskow, eds. *Weaving the Visions: New Patterns in Feminist Spirituality.* San Francisco: Harper, 1989.

———. *Womanspirit Rising: A Feminist Reader in Religion.* San Francisco: Harper, 1979.

Cixous, Helene. "The Laugh of the Medusa." Trans. Keith Cohen and Paula Cohen. *New French Feminisms.* Ed. Elaine Marks and Isabelle de Courtivron. Amherst: University of Massachusetts Press, 1980. 245–64.

Coates, Jennifer. "Gossip Revisited: Language in All-Female Groups." *Women in Their Speech Communities.* Ed. Jennifer Coates and Deborah Cameron. New York: Longman, 1988. 94–122.

Delbanco, Nicholas. *Group Portrait: Joseph Conrad, Stephen Crane, Ford Madox Ford, Henry James, and H. G. Wells.* New York: Morrow, 1982.

Dorris, Michael, and Louise Erdrich. *The Crown of Columbus.* New York: HarperCollins, 1991.

Ede, Lisa, and Andrea Lunsford. *Singular Texts/Plural Authors: Perspectives on Collaborative Writing.* Carbondale: Southern Illinois University Press, 1990.

Elbrecht, Joyce, and Lydia Fakundiny. "Scenes from a Collaboration: or Becoming Jael B. Juba." *Tulsa Studies in Women's Literature* 13.2 (1994): 241–58.

Freire, Paulo. *Pedagogy of the Oppressed.* Trans. Myra B. Ramos. New York: Continuum, 1970.

Gilbert, Sandra, and Susan F. Gubar. Interview by Laura Shapiro. *Ms.* Jan. 1986: 59+.

———. *The Madwoman in the Attic: The Woman Writer and the Nineteenth-Century Literary Imagination.* New Haven, CT: Yale University Press, 1979.

Gilligan, Carol. *In a Different Voice: Psychological Theory and Women's Development.* Cambridge: Harvard University Press, 1982.

Hannon, Patricia. "A Politics of Disguise: Marie-Catherine d'Aulnoy's 'Belle-Etoile' and the Narrative Structure of Ambivalence." Singley and Sweeney 73–89.

Howe, Florence. "Feminist Criticism Revisited: Where Are We Going? Where Have We Been?" Modern Language Association Convention. San Diego. 29 Dec. 1994.

Hutcheon, Linda, and Michael Hutcheon. "Marital Methodologies or Heterosexual Habits." Modern Language Association Convention. San Diego. 28 Dec. 1994.

Irigaray, Luce. "When Our Lips Speak Together." *This Sex Which Is Not One*. Trans. Catherine Porter. Ithaca, NY: Cornell University Press, 1985. 205–18.

Kaplan, Carey, and Ellen Cronan Rose. "Strange Bedfellows: Feminist Collaboration." *Signs: Journal of Women in Culture and Society* 18.3 (1993): 547–61.

Koestenbaum, Wayne. "The Waste Land: T. S. Eliot's and Ezra Pound's Collaboration on Hysteria." *Twentieth-Century Literature* 34.2 (1988): 113–39.

Laennec, Christine Moneera. "Christine *Antygrafe:* Authorial Ambivalence in the Works of Christine de Pizan." Singley and Sweeney 35–49.

Leonardi, Susan J., and Rebecca A. Pope. "Screaming Divas: Collaboration as Feminist Practice." *Tulsa Studies in Women's Literature* 13.2 (1994): 259–70.

Michie, Helena. *Sororophobia: Differences among Women in Literature and Culture*. New York: Oxford University Press, 1992.

Miller, Jean Baker. *Toward a New Psychology of Women*. Boston: Beacon, 1976.

"On Feminist Collaboration: How Do We Work Together on Books, Articles and Activism?" Modern Language Association Convention. San Francisco. 27 Dec. 1991.

Rich, Adrienne. "Compulsory Heterosexuality and Lesbian Existence." *Signs* 5.4 (1980): 631–60.

———. "Women and Honor: Some Notes on Lying." *On Lies, Secrets, and Silence: Selected Prose, 1966–1978*. New York: Norton, 1979. 185–94.

Seymour, Miranda. *A Ring of Conspirators: Henry James and His Literary Circle, 1895–1915*. Boston: Houghton Mifflin, 1988.

Singley, Carol J., and Susan Elizabeth Sweeney, eds. *Anxious Power: Reading, Writing, and Ambivalence in Narrative by Women*. Albany: State University of New York Press, 1993.

Smith-Rosenberg, Carroll. "The Female World of Love and Ritual: Relations between Women in Nineteenth-Century America." *Signs* 1.1 (1975): 1–30.

Stillinger, Jack. *Multiple Authorship and the Myth of Solitary Genius*. New York: Oxford University Press, 1991.

Sullivan, Patricia A. "Revising the Myth of the Independent Scholar." *Writing With*. Ed. David Bleich, Thomas Fox, and Sally Reagan. Albany: State University of New York Press, 1994. 11–29.

Trimbur, John. "Consensus and Difference in Collaborative Learning." *College English* 51 (1989): 602–16.

Van Pelt, William, and Alice Gillam. "Peer Collaboration and the Computer-Assisted Classroom: Bridging the Gap between Academia and the

Workplace." *Collaborative Writing in Industry: Investigations in Theory and Practice.* Ed. Mary M. Lay and William M. Karis. Amityville, NY: Baywood, 1991. 170–215.

Woolf, Virginia. "George Eliot." *Collected Essays.* Vol. 1. London: Hogarth, 1966. 196–204.

Helen Cafferty and Jeanette Clausen

5

What's Feminist about It?

Reflections on Collaboration in Editing and Writing

As we discussed how to write an article on this topic, one of our first thoughts was: *We've done feminist collaboration so often, we must know something about it.* In shaping that knowledge into an article, we chose to focus on our own evolution as collaborators in editing and writing because we believe our story brings into relief the many contradictions inherent in feminist collaboration within the academy. As far as we know, our attempt in the late eighties to coedit a juried academic journal as a feminist project incorporating feminist process was unique at the time. Placing our story, with its successes and failures, in a larger context of what others have written about collaboration has enabled us to view our own collaborative work more critically as we attempted to define what is feminist about it.

From the less than abundant literature about feminist collaboration, we learned that others are not sure what is feminist about it either. We believe that the question raised by Carey Kaplan and Ellen Cronan Rose—"Can there be a coherent theory of feminist collaboration?" ("Strange Bedfellows" 559)—will most likely be answered in the negative, for it seems self-evident to us that every collaboration, feminist or not, is uniquely shaped by the personal views and experiences of the participants and will differ in some ways from every other collaboration. At the same time, we assume it is possible to identify a range of qualities that characterize feminist collaboration, and that awareness of those qualities can play a crucial role in the feminist project of changing the academy.

Comparing our story with Kaplan and Rose's description of their collaborative work helped us see how we might build on our own experiences and insights as feminist academics to suggest a working definition of feminist collaboration. In "Collaborative Writing, Consciousness Raising, and Practical Feminist Ethics," students Angela Karach and Denise Roach describe their collaborative studying and writing as "a crucial learning and survival tactic" (308). Their passionate commitment to collaboration as solidarity and resistance within the patriarchal British university system confirmed our own sense of the potential of collaborative work to contribute to a feminist transformation of the academy.

Other sources suggested relevant analytical categories. Susan J. Leonardi and Rebecca A. Pope, in "Screaming Divas: Collaboration as Feminist Practice," provide an apt formulation of one of the challenges we grappled with in trying to define how our collaboration was/is feminist: "What we need to capture is what happens beyond the divisions of labor in collaboration—the process of negotiation, supplementation, and questioning interchange that goes into creating the product in the first place" (264). A useful vocabulary for capturing that process came from Lydia Plowman's article "Tracing the Evolution of a Co-Authored Text." Her categories for analyzing the importance of talk in coproducing a written document helped us see our own dialogues in a new light. Most helpful of all was Lisa Ede and Andrea Lunsford's *Singular Texts/Plural Authors*, in our view the best study of collaborative writing to date.[1] This book gave us the literature review, interdisciplinary grid, and theoretical framework we needed for situating our experiences as coeditors and coauthors in the context of various modes of collaborative writing.

Ede and Lunsford cite features of collaborative writing, distilled by Allen et al. from descriptions by experienced collaborators, that are broad enough to apply to both writing and editing: "(1) production of a shared document; (2) substantive interaction among members; and (3) shared decision-making power over and responsibility for the document" (15). Because every collaboration entails the construction of a relationship ("substantive interaction among members") that decisively shapes the progress and final accomplishment of the task, we can assume that the quality of the relationship will affect whether and according to what model decision-making and responsibility are shared; we also assume that the finished document will be affected by those decisions, though not necessarily in transparent ways. Perhaps less obviously, the goal of the collaboration will affect its form as well, for the desired outcome implies at least tacit acceptance of certain priorities, if not explicit agreement on a set of principles.

Our own collaborative work as coeditors of a journal was largely shaped by our understanding of the feminist context in which our project was situated. Initially, this meant that we attempted to conform our journal-editing practices to the feminist principles espoused by the sponsoring organization, Women in German (WIG). As long-time members of WIG, both of us had direct knowledge of those principles, based on our participation in the annual WIG conferences and at the association's business meetings; nevertheless, transforming our understanding of those principles into editorial policies and practices often forced us to confront uncomfortable choices. Looking back, we have come to see a crucial relationship existing between the feminist nature of the project and the kind of relationship created between the collaborators, that is, between the final product and the process. Thus, again in response to Kaplan and Rose, who wonder whether their own collaboration is "extraordinary, an accidental act of grace" (557), we believe that feminist collaboration does not "just happen," but is constructed with varying success through conscious and unconscious choices affirming the feminist politics of inclusion, power sharing, egalitarianism, consensus, and trust in the context of shared feminist commitments.

Coediting as Feminist Collaborators

The two of us did not know each other especially well, nor had we previously collaborated on a project, before agreeing to serve as coeditors of the WIG Yearbook for a three-year term. One of us had prior experience as coeditor (of one issue!) of the Yearbook; however, the journal was then still in its infancy; only four issues had appeared. There had never been an editorial board, so we did not inherit a long tradition of editorial policy. Rather, we faced the task of defining policies appropriate to the journal of a feminist association, WIG, that had been committed since its inception to collaborative work, and to egalitarianism, and consensus in its decision making, in the distribution of responsibility for organizing and presenting at conferences, and in producing its other publication, a quarterly newsletter.

Unlike other professional organizations dominated by the most senior members or star scholars, WIG's founding was embedded in the women's movement.[2] WIG's professionally established or well-published members problematized authority and their own status from the beginning. For example, more experienced, senior members have always been paired with graduate students or less experienced members as panel organizers or project contributors. Students just beginning their careers, women struggling to reenter the profession, and those teaching in high schools or at smaller postsecondary institutions where heavy teaching loads make the maintaining of an active research program very difficult have been encouraged to try their professional wings. WIG has had political goals from the outset: to open the profession to women by actively opposing discrimination, to overcome isolation and alienation, to help women find a voice and increase their influence, and to transform German studies. Of course, WIG has not always lived up to the utopian goals it set itself. The organization has experienced its own struggles and crises, some brought about by its successes, and it has evolved through the years to reflect the theoretical shifts and the changing role of feminist work within the academy. Nevertheless, some constants remain: WIG attempts to accommodate many different feminisms without glossing over the differences and tensions between them. The goal has always been to learn from and support each other, even in disagreement and contradiction, in a spirit of feminist solidarity and trust.

We began defining our editorial project by articulating our shared assumptions about the feminist principles of WIG and agreed that the journal should reflect these principles. This meant not only that the articles should be feminist but also that the process of editing the journal should reflect WIG's commitment to the politics of inclusion and egalitarianism. We saw our feminist academic project as having an acknowledged political dimension—that it should lead to positive change on behalf of women. In its challenge to traditional literary criticism, feminist academic writing would both open the German literary canon to analysis and correction and would contribute to the feminist education of our readers, many of whom were teachers of the next generation. We were also dedicated to WIG's avowed goal of advancing women in the profession. We aimed to produce a journal for the publication of theoretically defensible, substantive, well-written articles that would help authors get jobs or build successful tenure and promotion cases. How could we design criteria for the selection of articles and a process for editing them that would fulfill these various goals?

As we grappled with these larger questions of policy, we also faced the practical matter of how we would work together. For example, we had to decide how we wanted to present our own collaborative relationship. Because one of us had prior experience with the journal and would be teaching the other "the ropes," and because she had been and continued to be responsible for the more onerous tasks of communicating with the publisher, we decided to indicate her status by listing her name first on the first issue we produced and then to return in subsequent volumes to the convention of alphabetical order. We agreed, however, that for our coauthored editorial statements we would use alphabetical order. At the time we were not fully aware of the ambiguities involved. (Does the alphabetical order reflect a junior-senior or an equal authorship? Does a truly collaborative relationship allow for junior-senior status?) Our earnest attempts to negotiate our relationship fairly from the outset were thwarted, however: The publisher failed to follow our directive to change the order of the names on the subsequent volume, and the ambiguity of alphabetical order remains to this day in our collaboratively written pieces. While we eventually chose to ignore this problem in favor of the pleasure we take in collaboration and our growing appreciation of collaborative work as feminist practice, we would obviously welcome a convention that signaled the equality we feel characterizes our work.

Creating a collaborative relationship was complicated by the challenge we share with many other long-distance collaborators. Living half a continent apart, with no e-mail (much less widely available then) and only inconvenient access to fax machines, we did most of our work over the phone. In retrospect, we have come to understand more fully the role conversation played in shaping our project. We discussed in numerous and lengthy phone conversations many aspects of our personal lives as well as our editorial work. We were in some sense aware that our "off-task" talking, to use

Plowman's term, was important for establishing a basis for mutual trust. But at the time, we were not familiar with theories of collaborative writing or of collaboration generally, and it would not have occurred to us to apply to our conversations categories such as those developed by Plowman to analyze a group writing project. We find her analysis useful in formulating a working definition of feminist collaboration because of its emphasis on "talk" as process. Her categories of talk are: *"procedural* (deciding appropriate approaches for content and allocation of roles); *substantive* (asking questions and offering explanations concerned with the subject domain); *executive* (talk concerned with the writing process and style); and *group* (building group identity, jokes, off-task)." As Plowman observes, allocating statements to one category or the other is problematic because "the social and cognitive dimensions of collaborative writing are inextricably linked" (152). Although her focus is on collaborative writing, we find her discussion of the inseparability of social and cognitive dimensions to apply to collaborative editing as well: The quality of the cognitive dimensions of our collaborative work and the resulting product—our own evaluation of manuscripts, our interpretation and evaluation of referees' reports, our formulation of recommendations to authors—was directly related to the quality of the social dimension of our relationship.

To illustrate, let us look more closely at the stages of our editing process. The basic task was, of course, for the two of us to reach some kind of agreement on the quality of the articles submitted to the journal. To do this, we first had to set a date by which each of us would have read a given manuscript and be ready to discuss it over the telephone (procedural talk); in the process of making these arrangements, however, at this point we usually also talked about whether either or both of us knew a good deal, a modest amount, or not much about the topic of the article we were about to read (substantive talk). The next step, actually discussing an article, often involved some recapitulation or even expansion of how much expertise we had on the topic as well as evaluative comments about the article (substantive talk), and discussion of potential referees, to two of whom we would send the article (procedural and substantive). These steps—reading and planning to talk, then talking—were repeated after the readers' evaluations of the articles had been received, often in stages: first, upon receiving the readers' reports, we would discuss them with each other and decide how to reconcile (or not reconcile) disagreements we had with either or both of the evaluators, and sometimes with each other; second, we would discuss whether to recommend minor changes, extensive revisions, or resubmission after major revisions (rejection was a category we rarely used), and how to communicate the readers' (and our) evaluations and recommendations to the author. These stages of (primarily) substantive talk were usually interspersed with procedural talk (e.g., deciding who would draft the letter to the author), group talk (e.g., talking about our personal experiences of receiving criticism from journal editors, or about our respective work loads and other commitments that affected our ability to accept responsibility for a specific task), and executive talk, related to the tone and style of the author's contributions as well as our own letter. Next, a letter would be drafted by one of us, discussed over the phone and revised, and, finally sent to the author.

At this point, our readers may be wondering what's feminist about all this talk and communication. Wasn't it just the self-indulgent postponement of action so dear to the hearts of process junkies? While we agree that there was inefficiency, our labor-intensive process was our method of working collaboratively in a feminist way by reaching consensus as opposed to making compromises or coming to terms by power brokering and making tradeoffs. At worst, our agreement resembled compromise; at best, and this was most of the time, it was a consensus informed thoroughly by an understanding of the feminist principles articulated by Women in German. Thus our commitment to consensus and power sharing decisively affected our interactions with each other.

Editing as Feminist Collaboration with Authors and Referees

We faced various difficulties in attempting to create policies and a *modus operandi* that would reflect the feminist principles of WIG. As described in our article "Journal Editing: Issues for Feminists," we knew that challenging the established practices of the profession ran the risk of relegating the journal to obscurity. Some of our compromises with convention also reflected the contradictions within feminism itself. For example, it seemed obvious that striving to treat all potential contributors to the journal equally would require a policy of open submissions, yet the goal of inclusiveness—the responsibility we felt to represent a range of different feminist perspectives that would adequately reflect the different needs and concerns of our diverse readership—sometimes necessitated soliciting contributions from people whose work we knew. The goal of inclusiveness also demanded a policy of choosing reviewers who were sympathetic or neutral toward the particular feminist approach used by the author.

The goals of democratic inclusiveness and advancing women in the profession were also difficult to reconcile. Although we understood that blind review could be an invitation for cavalier, hurried, or harsh dismissals of inexperienced efforts as well as a guarantee of an objective reading unbiased by knowledge of the author's other work or status, our desire to have the journal count with the profession necessitated our continuing the policy of anonymous review of manuscripts established by the previous editors. As others who have written about collaborative writing in our discipline confirm, publications not subjected to such a review process would in all likelihood be discounted at tenure and promotion time. The goal of inclusiveness also demanded a policy of choosing reviewers who were sympathetic or neutral toward the particular feminist approach used by the author. To compensate for the lack of trust and openness implied by anonymous review, and to establish a kind of second-degree power sharing, we proposed to provide "supportive criticism" to the author, that is, constructive criticism that stated positively the strengths or potential strengths of the piece; our hope was that the author would be encouraged to realize her own vision of her article.

Although we did not fully realize it at the time, we were extending the range of collaboration beyond our own relationship as coeditors to include the authors and referees as well. Our mode of extended collaboration was shaped by our goal of producing a journal that had intellectual integrity in professional terms and our commitment to guaranteeing everyone democratic treatment and respect for "where they were" as feminists. Thus, despite the contradictions involved, we consciously embraced a feminist view of this combination of traditional evaluation and feminist mentoring.

What we discovered, however, was that many members of our discourse community—mostly Women in German members who were comfortable with the efforts the organization had made in the direction of consensus and power sharing—were not nearly so comfortable with expanding the evaluation of manuscripts to include mentoring, and that expertise in feminist research and theory was not always accompanied by an understanding of or commitment to feminist process, at least in this arena. With the clarity of hindsight, we do not find this to be surprising. The referees had not, after all, had the opportunity to discuss at length the implications of our policies as we had and thus may have attached little importance to our short statements on the referee form about "constructive criticism." While many referees did express their criticisms of the manuscripts sent to them in supportive terms, others did not. In such cases, we felt an obligation to mediate and to mentor by default, as it were, by transmitting the substance of a harshly or perfunctorily expressed evaluation in more gentle terms to the author, whose work, regardless of its quality, did reflect an interest in feminism and thus merited, from our perspective, a supportive review. Indeed, we received many papers from authors who were not well versed in feminist theory and/or lacked experience in formulating feminist analysis. Rather than simply rejecting work from such authors, we sought to give them an honest evaluation, but expressed in a manner that we hoped would empower them to make the improvements *they* saw as necessary to produce a feminist article.

Our commitment to feminist process did not always lead to the productive interactions with authors that we were hoping for. While we, the editors, saw ourselves as engaged in and constructing a feminist collaboration between ourselves and the authors, they did not necessarily share that vision. Many (perhaps most) did not expect a nonhierarchical editor/author relationship, nor did they necessarily perceive as nonhierarchical our efforts to interact with them in a more egalitarian way. Authors did not always welcome our attempts to provide supportive criticism, or did not see the criticism as supportive despite our efforts to make it so. In a few cases, our good intentions led to our becoming overly directive (and too teacherly) in our role as editors/mentors—without achieving the desired results. Thus, neither our efforts to communicate with authors nor their efforts to apply to their papers our recommendations for revision were always successful. With hindsight, we see that we underestimated the difficulty of establishing a solid basis for trust with each author—for no matter how strong our commitment to an egalitarian process, we were still the editors with the authority to make decisions affecting their ability to publish. It seems likely that our very success in establishing trust between the two of us may have led us to assume that it would be easier to establish trust with authors than turned out to be the case. Our success in arriving at a consensus on most points of disagreement may have blinded us to how long and hard we had to work to reach that consensus.

Another reason for the gap between our theory and our practice is, surely, the dearth of models for feminist collaboration between authors and editors. The one model we could draw on from our own experiences was the feminist classroom, in which the teacher is ideally the facilitator of a learning experience to which all contribute. The collaborations with authors that we viewed as most successful did reflect this ideal to some extent. At their best, these collaborations resulted in a finished article that had built on the original paper's strengths, lacked the original paper's weaknesses, and yet clearly represented the author's translation of the criticisms and recommendations she had received into a product that was distinctly hers, that is, an article that none of the evaluators/collaborators (referees and editors) would or could have written the same way. In such cases, we had a sense of having succeeded in empowering the author to realize her own vision of her article; at the same time, it is clear that the author's motivation, ability, and sensitivity to "what was wanted" were just as important to improving her paper as our intervention, if not more so. At least, the successes could show us that we had not *dis*empowered those authors—perhaps a more significant aspect of our collaboration than we realized.

The significance we attached to a revised article that answered our editorial criticisms while remaining distinctly the author's own work brings us to another contradiction inherent in the task we had set ourselves. In attempting to reconcile the advantages of traditional evaluation with power sharing cum mentoring, we had not consciously questioned the concept of individual authorship. Thus, although we were in a sense collaborating in the writing of some of the articles (that is, our intervention went beyond making editorial suggestions), we discouraged the authors from, for example, formally acknowledging our role in the development of their papers. In this case, we preferred to be seen in a traditional editorial role, because undiluted individual authorship of articles was and is what is rewarded within the academy. In other words, because we wanted the journal to be taken seriously by the academic community, we could not avoid constructing ourselves as authorities rather than collaborators and then were trapped between those two conflicting modes of interaction.

Nevertheless, our successful collaborations with authors confirmed for us that it was possible to translate the feminist principles that informed WIG's other projects (conferences, governance, newsletter) into another form. Obviously the WIG Yearbook was different from those previous projects in several ways: A journal issue is of greater permanence and subject to more rigorous scrutiny than a conference presentation or a newsletter; it also has the potential to reach readers outside the particular feminist discourse community that forms its primary audience. Awareness of multiple audiences made our self-imposed task of trying to work collaboratively with authors more difficult as well as making it seem more important. In the end, our collaboration as coeditors did not publicly "challenge the hegemony of single originary authorship" (Ede and Lunsford 119). Yet, although we were working in an essentially hierarchical mode with the authors, there were instances, as described above, in which our compromised method of power sharing seemed liberating. We and many of the authors we worked with found the process vitally important, even exhilarating, because for all the contradictions (and perhaps because of them), we experienced these collaborative interactions as overcoming to some degree the cleft between feminist theory—the political implications of what was revealed by the articles written for the journal—and feminist practice—the process through which these articles were produced and published.

Writing as Feminist Collaborators

As we struggled to find the right mix of support and criticism in interactions with authors, we increasingly felt the need to communicate our editorial expectations to readers of the WIG Yearbook. This led to our first collaboratively written piece "Who's Afraid of

Feminist Theory?" published as a postscript to volume 5. In addressing some of the highlights of the feminist theory debate within WIG at the time, we wanted to make clear that although all contributions to the Yearbook were expected to reflect a degree of theoretical sophistication, we did not want to privilege any one theoretical orientation over others, nor did we want to shut out potential contributors who were not yet well-versed in theory. We did not want to replicate the models we saw elsewhere that essentially promote a "star" system, in which proponents of currently fashionable theories dominate and, in effect, control what can be published. On the other hand, we wanted the journal to be a place where "stars" might want to publish. We were attempting to negotiate the rocky ground between our commitment to feminist egalitarian politics and the theoretical sophistication that was increasingly becoming necessary for women doing feminist criticism to gain credibility within the profession. We wanted to clarify these issues and to communicate with our readers insights gained in our attempt to ensure our editing process had been informed by feminist politics. But now we embarked upon a process of collaboration that was much more intensely focused on ourselves and how the two of us could share the writing of the article. What we had considered to be nonhierarchical before—the attempt to be inclusionary, democratic, and supportive in our editorial practice—still left us essentially in charge of the process and in final agreement with each other on how to proceed regarding other people's work. Now we would be focusing on our own writing and would be collaborating in the articulation of shared insights and experiences. At this point the "off-task" talk we had engaged in from the outset became crucial in laying a basis for the increased trust we would need to collaborate as equals in the writing.

At the beginning of our editing work, we had made a conscious choice to trust each other—a choice we believe to have been grounded in feminist solidarity, where one may decide to support a "sister" one doesn't know personally because her cause is a feminist one. As committed feminists we saw such solidarity with each other and those with whom we worked as part of the effort. The choice to trust someone for political reasons always entails some risk, however. In our case, decreasing this risk meant more off-task talk—an intimacy-creating process that brought us into more and more sharing of our personal lives and finally into the realm of friendship in which trust is the natural context and not a conscious act. We talked about everything from personal and familial problems to crises in feminist politics to language pedagogy to food preferences and care of pets, which helped us to develop an associative and free-flowing mode of thinking aloud in which, to use Plowman's language again, the social and the cognitive dimensions of our interactions could merge. It was, we feel, the trust we had been able to establish that gave us the freedom to make provisional attempts at formulations and to give up proprietary feelings toward our own trains of thought and idiosyncrasies of expression.

Nevertheless, we found the actual writing difficult. Despite what we considered to be good communication between us, our thought and expression seemed to be very different and resisted meshing. Sometimes we didn't understand each other's approach regardless of general agreement about what we wanted to say. Despite our treating each other with the same respect we showed our authors, taking care to formulate criticisms or disagreement as supportively as possible, it was not always easy for one or the other of us to delete a paragraph she had labored over, or to rearrange a sequence of ideas to which she had given much thought. In retrospect, we believe our ability to overcome these problems depended in great part on our shared commitment to the feminist principles that defined our larger project; in other words, what was most important to us was to communicate to our readers the vision of a journal based on the feminist principles of WIG, and this made it easier to take the necessary risks and accept the inevitable false starts and miscommunications.

Although we belong to the same (1970s) "generation" of feminists as Kaplan and Rose, and share many of the same feminist values, we would not describe our collaborative relationship in such ecstatic terms or employ a lesbian metaphor to characterize it. Like Leonardi and Pope, we are uncomfortable with descriptive models that imply a merging or fusion of identities, or that are based in women's biological functions. Yet we share some of the euphoria expressed by all these writers in our conviction that the feminist collaborative experience has the potential to be a precarious kind of feminist *coincidentia oppositorum*—feminist practice and theory reconciled within the academy. Despite how laborious or tedious our own collaboration has seemed at times, we both believe it to be at the heart of overcoming the alienation and competition that so often characterize professional academic life. Indeed, one of us recognized aspects of her experience as coauthor of "Who's Afraid of Feminist Theory?" in the description by two poets, Mariam May and Jamie Shepherd, of their collaboration:

> What we have discovered in the process of composing the pieces is that, once freed from the restraints of individual authorship, we are also freed from the potentially debilitating effects of personal ownership in the work. Once we chose to separate ourselves from the personality of our own writing selves and personal agendas we could come to the creative space that [our poems] occupy. (qtd. in Ede and Lunsford 128)

The value placed on individual authorship by the academy is not experienced as restrictive by everyone, of course. But when individual authorship is privileged over collaborative work to such an extent that coauthorship is actively discouraged, an important avenue of creativity is closed off. The image of coming "to the creative space" aptly characterizes one of the most rewarding aspects of our collaborative writing experiences.

What's Feminist about It?

In trying to define what was, and is, feminist about our collaboration, we have found Ede and Lunsford's discussion of hierarchical and dialogic modes of collaboration to be central. Not surprisingly, the hierarchical mode constructs the collaborative relationship rigidly and is "driven by highly specific goals, and carried out by people playing clearly defined and delimited roles" (133). Productivity and efficiency are very high priorities, as well as the likelihood of a senior member or leader of the group exercising authority. The dialogic mode, on the other hand, is "loosely structured and roles enacted within in it are fluid. . . . the process of articulating goals is often as important as the goals themselves . . . those participating . . . value the creative tension inherent in multivoiced and multivalent ventures" (133). Our own experiences represent various points along a continuum between these two seemingly opposite extremes.

The process we have privileged as feminist in this discussion of our collaboration negotiates between hierarchical and dialogical modes. Examples are the ways we attempted to mediate between referees and authors in coediting the WIG Yearbook and sought to resolve inequalities in the initial stages of our collaboration with each other. Although we see our present collaborative relationship as embodying the dialogic mode, we are still not impervious to deadlines and other external demands of academic publication, and we remain goal centered in our commitment to a product. At the same time, we are convinced that our own dialogic collaboration, and to some degree the semihierarchical collaboration that we had with the authors we mentored, constructed various dimensions of emanicipatory space within which we could experience an alternative to the competitive, instrumental, and ultimately lonely modes of producing research that prevail in the academy. Like Ede and Lunsford we found that our own dialogic relationship began to bridge the gap between "public" and "private," and to contain an intimation of the utopian reconciliation of the two within professional life.

Distinguishing between feminist and nonfeminist collaboration does not prove to be an easy task in the end. Considering collaboration undertaken in an academic, nonfeminist context, it seems clear to us that the practice of feminist politics can transform a collaborative mode and the project to some extent. In collaborating with (feminist and nonfeminist) colleagues on academic projects such as curriculum review or development, creating or revising university policies, the writing of committee reports, and so on, we have often found that our commitment to feminist politics has enabled us to affect the process or even the outcome of the project. For example, participation in decision making may become more egalitarian and consensual than it would if no feminist principles were involved. Work may be shared relatively equally through consensus (in contrast to the more traditional hierarchical model in which the committee chair either does most of the work or "delegates" it), or members of the collaborative group may assume responsibility unequally but according to a working formula reached by consensus. The questions that the group chooses to address (within the parameters allowed by the institution) may lead to expanding the scope or altering the goals of the project, usually by making them more inclusionary than a traditional decision-making mode would allow, yet the collaborators themselves would not define the project as a feminist one.

However, in documenting the potential of feminist politics to transform a collaboration and even affect the product, we believe it is important to recognize that feminists can be joined in their commitment to a nonhierarchical collaborative style by groups or individuals who might not identify themselves as feminists. Here, we focus our lens differently than do Leonardi and Pope, who state, ". . . given that single-author texts are the only kind our discipline seems to know what to do with, and hence to value, collaboration, whatever the subject, whatever the agenda, becomes a political act with political consequences" (259). We would argue that the political consequences are limited by the politics of the agenda: Does it support or challenge the exclusionary status quo? Is there a goal of transformation? Although collaboration per se may challenge entrenched academic practices to some extent, it will not necessarily lead to change that opens the academy to women and other "outsiders."

The possibility of feminist collaboration on a nonfeminist project leads to the obverse question: Can there be nonfeminist collaboration on a feminist project? We would answer that, in order to meet our definition of a feminist project, collaborators must in some way negotiate the distance between hierarchical and dialogic modes. A commitment to feminist politics *within the collaborative relationship* as well as with respect to *how others are affected by the project* will, we would claim, inevitably push the collaboration in the direction of the dialogic. Only through dialogue is it possible to recognize the contradictory ways a collaborative project affects both the collaborators *and* those who "consume" the finished product, and only dialogue can establish a critical basis for making feminist choices in shaping the project. A range of communicative interactions makes possible a consensus that can function as "an oppositional practice that challenges prevailing conditions of production" rather than as "an acculturative practice that reproduces business as usual" (Ede and Lunsford 119). The more conscious the commitment to process and the more dialogic the process is, the greater the chance to translate feminist political theory into feminist practice. The politics of transformation central to feminism have the potential to construct a feminist collaborative process as well as product—be it in the design for a Women's Studies major, the organization of a rape-crisis hotline, the coediting of a journal, or the collaborative writing of an article on feminist collaboration.

NOTES

1. We note that Ede and Lunsford's work is often cited as a "pioneering" study, for example by Holly Laird in her preface to the special section on collaborations in *Tulsa Studies in Women's Literature* 13.2 (Fall 1994). Laird comments on the sparseness of theoretical writing on feminist collaboration prior to the 1991 MLA session on feminist collaboration (where an early version of Kaplan and Rose's "Strange Bedfellows" was presented); this event helped launch other projects analyzing "the practice and consequences of feminist coauthorship" (235–36). However, we know of no studies other than our own that address feminist journal editing, a gap that is all the more surprising because so many feminist journals are coedited.

2. The Coalition of Women in German (WIG) was founded in 1974 and became an allied organization of the MLA in 1977. At present, there are some 600 members. In addition to the Yearbook and Newsletter, the organization has sponsored several undertakings, including a project on exposing sexism in language textbooks and the publication of course syllabi in literature and film. WIG now maintains a list on the internet. Since 1991, the *Women in German Yearbook* has been published by The University of Nebraska Press. For a description of the first ten years of WIG, see Jeanette Clausen, "The Coalition of Women in German: An Interpretive History and Celebration."

REFERENCES

Cafferty, Helen, and Jeanette Clausen. "Journal Editing: Issues for Feminists." Editors' Notes. *Bulletin of the Council of Editors of Learned Journals* 9.2 (1990): 28–32.

———. "Who's Afraid of Feminist Theory? A Postscript from the Editors." *Women in German Yearbook 5. Feminist Studies and German Culture.* Lanham, MD: University Press of America, 1989: 131–35.

Clausen, Jeanette. "The Coalition of Women in German: An Interpretive History and Celebration." *Women in German Yearbook 1. Feminist Studies and German Culture.* Ed. Marianne Burkhard and Edith Waldstein. Lanham, MD: University Press of America, 1985: 1–27.

Clausen, Jeanette, and Helen Cafferty, eds. *Women in German Yearbook 5. Feminist Studies and German Culture.* Lanham, MD: University Press of America, 1989.

———. *Women in German Yearbook 6. Feminist Studies and German Culture.* Lanham, MD: University Press of America, 1991.

Ede, Lisa, and Andrea Lunsford. *Singular Texts/Plural Authors: Perspectives on Collaborative Writing.* Carbondale: Southern Illinois University Press, 1990.

Kaplan, Carey, and Ellen Cronan Rose. "Strange Bedfellows: Feminist Collaboration." *Signs: Journal of Women in Culture and Society* 18.3 (1993): 547–59.

Karach, Angela, and Denise Roach. "Collaborative Writing, Consciousness Raising, and Practical Feminist Ethics." *Women's Studies International Forum* 15.2 (1992): 303–308.

Laird, Holly. Preface to Forum on Collaborations Part I. *Tulsa Studies in Women's Literature* 13.2 (1994): 235–40.

Leonardi, Susan J., and Rebecca A. Pope. "Screaming Divas: Collaboration as Feminist Practice." *Tulsa Studies in Women's Literature* 13.2 (1994): 259–70.

Plowman, Lydia. "Tracing the Evolution of a Co-Authored Text." *Language and Communication: An Interdisciplinary Journal* 13.3 (1993): 149–61.

Kimberly A. McCarthy and Sandra A. Steingraber

6

Self-Connection Shared

Integrating Collaborative and Autonomous Impulses within Feminist Projects

---

> The sharing of joy, whether physical, emotional, psychic, or intellectual, forms a bridge between the sharers which can be the basis for understanding much of what is not shared between them, and lessens the threat of their difference. . . . Self-connection shared is a measure of the joy which I know myself to be capable of feeling. (Lorde, 1984, pp. 56–57)
>
> To make a difference (to Make Difference, one might say), women have to do impossible things and think impossible thoughts, and that is only done in community. . . . We call each other to creative acts of courage, imagination, and memory, but they are literally impossible without a community of women which recognizes and authorizes women's initiatives. (Frye, 1992, p. 8)

In the 1991 Hollywood comedy, *Switch,* Ellen Barkin plays Amanda ("A-MAN"-da), who is the reincarnation of a ruthless advertising executive named Steve. Punished by God for sexual chauvinism ("I can't get into heaven because I was such a shit to women"), Steve's mind and soul have been transplanted after his murder into the body of a beautiful woman. When Amanda/Steve then attempts to reclaim his old job at the firm, the laughter begins.

Switch can hardly be called a feminist film—Amanda is finally allowed into heaven after she is raped and dies in childbirth, a sequence of events the film attempts to portray with great hilarity.

Nevertheless, the comic elements of the workplace scenes turn on a catch-22 that is all too familiar to feminist women. As Amanda struggles to regain the power and prestige that Steve formerly wielded with ease, she discovers a double standard: the same project that she was developing in her previous life as Steve—and which had the potential to elevate him to the position of creative genius in the advertising world—she was now expected to expect no credit for. After Amanda's boss presents her ideas as his own in an executive meeting, she confronts him and is met with mock astonishment: "afterall, we work as a team; collaboration, not authorship, is what's important here, isn't it?"

As it has been for many real women, including both of us, this scene becomes a moment of enlightenment for our man "trapped" in the body of a woman protagonist. Abusive experiences similar to the one in *Switch* not surprisingly have caused many women to caste a suspicious eye on the notion of collaboration as a warm and wonderful creative process. Collaboration is a slippery concept that can conceal self-serving ends in a world which recognizes and rewards individual achievement.

Enforced selflessness is a term we have been using with each other to describe the potential of collaborative projects to replicate the kinds of servicing and self-denial into which women historically have been forced. For example, panelists at a recent forum on collaboration in the arts each argued that collaboration is necessary to dismantle the "disciplinary chauvinism" that serves as a barrier to community-based art. So far so good. The panelists then went on to contend that "obliteration of ego" and "diffusion of self" were essential prerequisites for successful collaboration. At this point, the hair on the backs of our necks began to stand up. Enthusiastic collaborators ourselves, we find such directives simplistic and regressive (and ironically inappropriate!) for projects that explore women's quests for autonomy and self-definition or, as suggested by Chodorow (1978) and Ostriker (1986), that are directly concerned with the tendencies of the female self to dissolve into its relationships. Models for collaboration that require a renunciation of authorship run counter to Carolyn Heilbrun's (1988, p. 18) definition of creative power—which we have taken to heart—as "the ability to take one's place in whatever discourse is essential to action and the right to have one's part matter."

For women in science, the danger of relinquishing one's rightful part within a collaborative discourse is acute (see, for example, Keller, 1985; Gornick, 1990). Laboratory science, by definition, is a social endeavor that requires collaboration at every level. As Gornick (1990) has documented, a woman scientist married to a man scientist very likely works without pay or without a formal position in a corner of her husband's laboratory, where it is often assumed that she does the subordinate, noncreative work—and for which she is also resented for seeming to receive unearned privilege. Scientist wives who do not work collaboratively with their husbands often sacrifice their working lives completely, while unmarried women scientists frequently occupy marginal, isolated positions within their departments and are denied the opportunity to collaborate altogether. Gornick (1990) cites the example of Rosalind Franklin, the x-ray crystallographer whose photographs contributed to the discovery of the structure of DNA and whose lab notes contain all the essential observations toward that discovery, but who had no one to talk to about her findings. Francis Crick and James Watson, working partners who have come to emblemize collaboration in science, went on to share the Nobel Prize for that discovery along with Maurice Wilkins—who worked in the same laboratory as Rosalind Franklin. Not part of their network, Franklin received no official credit for her contribution.

As women who each hold dual citizenship in the world of science and the world of art (Kim McCarthy is a psychologist and a music composer; Sandra Steingraber is a biologist and a poet), we see collaboration as necessary yet dangerous. Like Carolyn Heilbrun (1988) and bell hooks (1991), we are interested in theorizing through autobiography and require a model for collaboration that honors the authority of the individual, creative, female self. Even as we worry about the repressive potential of collaboration, we are excited by its liberatory aspects. By troubling the patriarchal notion that the individual is the sole authentic source of creativity, collaborative projects bear out at least two imperatives of feminist theory: that knowledge must be multi-authored, and that the relationship between Self and Other (artist and audience or scientist and the natural world) should be reflexive rather than binary (for review, see Bateson, 1990; Farwell, 1988; Frye, 1992; Harding, 1991; Hare-Mustin & Marecek, 1992; Jordon et al., 1991; Lorde, 1984; Rich, 1979; Wittig, 1992).

In 1991 we collaborated on a music composition that employed the principles of "autonomous connection" in its methodology and addressed them in its content (Sandra wrote the text; Kim wrote the music). Without presenting a formal model of collaboration, we discuss here the general evolution of the techniques and processes we used in addressing the vexing question that arose from this project: How can two or more people work on a project that examines autonomy without obliterating autonomy through the process of collaboration?

The Collaboration

> As we fear each other less and value each other more, we will come to value recognition within each other's eyes as well as within our own, and seek a balance between these visions. (Lorde, 1984, p. 173)

Content-Form Interplay: One Collaborative Tenet

Before moving on to the review of our collaborative process (the content), we should first discuss the manner in which it is reviewed in this essay (the methodology). The music composition and this essay are unique in one way: the use of ambiguity through "content-form interplay" (McCarthy, 1993b). Through this type of interplay, the message and the manner in which it is experienced are paradoxically interdependent: content shapes form which shapes content which shapes form, etc. Add to this a content that is itself paradoxical—as in autonomous connection—and one is left with a great deal of ambiguity.

For example, the traditional academic essay consists of the linear presentation of ideas. In contrast, the presentation of artistic ideas may or may not include linearity. It isn't the linearity or nonlinearity which distinguishes academic from artistic works but the degree of expectation associated with each type. Nonlinearity evades expectation and prediction, the result of which is ambiguity. Relative to the academic work, the artistic work invokes a high expectation for the unexpected, most often in either the presentation itself (the methodology or form) or the ideas and symbols being presented (the content). By evading objective interpretation, the artistic work calls for an increased emphasis on subjective interpretation—or at least a closer examination of subjectivity and objectivity in interpretation. This interplay between subjectivity and objectivity (self and other; content and form) sometimes results in ambiguity. And ambiguity and expectation are two sides of the same coin of creativity (McCarthy, 1993a).

The content-form interplay for our music composition consisted of an audience participation segment; the content-form interplay for this essay consists of the traditional, linear presentation of ideas juxtaposed with the interspersed presentation of "duologues"— two running dialogues presented as dual, parallel columns (more on duologues later). In each instance, ambiguity is experienced in terms of identity—who is the subject (or self) and who is the object (or other)? Or more concretely, who is the composer (or writer) and who is the audience member (or reader)?

The self-other relationship not only serves as the content (e.g., theoretical base) of our music composition and essay, but also as the form (e.g., the manner in which the content is experienced). Content-form interplay via audience/reader participation provides one opportunity to objectively and subjectively experience autonomy and connection: Am I now the composer *and* the audience member? Am I now the writer *and* the reader? In turn, play with the autonomy/connection boundary clarifies the nonambiguous autonomous or connected experience: I am now the writer and not the reader; we are now audience members and not composers.

Content-form interplay can serve as a catalyst for creative thought by introducing or amplifying ambiguity through context change (McCarthy, 1993b). Context change refers to the interchangeable perception of a piece of information as the point of interest or the supporting background. Take for example, the yellow faces/green vase optical illusion. If yellow is viewed as the background, we see the green vase; if green is viewed as the background, we see the yellow faces. By changing the context, the same information may be experienced as different. This "changeability" introduces ambiguity.

The experience of ambiguity (as the issue of authorship within collaboration) can be repressive or liboratory (McCarthy, 1993b). "Difficult problems require creative solutions." The reality of this saying is that difficult problems are often, if not always, ambiguous problems. The creative solution is a new solution. And to create (or creatively discover) a new solution, one must be willing to delve into uncertainty. The experience of uncertainty is difficult (repressive at times) because the outcome is unpredictable. Creativity requires autonomy: there are no absolute models for how to proceed toward a solution, nor are there absolute criteria or guidelines to reassure the individual that she or he is on the right track (for an interesting discussion on creativity and courage, see May, 1975). But while creativity demands autonomy, it also fosters connectedness.

According to Humanistic psychologists Cszikmenthalyi (1990) and Maslow (1971), creativity is valuable not so much for the products but for the ability of the process to make us better people; *we* are the products. As such, the creative process is inherently rewarding because through it we glimpse aspects of our potential as humans (we are liberated). Such glimpses have been coined "peak experiences"—moments of intense, ecstatic excitement in which time and place are transcended, accompanied by a feeling of unity with the world (autonomous connection?). Creative individuals do not withdraw from the world but immerse themselves in it, experiencing deeply profound relationships due to clarity of the self and the not-self or other, as well as the complex relationship *between* self and other.

The important lesson learned from the creative process is to question definitions, that which might normally be identified as a "failure" (or repression) may in fact be the hint of a creative solution (or liberation). After all, *success* and *failure* are simply adjectives whose meanings can change based on the context, a sort of "glass as half empty, half full" view. Content-form interplay is designed to facilitate this awareness.

The Connecting Seed: Steingraber's (1988) Original Prefatory

Prefatory

I am often unsure
   how to begin

as a bird who holds
in her mouth
the first twigs
of a new
nest

and not far below
the gray cat squinting
in the full sun

One of the first things to occur in our collaboration was the selection of *Prefatory* as the text (see "Duologue I" below). (The poem *Prefatory* was initially selected for reasons of content [subjectivity/objectivity and self/other, e.g., the boundaries between bird and cat] and form [its short length—each composer contributed a composition between five and fifteen minutes in length].) This was followed by a discussion of our individual past collaborative experiences, gradually focusing on the "wish list" we each had for the music project. We were both committed to exploring autonomous connection but were not sure how this might be accomplished.

In addition to a conceptual agreement on the desired focus of the project, there were other important factors influencing the initial decision making regarding the collaborative process in general. First were the differences in our collaborative experiences: Sandra had not collaborated with a musician before; Kim had collaborated with writers in both autonomous and connected capacities, but never in the collaborative examination of autonomous connection. Second, we were constrained by time since a date for the project had been previously set by our hosts. In turn, this date precluded the creation of a poem specifically for this project. Lastly, this was to be our first artistic collaboration. We would be learning more about each other's preferences and styles, and the development of this understanding needs time. With all these factors in mind, we agreed on a modified collaboration: final decisions regarding the musical setting would be made by Kim, but the composition process would include continuous dialogue with Sandra regarding the interpretation and musical setting of the text.

Our openness toward the exploration of process in collaboration (as opposed to product) introduced a fair amount of ambiguity: Sometimes we experienced autonomy, sometimes connectedness, and sometimes something in between the two, an ambiguous experience whose understanding we are still striving to achieve.[1] In hindsight, our collaborative process evolved into one of "connected autonomy," and consequently, the review of our process required a format capable of illustrating ambiguity, specifically linear and nonlinear ideas, which led us to the "duologue." (See figure 6.1.)

Duologue I: The Collaborative Beginning...

Sandra:	Kim:
When we first met as new faculty members at Columbia, Kim and I began a discussion of our lives in both science and the arts...our observations of other women's lives... I had written a couple of poems, metapoems that addressed, in a very encoded way, the conflicts I felt about being an author, and gave copies to Kim as a token of our new friendship... yes...Prefatory was one of them...a simple imagistic poem that "is about" the isolation and paralysis I feel when sitting down to begin writing...	After giving a presentation on my dissertation at the Science Dept. meeting, I was invited to contribute a music piece for a concert in the spring... ...Sandra and I had talked... I'd read some of her poems and thought it'd be nice to use them...she's in the Science Department, she's female.. so I picked Prefatory since I never know how to begin... anything...and my work focuses on uncertainty and the subject-object paradox, and it was a great poem on self-reference and beginnings.

Figure 6.1

The Duologue: One Collaborative Technique

The above dual-column text represents a "duologue": a performance technique introduced to us by John Malpede, director and founder of the theater company "Los Angeles Poverty Department" (LAPD) based on LA's skid row. Comprised primarily of homeless and formerly homeless people, LAPD employs a unique improvisational ensemble performance style in creating community art that articulates the reality of the streets (LAPD, 1994). The duologue functions as an important element of LAPD's improvisational style. It is an oral form of discourse that exists somewhere between monologue and dialogue. In a duologue two people speak on a given topic at the same time but also listen to each other. It is not a direct conversation between two people but rather two separate texts that indirectly comment on each other. The duologue is designed to foster creative associations among dispersed verbal material (largely autobiographical), as well as physical motion.

We have chosen to visually portray a duologue in this essay to illustrate the self-other paradox of our collaborative process, and its effectiveness as a tool for facilitating autonomy within collaboration. The duologue sections are an essential part of our essay, as opposed to an optional example. The reader is encouraged to read the duologues in two manners: (a) as a single, unified paragraph; and (b) as two autonomous paragraphs. Note the shift in attention necessary to comprehend the unified version, as well as the different interpretations afforded because of the strain on attention.

The production of duologues works best when people have a moderate chunk of time, say at least fifteen minutes, and improves with practice. It is over time that the autonomous connections begin to take place, with sometimes very funny results! (See figure 6.2.)

Duologue II: Beginning Shifting Beginnings...

Sandra:	Kim:
Later on, I came to see the poem itself as an important utterance--as a prayer <u>against</u> futility, and gave it the title <u>Prefatory</u>...after all...if this is a prefatory then the writer must have gone on to finish her work right?!!.... this is how I understood the poem...as a little puzzle ...before Kim read and responded to it...she said she saw the inherent paradox of the poem reflected in "learned helplessness," which I was only vaguely familiar with, she gave me some readings which described the experiments to demonstrate it..this gave me a whole new way of looking at the piece...	I still suffer writer's block...or at least writer's obstacle course...I don't know how to begin, but you know what's worse? I don't know how to end either...prayers...I've always liked chants...anyway, I was saying how I can't begin, can't end, you know...feeling exasperated and frustrated...and I asked Sandra to write another poem for those of us who can't begin or end!...and how come we don't get to see that she finished the work?!...learned helplessness...very tricky...the cat-bird seemed to parallel it somehow

Figure 6.2

Psychology of the Duologue

Psychologically the duologue participant experiences a dual draw on attention: attention toward their own monologue and attention toward their partner's monologue. However, attention—whose function is to select from incoming information and regulate the flow of novel information—has a limited capacity: it can hold only so much information at any one time (Baars, 1988). Consequently, the duologuer's attention is continually shifting between their material and that of their partner. But competing information takes more time to process, more time for attention to select a small amount of information. And until attention is established, the information is perceived as ambiguous. For example, the artwork of M. C. Escher is full of "competing information" in the form of optical illusions. What usually happens when looking at optical illusions is that habit response kicks in, we dismiss the ambiguity and move on to a different task, or we spend more time viewing the illusion, trying to resolve the ambiguity, like the stairs that never have a top or bottom step.

But the suspension of attention, otherwise known as unconscious perception, does serve a purpose: it has been proposed that unconscious perception is the source of creative thinking (for general review of creativity theory, see Glover, Ronning, and Reynolds, 1989; Rothenberg and Hausmann, 1975; Runco and Albert, 1990; Sternberg, 1988). Unlike conscious perception, in which attention is engaged, unconscious perception has no identifiable limits (Baars, 1988). Not only does the amount of information perceived increase on the unconscious level, but, with the relaxation of attention, this information is perceived bias free (McCarthy, 1993a). In this manner remote associations may be made which might otherwise be dismissed as "ridiculous," "impossible," or "crazy."

What does all this mean for the duologue experience? Immersed in a cycle of clarity and ambiguity, the duologuer shifts in and out of intentional and unintentional dialogue. The experience of ambiguity not only evades attention, but may also evade defense mechanisms (McCarthy, 1993a): the duologuer may find themselves discussing topics they had not intended to discuss, as well as discussing them in new and creative ways. In the best instances, over a period of time, the duologue experience can facilitate insight, on a variety of levels, in one's personal life and relationships.

The immediate (and very difficult) goal of the duologuer is to remain in the paradoxical space in which self and other are simultaneously autonomous and connected: to emphasize one's text or your partner's is counterproductive to the process. In this manner then, the duologue functions as a technique in which the individual may experience and develop autonomy within collaboration. (See figure 6.3.)

Duologue III: Shifting Conceptions . . .

Sandra:	Kim:
I especially wanted to hear more from the cat, who seemed now to be the personification of some kind of internal censor...after talking with Kim, I was also now fascinated with the idea of knowledge...did the bird learn how to build a nest and then unlearn it? is the knowledge of nest-building instinctual but thwarted?...why is the bird helpless? If the bird is Self and the cat Other, what if the boundary between them began to blur?...so I roused the cat from his sleep and had him climb the tree and enter the very twigs the bird held in her mouth!...and isn't the bird holding the twigs in its mouth a very cat-like image in the first place?!!...	...discussing how, from a psych perspective, it is easiest to work on yourself...what makes beginnings and endings hard for me? a large portion of it is my fear of what might happen...it's the old internal censor!...At least for me, getting pissed off seems to be my mode of coping...which is probably why I like verse three!!! I don't know...it's the old nature vs. nurture debate...question. Why are any of us helpless...and how do we manage to make the self "other"? How are we like the cat...the bird? how are we like the twigs?...what was ever meant by the "cat-bird" seat?...it was supposed to be somehow advantageous...

Figure 6.3

The Product

The music project began with the original, single-stanza poem, but soon evolved into five stanzas. Through our discussions regarding the meaning of the poem, we experienced boundary shifts in a variety of contexts, both invoked and uninvoked. When were we "self," "other"? How were we the bird, the cat, the twigs? What is the "natural" behavior of birds and cats? How does instinct differ from learned behavior? Why are beginnings sometimes so difficult? Why don't we, as recent commercials state, "just do it"? And so on. The additional stanzas of *Prefatory* developed as part of our collaborative project reflect some of these discussions.

Prefatory Shifts: Additional Conceptions

ii
I don't know how to begin

I'm like a bird
holding in my mouth
the first twigs of a new nest

and not far below
the cat

    just sitting there

iii
I don't know how to begin
I don't remember how to begin
I'm sitting in the tree
with a mouthful of twigs
and I can't remember how
to make a damn nest

I used to know
I was born knowing how to begin
I learned how to forget how to begin

Well, it doesn't matter anyway
the cat's always down there
just waiting for me to screw up

so what's the point

iv
I'm terrified of beginning
I don't know if the cat

is still down there or not
It doesn't matter
because the cat   is always there

the cat is inside this tree inside these twigs
inside my own mouth inside this tree
inside these twigs   inside my own mouth

v
I am the cat
the teacher of helplessness
foreshadowed in all beginnings

In the end I devour her first born

Connected Separateness

While each of us came to the project with considerable knowledge in our respective areas, sharing this knowledge provided us with new interpretations for the poem and music. For example, the poem contains organic images reflecting Sandra's experience as a biologist; Kim's interpretations of the bird-cat relationship reflected psychological theory. The poet's visual display of language and the repetition of certain words influences the semantic, rhythmic, and aural interpretation of the poem. The composer's selection of text is influenced not only by aesthetic factors but by the composition of the audience, the projected duration and instrumentation of the composition, and the availability of musicians receptive to a particular musical style. Resolution of various practical issues (e.g., revision of the poem, program notes, rehearsal time and space, musicians' response to the work) presented the opportunity for discussion of theoretical, philosophical, and personal issues such as the juxtaposition of self-other (e.g., musician-audience), the function of "explanation" in the arts, and the development of communication skills in addressing delicate self-esteem issues. We wanted the audience to experience the blurring of boundaries, as we were, but also the continuing separateness, as we were. So we agreed on incorporating an audience participation segment into the music composition. (See figure 6.4.)

Duologue IV: Shapeshifters . . .

Sandra:	Kim:
well, as Kim told me more about her work with sound and music, we decided to collaborate on a piece that would be both collaborative in our creation (co-authored) and collaborative in its relationship between us and the audience...they would help create the piece during the moment of performance...in this way we were blurring the boundaries between self in several ways at once...	Sandra also told me about field training and how female birds will perch very quietly, with twigs in their mouth...for hours...how do they know where to put that first twig or piece of grass?...hey--if the birds have problems starting!!...quantum physics states some uncertainty is inherent in nature...so we incorporated an audience participation segment...

Figure 6.4

The Music Concert

> To really know something is to lose awareness of its name. When we name something we make it "other." Losing awareness of its name is part of the appropriation of "other" into "self." (*Prefatory Music Concert Program Notes*)

The music composition was introduced with a short review of the structures and functions of attention. In short, the audience was referred to a program insert that contained an illustration of a two-inch circle with a dot in the center (you can try this at home). They were then instructed to stare at the dot and describe what they saw: "the circle fades or disappears."

The disappearance of the circle occurs not because of any physiological limitation, such as the blind spot in vision, but because of the psychological limitation of attention. Once attention is focused on the dot, we are no longer "aware" of the circle, just as you, the reader, have been unaware of the feel of this book in your hands, until, of course, our prompt shifted your attention. However, studies have shown that on the unconscious level, in which attention is relaxed, information may be perceived without limitation, and this information is capable of influencing our thoughts, feelings and behavior, without our awareness (Bornstein and Pittman, 1992; Oakley and Eames, 1985). Therefore, on the unconscious level we perceive the circle but without awareness. Such experiences occur because of attentional shifts.

Conscious perception—that is, perception with attention—is often associated with the self: I am looking at that (McCarthy, 1993a). Therefore, to lose awareness of the separateness between observer and observed is to experience the self-other relationship as blurred. However, this does not mean that the self always merges into its relationships, but that a space exists in which the self may be experienced as simultaneously autonomous and connected. (See figure 6.5.)

Duologue V: Self-Connection Shared...

```
Sandra:                          Kim:
so, we discussed
collaboration and                it was important that we
collaborative experiences        each kept some creative
we had in the past.              autonomy so we decided to
yes...to work                    work in turns...once
sequentially...creative          Sandra finished the extra
autonomy was very                verses, the final version
important...and once I           went through about two
finished a series of             drafts, she gave them to
verses I handed the poem         me...plus her permission
over to her...were there         to play with them, which
two drafts?...anyway, Kim        isn't always an easy
had my permission to             thing for a writer, but
deconstruct and                  yes, I could focus on the
reconstruct their sounds,        sounds of the words or
their order, their               change the order...as it
linearity as she composed        turned out we didn't use
music and the words              the entire text although
became lyrics for the            it was printed in the
singer...my text, as I           program and the audience
had written it, would be         was free to use any or
printed in the program           all of it in their
notes, and would become          participation section...
material for the audience
to use however they
chose...
```

Figure 6.5

The music began and approximately three-fourths of the way into the piece, the audience was cued to participate in either repetitive recitation of self-selected parts of the poem or through improvisation on the form (vowel or consonant sounds) and the content (audience members could incorporate autobiographical material into the piece, e.g., their experience of certainty or uncertainty in creating at that very moment). In providing the audience with an opportunity to engage personally with the material, the boundaries traditionally distinguishing creator and audience were temporarily disbanded. It was our hope that the audience, having been conditioned to expect not to participate in a music concert, would experience some of the tension or excitement associated with uncertainty in beginnings, as well as uncertainty regarding their identity as audience or composer, a sort of performer's "stage-fright/performance-rush." Ideally, this would lead to an experiential understanding of the poem and the music distinct from either a traditional separate reading of the poem or hearing of the music. The audience was provided with an opportunity to experience autonomy within collaboration.

Authorship Revisited

Where does that leave us in terms of authorship? In terms of the products (the revised version of *Prefatory;* the music composition), the poem is Sandra's, and will be included in her book of poems, *Post Diagnosis* (in press); the music composition is Kim's, with special permission from Sandra to use the text.

Each collaborative team must come to their own process for dealing with the struggles for autonomy and connection. The "duologue" may be helpful in that through its process one experiences autonomy (e.g., how involved you become depends, in large part, on how involved you want to be), and connection (e.g., the "who" you want to be involved with and the "who" who wants to be involved with you). To start with how you feel at the very moment—for example, you don't know how involved you want to be—is a good starting place, which could lead to clarification of your indecision or that of your partner's toward collaboration. But it is important to remember that each clarification sometimes brings with it additional sources of ambiguity in terms of new or revised objectives introduced or discovered by you or your partner.

It is also essential to share that not all of our collaborations have been satisfactory or productive. We have yet to attempt an artistic collaboration in which we start from scratch, as we might have if we had created a poem specifically for this project. The one benefit of collaboration, however, is that it can lead to other projects. In this way authors may take turns for primary responsibility or control, with autonomous connection the long-term result.

The Music Composition

The following is a musical example derived from the opening stanza of Prefatory—the words and sounds used are similar to those notated for the soprano in the original score and those improvised by the audience during the premiere performance. This particular type of art form is also known as a sound-text composition or sound-poem (for review, see Hultberg, 1994). It is included here so that the reader might experience first hand the musical and self-other experience of the music composition *Prefatory,* in particular, the issue of authorship in collaboration. Ideally, each individual reader will find others to collaborate with in experiencing the musical example.

The reader(s) is instructed to sing/speak in a variety of ways (e.g., whispered, shouted, determined, stuttered, psychotic), the words/sounds as notated. The unparenthesized words/sounds form the primary "melody"; the parenthesized words/sounds form a complementary "melody." Traditionally, "melody" has been defined as a sequence of pitched tones. Contemporary ideas free melody from the confines of pitch as sole identification. As part of the improvisation, the reader(s) makes decisions (expresses autonomy and connection) regarding all aspects of sound—pitch, volume, duration, emphasis, and color, among others.

For example, the repetition of vowels or consonants shows relative duration of that particular sound: "I" is much shorter than "Iiiiiii" though both are based on the pronoun "I" phonetically sounded as "eye"; "ahhhhIiiiii" is the stretching out phonetically of the word "I." Capitalized letters are louder or accented; lower-case letters are softer or smoother. Sometimes the sounds/words are treated semantically, other times as pure, abstract sounds.

The parenthesized words indicate a complementary "melody" in which the reader is encouraged to describe musically his or her subjective experience with beginnings and endings. The complementary melody is performed by a separate individual(s) who merges in and out of the primary melody at random. In addition, the speed of the performance may be manipulated, starting slowly and gradually working up to a frenzied pace, which we did, or switching at random between fast and slow paces.

The following musical example serves as a map from which to experience uncertainty in beginnings and endings. The more performers, the more variations and interpretations may be experienced. This is one way the reader may experience, in some way, the musical and self-other experience of the composition *Prefatory* and the issues of collaboration discussed in this chapter. (See figure 6.6.)

Prefatory
(An example from the Music Composition)

```
i, i, ahhhii, ahhhhii, (don't know) i, ahhhhii, i, i, i, ahhIia,
(I can't sing) ahhIIiaa, I, ahhIiaam, mmmm, ahhIiammm, (what am I
supposed to do?) ahhIiammmm, mmmmmm, aaahhI, aahhIammmm, Iiiamm,
mmmm, (this sounds psychotic) ahhhhIiammm, Iimmm, mmmmmmof,
(gotta focus, gotta focus) IiammOften, of..ten, OFten,
IiiaammmOFten, (this is music?) OFten, OFF..TEN, OFten,
Iiaammmoften, un, un, (I shouldn't be critical) unsure, unsure,
unSHure, (how did I get into this?) OFFten, unSHure  Shure,
unSHure, (what will my friends think?) UN, SHure, UNsure, (I
don't know) UN...SHure, Unnnn, IiaammmUNsure, mmmmmmUNsure, (no
one is going to understand this) UN...SHure, Iiiiii, ammmmm,
UNsure, OFF...TEN, UNshure, UunnnnSHuure, UnnnnnnSHuuuuuure,
Unnnnnnnnn, (this is wierd) mmmmmmUnnnnnnSHuuuuure, Iam, Iam,
Iiiiiaaammmooooftennnn, (how do we end this?) Unnnnsuuuure,
sshure, Iiiii, aaaammmm, sure, unnnshhuuurre, shhhh,
unnnnnshhhuuure,  un..sure, (how is this going to end?)
Uunnnnshhuurre, SH, SH, SHuurree, unnshuure, unnshhuure,
ssssSSSHSHshshshshshhhhh, (at least I'm certain about feeling
unsure) ssssssSHshshshshhhh, ssssssshhHHHHHAAAAAaaaaaaaa
```

Figure 6.6

"We are often unsure . . . how . . . to end . . ."

In this chapter we described the collaborative process we used in creating a music project. Why have we contributed this chapter? Because we have experienced the power of collaboration to liberate and oppress. Problematic for women is the issue of authorship within collaboration. The question of authorship for a woman goes deeper than acknowledgment of her solitary signature. Even if she retains complete authority for her ideas, the woman is vulnerable to accusation that her creativity is "not her own."

Cross-sex collaboration is particularly problematic: women who collaborate with men are vulnerable to having their work relegated to the level of "support," or worse, a threat to "his" productivity (Chadwick and Courtivron, 1993). Even when cross-sex collaboration does not occur, the creative woman partnered with a creative male is vulnerable to being viewed as a pale copy, incapable of "serious" work, an imitator with little originality of her own. This view is intensified if the partnership is beyond professional colleagues, as with sexually partnered collaborators such as the married couple.

According to Chadwick and Courtivron (1993, p. 12) same-sex collaboration is no less challenging in that the "partners are called upon to reinvent, to refigure the myths [about creativity] into new realities." While same-sex collaboration possesses the potential to transcend the limitations of heterosexual models, it is not entirely free of social expectations regarding sex roles. Aside from gender, motivation is influenced by other identity characteristics, such as race, class, and age, from sources both intrinsic—the task itself is reinforcing—and extrinsic—the reward for the completion of the task is reinforcing, as opposed to the task itself (McCarthy, 1993a).

"Enforced selflessness," another problem area for women, is alive and growing within some academic circles. In the past two decades higher education has become more sensitive to the importance of women and minority representation. Consequently, women and minorities are often invited to serve on many committees. However, while minorities and women "work for the team," making "important contributions," their colleagues forge ahead with independent research or professional arts production. When it comes time for tenure, minority and women faculty may not be promoted due to lack of "professional development" (Chamberlain, 1991; Hensel, 1991; Jarvis, 1991; Schoenfeld and Magnan, 1992; *Women and tenure at Albany*, 1987).

The problem has been that while many institutions are "sensitive" to women and minority representation in committee work, the number of committees outnumber the available pool of minority and women faculty. The desire (or demand, in some cases) to "serve your college" has impinged upon the requirement to develop professionally, whether in research or artistic production. In contrast, women and minority faculty who are protective of their independent project time may be viewed as "selfish" and "anti-community," promoting their personal research over that of the department, institution, or political cause.

The situation is compounded for minority women who may be in the paradoxical position as both overburdened and overlooked (Sandler, 1992; *Women and tenure at Albany,* 1987). Minority women and lesbians may be in more demand, especially for their affirmative action "two-for"-ness as "female minority" or "three-for"-ness as "female minority lesbian." On one hand, they are more likely to be seen as "tokens," despite their qualifications, and on the other, as "experts" on their particular identity characteristics. In being viewed as nontraditional, minority women may be excluded from informal contact and therefore learn less about the informal politics and professional opportunities of a department or institution. As a result they may be more isolated from their colleagues, both caucasian and minority men, as well as caucasian women.

Although any type of authorship or collaboration can be repressive for women, success is possible. We each have been the recipient at various times in our careers, of concerns that *"others* will wonder who did the actual work," the implication of which is that the other partner did the actual work, especially if that partner is male. To counter this accusation, women academics are advised to coauthor with a variety of people and to balance coauthored work with single-authored work (*Women and tenure at Albany*, 1987), advice we extend to collaborative projects.

Women academics, especially those seeking tenure, are also advised to share their professional accomplishments (e.g., publications, conference presentations) with colleagues and chair: "Merit is obviously necessary for survival and success, but merit alone is not enough. Because women and the work they do is often either ignored or devalued, it is even more important for women than for men to be sure that others know how good their work is" (Sandler, 1992, p. 8). From this standpoint, authorship and collaboration present important concerns for women.

Because of the above challenges for women in collaborative work, it is important that we note some of our areas of consensus or agreement before our collaboration. Decreased commonalities before collaboration may increase the challenge for attaining autonomy within collaboration, but the results may be more dramatic. In addition to personal characteristics, we shared three areas of concensus helpful for collaboration: (a) a background in two fields—in our case, art and science; (b) a background in interdisciplinary work; and (c) a shared interest in feminist theory, and the relationship between autonomy and connection. The first area of consensus, a background in two or more fields, helps one develop an appreciation for multiple perspectives, even though those perspectives may conflict. A background in interdisciplinary work, most of which is collaborative, is useful in the development of perseverance necessary for rising to the challenge of autonomous connection (for review of interdisciplinary research, see Chubin, Porter, Rossini, and Connolly, 1986). Lastly, shared interests provide meaning and purpose for the project, which in turn serves as powerful sources of motivation.

But maybe similarities and differences were not at all important to our collaborative project. Maybe what gave this project meaning was the central placement of an issue we were each currently dealing with, in this case autonomy and connection. Perhaps by starting with a paradox, we were better able to focus on the process; or was it because we focused on the process that we were better able to address the paradox? By continually questioning various theories on—such as feminist, scientific, psychological, and aesthetic—and personal experience with autonomous connection, we were able to keep moving forward. Our questions and answers shaped the project, which in turn shaped the questions and answers. The boundaries were shifted between self and other, between individual and collective. In Ferguson's (1993) terms, we did not avoid irony nor dismiss it, but embraced it. Perhaps that is what kept us this time from the twin dangers of paralysis.

> To initiate, change and create are manifestations of power. (Helson, 1990, p. 47)
>
> The politics worth having, the relationships worth having, demand that we delve still deeper. (Rich, 1979, p. 193)

NOTE

1. While this chapter focuses on the collaboration between composer and poet, a second layer of collaboration existed between composer and the musicians—three flautists and one soprano, all female, and a third layer

between musicians on stage and the audience. The composition was altered or adjusted to fit the particular performance strengths of the musicians. In addition, our piece was one of six on a concert of new music. Ironically, all other musicians and composers were male, which added a unique feature to our collaboration all around!

REFERENCES

Baars, B. J. (1988). *A cognitive theory of consciousness*. New York: Cambridge University Press.
Bateson, M. C. (1990). *Composing a life: Life as a work in progress—the improvisations of five extraordinary women*. New York: Penguin.
Bornstein, R. F., and Pittman, T. S. (eds.). (1992). *Perception without awareness*. New York: Guilford.
Chadwick, W., and de Courtivron, I. (1993). *Significant others: Creativity and intimate partnership*. London: Thames and Hudson.
Chamberlain, M. K. (ed.). (1991). *Women in academe: Progress and prospects*. New York: Russell Sage.
Chodorow, N. (1978). *The reproduction of mothering: Psychoanalysis and the sociology of gender*. Berkeley: University of California Press.
Chubin, D. E., Porter, A. L., Rossini, F. A., and Connolly, T. (eds.). (1986). *Interdisciplinary analysis and research*. Mt. Airy, MD: Lomond.
Cszikmenthalyi, M. (1990). *Flow: The psychology of optimal experience*. New York: Harper and Row.
Farwell, M. (1988). Toward a definition of the lesbian literary imagination. *Signs* 14(1), 100–18.
Ferguson, K. E. (1993). *The man question: Visions of subjectivity in feminist theory*. Berkeley: University of California Press.
Frye, M. (1992). *Willful virgin: Essays in feminism*. Freedom, CA: Crossing.
Glover, J. A., Ronning, R. R., and Reynolds, C. R. (eds.). (1989). *Handbook of creativity*. New York: Plenum.
Gornick, V. (1990). *Women in science: One hundred journeys into the territory*. New York: Simon and Schuster.
Harding, S. (1991). *Whose science? Whose knowledge?: Thinking from women's lives*. New York: Cornell University Press.
Hare-Mustin, R. T., and Marecek, J. (1992). The meaning of difference: Gender theory, postmodernism, and psychology. In J. Bohan (ed.), *Seldom seen, rarely heard: Women's place in psychology* (pp. 227–50). Boulder, Co: Westview.
Heilbrun, C. (1988). *Writing a woman's life*. New York: Ballantine.

Helson, R. (1990). Creativity in women: Inner and outer views over time. In M. A. Runco and R. S. Albert (eds.), *Theories of creativity* (pp. 46–60). Newbury Park, CA: Sage.

Hensel, N. (1991). *Realizing gender equality in higher education: The need to integrate work-family issues.* ASHE-ERIC Higher Education Report #2. Washington, DC: George Washington University.

hooks, b. (1991). Interview with Andrea Juno. In *Angry women* (#13). San Francisco: Re/Search Publications.

Hultberg, T. (ed.). (1994). *Literally speaking: Sound poetry & text-sound composition.* (P. Pignon and T. Geddes, trans.). Goteberg, Sweden: Bo Ejeby Edition.

Jarvis, D. K. (1991). *Junior faculty development: A handbook.* New York: Modern Language Association of America.

Jordan, J. V., Kaplan, A. G., Miller, J. B., Stiver, I. P., and Surrey, J. L. (1991). *Women's growth in connection: Writings from the Stone Center.* New York: Guilford.

Keller, E. F. (1985). *Reflections on gender and science.* New Haven, CT: Yale University Press.

Lorde, A. (1984). *Sister outsider: Essays and speeches by Audre Lorde.* Freedom, CA: Crossing.

Los Angeles Poverty Department (LAPD). (1994). *Change/Exchange* [Brochure]. Los Angeles: Author.

Maslow, A. H. (1971). *The farther reaches of human nature.* New York: Viking.

May, R. (1975). *The courage to create.* New York: Bantam.

McCarthy, K. A. (1993a). Indeterminacy and consciousness in the creative process: What quantum physics has to offer. *Creativity Research Journal* 6(3), 201–19.

McCarthy, K. A. (1993b, March). Creativity and transcendence. In D. Chatterjee (Chair), *Creativity and transcendence.* Symposium conducted at the meeting of the Fourth International Congress of Vedanta, Miami University, Oxford, OH.

Oakley, D. A., and Eames, L. C. (1985). The plurality of consciousness. In D. A. Oakley (ed.), *Brain and mind* (pp. 217–51). New York: Methuen.

Ostriker, A. (1986). *Stealing the language: The emergence of women's poetry in America.* Boston: Beacon.

Rich, A. (1979). *On lies, secrets, and silence: Selected prose, 1966–1978.* New York: Norton.

Rothenberg, A., and Hausmann, C. R. (eds.). (1975). *The creativity question.* Durham, NC: Duke University Press.

Runco, M. A., and Albert, R. S. (eds.). (1990). *Theories of creativity.* Newbury Park, CA: Sage.

Sandler, B. R. (1992). *Success and survival strategies for women faculty members*. Washington, D. C.: Association of American Colleges.

Schoenfeld, A. C., and Magnan, R. (1992). *Mentor in a manual: Climbing the academic ladder to tenure*. Madison, WI: Magna.

Steingraber, S. (1988). Prefatory. In *Benchmark: Anthology of contemporary Illinois poetry* (p. 240). Illinois: Stormline.

Steingraber, S. (1995). Prefatory (revised version). In *Post-Diagnosis*. Ithaca, NY: Firebrand.

Sternberg, R. J. (1988). (Ed.). *The nature of creativity*. New York: Cambridge University Press.

Wittig, M. (1992). *The straight mind: And other essays*. Boston: Beacon.

Women and tenure at Albany: A guide for faculty. (1987). New York: State University at Albany, Women's Concerns Committee of the University Council on Affirmative Action.

Mary Alm

7

The Role of Talk in the Writing Process of Intimate Collaboration

"If you can imagine the words *talk* ... *write* ... *talk* ... *read* ... *talk* ... *write* ... *talk* ... *read* ... written in a large looping spiral—that comes closest to a description of the process as we know it." The process referred to is that of collaborative writing, and the speakers are composition scholars Lisa Ede and Andrea Lunsford ("Why Write" 151). The writings of these two professors sparked my own interest in the collaborative writing process and the role of talk within that process. As you read this, you will frequently see references to the work of Lunsford and Ede, but you also will hear the voices of other women who are thinking and writing about women and/or collaboration and/or writing. I bring these voices together both to demonstrate how these topics are interrelated and to illustrate my own claims about talk in the collaborative writing process of certain women.

In my field of composition studies, collaborative writing has been treated primarily as a matter of either theoretical or pedagogical interest. Kenneth Bruffee has theorized that all writing is collaborative because writing communicates thought, and thought is internalized conversation. Bruffee's "conversation of mankind" [sic] is the mingling of all the voices of people with whom we've been in contact, either face to face or through communicative media. He recommends creating more opportunities for talk in the composition classroom; he would have students talk with one another about their ideas for writing and review one another's written drafts, but he never goes so far as to suggest the coauthorship of text. Composition teachers who *do* organize their classrooms for coauthorship most frequently teach business or technical writing. In these areas, collaboration is the accepted means for document production, and the curricula give students opportunities to practice collaborative writing.

Lisa Ede and Andrea Lunsford document this tendency to treat collaborative writing either theoretically or pedagogically in *Singular Texts/Plural Authors*, the report of their extensive research into collaborative writing. Lunsford and Ede surveyed 1400 members of professional and business associations to discover the extent to which their on-the-job writing involved collaboration. The scholars followed up with a second survey, asking more open-ended questions of eighty-four of the respondents to their first survey. Lastly, Ede and Lunsford identified and conducted in-depth interviews with seven professionals who frequently collaborated and who were enthusiastic about their collaborations. About the relationship of theory and pedagogy to collaborative writing, they concluded: "[C]ollaborative writers in the professional world tend not to reflect on or to recognize the theoretical implications and problems raised by their practice [e.g., issues of power and ideology]." However, Lunsford and Ede also noted that "many of the theorists . . . tend to lean in the opposite direction. Too often, that is, they seem not to recognize the practical implications of or the need to develop methods consonant with their theories" (138).

I agree with this criticism and add a concern of my own. I am disappointed in how few scholars in composition and rhetoric turn their attention to their own writing practices or the writing practices of scholars generally. I believe our work as theorists and as teachers is made better by critical self-reflection; before we can assist others toward understanding or skill development, we must analyze our own experiences with coming to knowledge or competence. In my discipline, we too often make assertions about the nature of writing or methods of teaching without examining (much less revealing) our own experiences with writing and teaching. My longing for more testing of ideas through self-study is an outgrowth of my contact with feminist scholarship. As Sandra Harding has written, "[t]he best feminist analysis . . . insists that the inquirer her/himself be placed in the same critical plane as the overt subject matter, thereby recovering the entire research process for scrutiny in the results of research" (9).

Ede and Lunsford are an exception to my generalization concerning self-reflexivity among compositionists and rhetoricians, having written and spoken often of their own experiences with collaborative writing. They also are aware of the possibility that gender influences the writing process. When they studied collaboration in the workplace, they found that most collaborative writing is done under highly structured circumstances, with clearly delineated roles for participants as they pursued a calculated outcome. Lunsford and Ede call this mode of collaboration "hierarchical" and add, "in our experience, [this is] a masculine mode of discourse" *(Singular* 133). However, they also found "glimpses" and "traces" of a mode of collaboration which is "loosely structured," where "the process of articulating goals is often as important as the goals themselves and sometimes even more important" (133). They call this "dialogic" collaboration, and say that because "most who tried to describe it were women, and because it seemed so clearly 'other,' we think of this mode as predominantly feminine" (133).

I am focusing my own research on this latter sort of collaborative writing as practiced by women professors in the humanities. As a female composition scholar, I obviously have an investment in the subject of my research and its outcomes. Also, I confess a preference for collaborative work situations even though I currently work by myself on researching and writing about collaboration. In the present text, then, I (en)act my preference by inviting other voices to join me through quotation.

The purpose of my research is to describe the writing process of Ede and Lunsford's "dialogic" collaboration, a collaborative mode requiring each participant to be fully involved at all stages of the writing process, from conceptualization to final editing. I am in the midst of my research, collecting reports from collaborative writers about *how* they do it, how they write together from beginning to finish, creating one set of words to express one set of thoughts. Some of these reports are written into the prefaces and introductions of books while others appear in journal articles. These published stories of collaboration come primarily from scholars in the humanities, but occasionally come from social scientists; I found almost all in either feminist or composition publications. I gather other reports by interviewing women professors working together on scholarly writing projects. I have conducted interviews with three collaborative pairs and observed two of the pairs working together. All of these sources, published and unpublished, provide data for this article. To maintain confidentiality, I do not name the women I interviewed; all quotations from them are my transcriptions from tape recordings of my time with them.

I have chosen *intimate collaboration* as the general term for the process of writing in the "dialogic" collaborative mode in order to emphasize the emotional and social dimensions of such collaboration. Unlike persons who choose to collaborate because they seek an efficient way to divide the work of a large project, intimate collaborators experience the process as intense and demanding; both individuals give their whole selves to all phases of the work. For instance, in talking about how *Women's Ways of Knowing* was written, Mary Belenky describes the drafting process as both "sensuous" and "loving" (Ashton-Jones and Thomas 280). Carey Kaplan and Ellen Rose describe their "hours of working together" as "physically, emotionally, and mentally intimate" (549) and adopt "the metaphor 'lesbian' to describe what [they] experience in the connectedness of collaboration" (550). And, finally, during a roundtable discussion about writing collaboratively, Kate Ronald stated simply, "Collaboration ends up being a very intimate thing to do" (Kutz et al.).

That women professors use these terms when describing their collaborative process is not surprising given what is known about women's interactions with one another. Barbara Bate summarizes the findings of Mary Jeannette Smythe, a communications researcher who reviewed "the few quantitative studies of female dyads." I quote Bate's summary in its entirety because Smythe's conclusions apply to intimate collaborative exchanges as I have observed them and as they have been described to me.

> [Smythe] found evidence (a) that in conversations with one another women exhibit lower levels of dominance, dealing with each other in a more cooperative or synergistic manner than they do with men; (b) that during initial interactions with each other, women are less guarded and more relaxed than are men with men; (c) that women together discuss more personal matters, focusing on family, relationship problems, and (hence) men; and (d) that women talking with women exhibit a high rate of verbal back-channel cues, behaviors demonstrating active attentiveness and perhaps supportiveness. (Bate 306)

Bate reviews Smythe's work in the context of her own collection of communication studies about women, *Women Communicating: Studies of Women's Talk*, jointly edited with Anita Taylor. Introducing their work, Bate writes, "Communication of women with each other has rarely been treated as a serious research subject" (1). Eight years earlier Dale Spender made a similar observation: "Little or no reliable work has been done on the talk of women" (120). My current study of collaborative writing contributes to our understanding of women's talk because intimate collaboration, as I have come to know it, is grounded in talk. Lisa Ede and Andrea Lunsford write that "talk is central to our collaboration in a way that it seldom has been for us as individual writers" (Lunsford and Ede 125). Hephzibah Roskelly declared, at that roundtable discussion of collaborative writing referred to earlier, "Good collaboration depends on good talk." And Roskelly's most frequent collaborator, Kate Ronald, concurred: "Our collaboration was born in talk and continues to live in talk" (Kutz et al.).

Unlike Bruffee's abstracted notion of the "conversation of mankind," this is actual talk exchanged between two fully present women. As a part of the collaborative *writing* process, talk challenges the stereotype of conditions under which writing gets done, conditions expected to be like those existing as I write this article—an office, silent but for the mechanical hum of the heater and the clicking of the keyboard, with one writer, isolated from contact with both intimates and strangers. But others before me have noticed the centrality of talk to the collaborative writing process. In a text intended to guide academic authors, Evelyn Ashton-Jones points out that "Conversation . . . is not a luxury but a crucial element of collaboration" (276). My own observations provide evidence for that claim. I was with one collaborative pair for three consecutive days, and only on the third day did their work include the written recording of the ideas they had been developing. For another pair, the day set aside for writing together began with two hours of on-task talk, followed by a lunch break of an hour and a half. When they came back from lunch, they immediately started writing a detailed outline for their article. Without explicitly acknowledged turn-taking, each contributed sections to the outline which was created on a whiteboard with marking pens.

Finding talk so integral to the writing process of intimate collaboration, I have started paying attention to the various functions it serves in the collaboration. Marie Wilson Nelson has written of the interpersonal dynamics she strives to realize within her research teams, dynamics which I recognize as representative of intimate collaborations as well.

> I knew from other women that the kinds of interactions I sought were widely perceived as more typical of female than of mixed groups. The sewing circle, for example, and the quilting bee, were often mentioned as examples of traditional women's groups having collaborative *production* and mutual *support* as their primary goals and a lateral rather than hierarchical pattern of organization. (203; my emphasis)

Barbara Bate mentions the same dual purpose as she sums up the various studies reported in her collection. "The material gathered in this volume," she concludes, "supports strongly the claim that women communicating with each other try to nourish joint values and to pursue goals cooperatively" (312). My work with intimate collaboration demonstrates the same phenomenon: the ubiquitous talk of intimate collaboration allows the participants to "nourish" each other as friends and as scholars and to "pursue" the goals of friendship and scholarship.

The talk of intimate collaborations reflects both activities, support and production, both maintaining the interpersonal relationship between the collaborators and generating knowledge. Academic women have reproduced the conditions of Nelson's sewing circle within intimate collaborations where they stitch together their academic wardrobes, that is, conference presentations, journal articles, and books. They use their friendship to support their intellectual work. As one pair of collaborators put it, "Work and friendship. From our first encounter, we have been able to distinguish between the two" (Kaplan and Rose 547).

Maintaining a friendship requires conversation, and not just conversation about the work to be done. When I sat down with two of my friends to interview them about their collaboration, we began with twenty-five minutes of chitchat about our activities since we had last seen each other. When the tape recorder was turned on to begin the interview officially, one of the women said, "I have something on my mind that I really want to say first. That all of this talk that we've just done for twenty-five minutes is a part of the collaboration. That's what we always do, too, is clear the air about what's been going on as a way of getting to the work." Her partner agreed: "Yeah, I don't think we ever start a collaborative session without kind of doing a check-in . . . in terms of what's been going on in our lives." Another pair, who became friends in graduate school and are now separated by geographic distance, use their collaboration as "a way to keep us together." Carey Kaplan and Ellen Rose are also separated by distance; they "now write diary letters to one another each week, letters that include gossip and dailiness as well as intellectual exchange" (555).

The intellectual component is important to these friendships; they are, after all, friendships between college professors. One woman called her collaboration "a thought adventure," while her collaborator named their friendship an "intellectual friendship." This latter woman continued by contrasting the "intellectual friendship" she enjoys with her collaborator to the friendships she sees among men in her department; she sees the men's friendships as "built on a common ground of negativity and disdain and competitiveness." Her own collaboration, on the other hand, is "a safe place," a place she uses "to think big thoughts."

The collaborative friendship is also a place for women to deal with problems arising from their academic situation. As one pair told me, "And then we had some stuff happen in the department . . . that we were both really angry about. We decided that maybe a thing we could do about that would be to try to just get together and process that, to try to figure out how these events had unfolded, and what part we played in them. As that went on, we said. . . . " At this point, her partner broke in, saying, "We said, 'There's an article in this. This is how we can transcend this.'" And the first speaker resumed, "Actually, that's how it usually works between us. We'll be going along and talking about something, and [she] will say, 'There's an article here.'" Here is an intellectual friendship at work; two professors discussing an internal political matter and then stepping back to recognize the universal elements which make the situation one of interest to colleagues outside their institution. This is how the work of intimate collaborations gets done.

Pauline Adams and Emma Thornton are two more intimate collaborators who became curious about the nature of collaborative relationships after they had been working together a while. They conducted an informal survey of thirty-five writers with collaborative experience, mostly male but some female, and only one nonacademic. Their results paralleled Lunsford and Ede's findings. They found that though most coauthors focused on the attainment of a goal, a minority "were motivated more by the need to nurture a relationship, to alleviate loneliness, to achieve companionship. This last group appeared to be more concerned with the process than with the product" (25). Such social goals are important reasons for engaging in intimate collaborations, often serving as the major motivation for continuing to work together. Some of the women I interviewed live far apart and must put forth considerable planning and effort to get together for writing sessions. One of these told me, "I don't mean [to suggest] we don't believe in the work we're doing, but the bottom reason for doing it is to stay together." And another, who works in the same department as her collaborator, said simply, "the friendship is probably more valuable than anything in [our work]." The experiences of these intimate collaborators confirm Jane Hood's speculation in her article, "The Lone Author Myth," that is, "creative scholarship appears to be as dependent upon positive social support as it is upon persistence" (114).

The talk described by intimate collaborators, the talk I've engaged in with them and observed between them, is the "real talk" of constructivist knowers as described by Belenky, Clinchy, Goldberger, and Tarule. This is talk which creates the conditions for real scholarship, the making of knowledge: "'Really talking' requires careful listening; it implies a mutually shared agreement that together you are creating the optimum setting so that half-baked or emergent ideas can grow. 'Real talk' reaches deep into the experience of each participant; it also draws on the analytical abilities of each" (144).

Many intimate collaborators have commented on how their talk becomes a collaborative *thinking* process. Carey Kaplan and Ellen Rose have written that their "ideas and words—like sounds—meet, mingle, harmonize, and emerge conjoined, saying more than either of us would have said alone" (550). Mary Belenky claimed the "scope," "clarity," and "bold ideas" of *Women's Ways of Knowing* "could not have [come from] any single one of us without this broader conversation" (Ashton-Jones and Thomas 280). Lisa Ede and Andrea Lunsford also testified that by talking/working together, they "were more likely to achieve a better understanding, generate potentially richer and fresher ideas, and develop a stronger overall argument than [they] might have done working alone" ("Why Write" 154). Like others, they chose the word *synergy* to represent this outcome of collaboration.

One team I interviewed has collaborated on only a few writing projects, and they struggled for language to describe their experience with this synergy. Their process has one talking out loud while the other writes, and these roles are fairly stable in their working relationship. Of the draft produced by her partner, the one who does the talking explained, "What she wrote is what I said, but it isn't what I said. I mean, the ideas are mine, but those are not the words." But the partner believes the words she has written couldn't have come into being without the spoken words, and she doesn't think of the writing as "her" words either. They called the experience their "discovery process" and later referred to it as "getting into sync." But they also revealed they were not fully in control of the process, yet: "We never know when this is going to happen."

Talk and thought are also recognized as going hand in hand by another collaborative pair I interviewed. Responding to a prompt about the first time they worked together, one reported, "I remember, always, the discussions, the getting together and talking and just letting the conversation flow, to follow ideas, and the excitement of ideas." This is the woman who calls her collaboration a "thought adventure." Her partner said, "I think sometimes I'm kind of crazy in some of the things that I think. But, then I can talk to [her] and she is adventurous and willing to go with me and be crazy. And so I feel like, gee, maybe I'm not so crazy, or maybe I might fit in academia. I'm not sure. I was never sure, and I'm still not quite sure. But I feel that if there were more people like [my collaborator] around, maybe I would." They also believe that when they work together, they "get a richer written product." One said, "I think it is part of collaboration, the sense of it being a safe place to think big thoughts." In fact, "big thoughts" surfaced in my conversation with another pair as they reminisced about the moment they first thought of their edited book project: "This was a big thought," said one, and she repeated, "It was a big thought."

Intimate collaborations do provide a "safe place" for thinking, and that thinking is done aloud, in a conversation that flows between the two collaborators; not an imagined "conversation of mankind," but the "real talk" between women friends. Like Kenneth Bruffee, Lydia Plowman avers that "Most non-fiction texts are written collaboratively whether attributed to one author or not" (149). However, in contrast to Bruffee, Plowman tests the principle of social construction of knowledge in an actual collaborative writing situation. Her study focuses on the transformation of talk to text; she traces the passage of ideas generated during discussion among a group of students working on an assignment to the appearance of those ideas in the final text jointly authored by the group. She concludes that both "talking and writing shape meaning" and that either "spoken or written text . . . not only *conveys* meaning, it also *generates* it" (151). Even though Plowman admits that group authorship "is an untidy, protracted and, at times, frustrating process," she points out that her "study demonstrates the importance of talking for the generation and reformation of ideas and their subsequent capture as text" (159). Furthermore, Plowman, like Bate and Nelson, observes that group talk is "multifunctional," serving both social and cognitive ends (152).

Through her study of the student writing group, Plowman saw that "much of the thinking and formulation of ideas is distributed between two or more people in the ways they finish sentences for each other, and ask questions to draw out responses" (159). At another point, she observed how members of the group "'talk in text,' as opposed to usual talk which is full of hesitations and does not conform to the conventions of continuous prose" (158). These observations suggest to me the formation of a collaborative mind and a collaborative voice, neither of which is the mind or voice of any one member of the collaboration. Finishing each other's sentences, eliciting responses from one another, "talking in text"—all are evidence that collaborators are "in sync" with one another, participating in a synergistic relationship. Carey Kaplan and Ellen Rose described what happens in their collaboration as follows: "'She' and 'I' metamorphose into 'we,' hypothetical, invisible, yet nonetheless articulate. 'We' emerges from the space between our individual, different voices, its meaning elusive, dispersed, always deferred, never unitary" (549). Lisa Ede and Andrea Lunsford have experienced this same metamorphosis which they represented visually by running their names together in print across the title page of their book.

The collaborative mind is that synergistic entity capable of work beyond the reach of the two individual minds. It is as Emile Durkheim has written: "[W]hen individual minds are not isolated but enter into close relation with and work upon each other, from their synthesis arises a new kind of psychic life" (qtd. in Roen and Mittan 295). One of my interviewees called her collaborative work "another mode of being" and reported that she had "an almost physical sense of how different it is." Her partner agreed, and added that entering that mode was "almost scary." Business and professional collaborative writers told Nancy Allen and her colleagues that one benefit of writing together was that "the documents they produced were definitely better than those any one of them could have produced alone" (82). Lisa Ede and Andrea Lunsford report that working together enabled them "to achieve a better understanding, generate potentially richer and fresher ideas, and develop a stronger overall argument than [they] might have done working alone" ("Why Write" 154). And Carey Kaplan and Ellen Rose give us a wonderful dreamlike image as emblem of the collaborative mind: "Our minds meet in the air between us" (556).

Andrea Lunsford and Lisa Ede have explored the difference between themselves as individuals and their collaborative self. "[W]e feel less ego involvement with the pieces we have co-authored than those we have written alone. Hence, we have a greater distance from the work" ("Why Write" 154). This does not mean they feel less ownership of the final written product. It does mean they are able to interrogate the writing with greater freedom because it "belongs" to some other entity than either of them personally. The same idea was articulated by two of the women I interviewed:

> **A:** [E]very section bears the imprint of both of us. And, not of us as individuals, but of us as a collaborative mind, in a way. I don't know how to express that.
>
> **B:** Yeah. The two of us together are one entity when it comes to that document.
>
> **A:** And that one entity is different than the separate entities that we are.
>
> **B:** (interrupting) Yeah, yeah.

This collaborative mind has a collaborative voice, too, different from the voices of either of the collaborative partners. Jill Dillard and Karin Dahl noticed this in their own intimate collaboration: "We found a 'we' voice, different from our separate voices" (274). Other collaborators have used other terms for this phenomenon. At the roundtable about collaborative writing, Keith Rhodes called it the "third voice grown out of collaboration," while Eleanor Kutz referred to it as the "common voice," and Hephzibah Roskelly used the term, *shared voice*. They discussed how the collaborative voice could accompany an individual into other collaborations. For instance, Keith sometimes felt as though the collaborative Kate-and-Hepsie were present when he was writing only with Kate Ronald, who has enjoyed a longstanding collaborative relationship with Hepsie Roskelly (Kutz et al.). One pair of intimate collaborators told me about the voice they have developed as a collaborative unit and spoke of hearing that voice as they write together: "[W]e just hear what we need. And we add what is missing. We might read it back to each other with the amended version, and the other one will hear that change and realize that it's in service of that voice."

When Jill Dillard and Karin Dahl investigated how five other pairs of academic collaborative writers, including both men and women, approached the task of writing together, they found that "within the act of collaboration, the wordings, sentences, and paragraphs become a synthesis of both writers' thoughts and feelings" (277). Dillard and Dahl decided that the collaborative voice became possible for collaborators who worked together for an extended period of time. When a "we" voice was not reported as part of the collaborative experience, Dillard and Dahl posited two options; sometimes one writer became the dominant voice, and, at other times, both writers suppressed their individual voices and adopted a style in which both of them could write. I want to emphasize that this latter approach, the adoption of a common *style*, is markedly different from the development of a collaborative *voice* because the collaborative voice speaks for the collaborative mind. Those individual writers who are adopting a common style are using that style to tie together their individual thoughts; their collaboration consists of a collection of thoughts rather than the synergistic transformation of those thoughts through collaboration. Intimate collaboration is synergistic, transforming individual thoughts and words into "another mode of being."

Accepting the possibility of a collaborative mind and voice is difficult for many academics. For those schooled in individual scholarship, it is hard to understand how an intimate collaborator can abandon Ego in a creative encounter with an Other. Not only do those with no experience of intimate collaboration fail to comprehend the process, they all too often reject the experience as outside the bounds of scholarly practice. One of my interviewees commented, "The very same people who know all about social construction theory and support the notion of collaboration in theory are the very ones who, not only don't do it themselves, but demean it . . . professionally." In the competitive environment of the university, our experience as both students and professors has taught us to establish relationships of trust before daring to lower our defenses, disclose our Selves. Because of this competitive reality of the academy with its attendant exaltation of individual achievement, intimate collaboration is a mode best suited for those sharing equal access to power and privilege; truly equal participation and ownership may be jeopardized when professor and student or senior professor and junior professor write together. But clearly the rewards outweigh the risks for those who choose this route to scholarship. Carey Kaplan and Ellen Rose tell us, "we experience ourselves as individually empowered by our work together" (553), while Lisa Ede and Andrea Lunsford have written that the experience is "not one of loss of self or subjectivity but instead a deeply enriching and multiplicitous sense of self" (*Singular* 142).

Individual empowerment through collective voice is a truism of the women's movement and is one explanation for the success of consciousness-raising groups. To hear it invoked here as an outcome of intimate collaboration is most fitting. The intimate collaborations of female professors partake of the tradition of quilting bees and sewing circles; all are sanctuaries where women can "really talk." In these settings, women simultaneously work and build a supportive network of friends. Although not restricted to women, intimate collaboration is a mode of writing which fits the profile of how women communicate, think, and work (Bate, Belenky et al., and Nelson).

Risk, nonetheless, does exist for women choosing intimate collaboration as a scholarly method. They risk having their work misunderstood by those outside the collaboration, particularly at those times when one of them is being judged as worthy of either tenure or promotion. In 1991, the Smithsonian Institution sponsored a series of seminars about collaboration as a way of making knowledge in the arts, sciences, and humanities. Because of my focus on the humanities, I draw attention to the remarks of George Lucas who, at that time, was Assistant Director in the Division of Research Programs at the National Endowment for the Humanities: "There is little in the way of either precedent or encouragement for collaboration in the humanities; in fact, collaboration is sometimes actively discouraged. There is a tendency among humanities scholars to denigrate the significance of multiauthored works as somehow representing a 'shortcut' to publication" (qtd. in Borden 116).

Many of the women professors who write or talk about their experiences with intimate collaboration report encountering such misunderstanding. They are asked by T & P committees to make Solomonic decisions about how to cut up their collaboratively produced scholarship. They face incredulity when each claims, as expressed by one of the women I interviewed, "I am 100% responsible for everything that we've written, and so is [my collaborative partner]." Rebecca Burnett and Helen Ewald are two intimate collaborators who have expressed concern for what they perceive as the "typical" practice of awarding more status to "single-authored texts." They recommend that "when collaboration has been reciprocal and equal, coauthors should be accorded credit equal to that of single authors" (23).

Elizabeth Ervin and Dana Fox, who examined a series of documents from the University of Arizona "that detail policies and expectations for students and faculty" (55), concluded that "*all* the documents we examined suggest, subtly or explicitly, that independent scholarship is safe and collaboration is dangerous" (59). Michelle Violanti reviewed "'research methods' books designed for communication and social scientific research" (70) and found the same devaluation of collaboration: "[A]dvice on conducting scholarship often excludes mention of collaboration as part of the research process . . . [and] in books about authorship, collaborative writing and coauthorship typically are presented in a negative light" (82).

Violanti, as a feminist scholar, also points out that "Collaboration [is] frequently associated with women and research done by women"

(82). Choosing to engage in intimate collaboration, then, becomes one more way in which women become marginalized within the academy. In 1986, the Association of American Colleges published its report on the status of women faculty, administrators, and graduate students on American campuses; it is this report that gave us the description of campuses as "chilly climates" for women. Among the many chilly findings detailed in the report is the conclusion that *"Women often find it more difficult to have their scholarly work taken seriously. It may be devalued, trivialized, or ignored"* (Sandler 15). In 1988, Nadya Aisenberg and Mona Harrington published their interview study with academic women, both those who had succeeded and those who had failed in securing a place for themselves on the tenure track. The authors confess to being "astonished" at finding more similarities than differences in the stories of these women; "Taken together, the stories reveal a continuum of outsiderness—literal in the case of the deflected women but nonetheless real for the tenured women as well" (xii).

Understanding why women scholars engage in intimate collaborations when the practice puts their scholarship at risk of being trivialized or ignored requires appreciating the potential rewards from the perspective of the collaborators themselves. Working closely with another woman scholar allows a female professor to experience both the intellectual excitement of exploring "emergent" (Belenky et al.) or "crazy" (one of my interviewees) ideas as well as the emotional uplift of friendship. These experiences are incarnated in the stimulating talk which is the very substance of intimate collaboration; this talk enables the synergistic transformation of individual thought and words into the collaborative mind and voice of an entity with more authority and more daring than either of the collaborators. Individuals *are* transformed in the collaborative experience. As Donna Qualley and Elizabeth Chiseri-Strater put it, "The paradox of collaboration is that through the process of interacting with others, individuals (re)discover their selves" (111).

I understand intimate collaboration as a powerful energy source for women academics. As women work together, defying expectations for how academic work is accomplished, their relationship warms the chilly climate of the university structure. As they acknowledge and celebrate their collaborations in publications and conference presentations, they are using that energy to reshape the structure itself. In the hypercognitive environment of the academy, intimate collaborations invite women to develop not only as intellects but as emotional/social beings. The omnipresent, rich conversations of intimate collaborations allow women to address concerns arising from any aspect of their lives. To participate in an intimate collaboration is to be willing to be present to an Other as a whole person. This wholeheartedness/wholemindedness of intimate collaboration is perhaps what sparks the synergistic combustion between the two individuals. "Intellectual friendship" takes on new meaning in this context, too; it comes to represent *both* the process and the product of intimate collaboration—the pursuit *and* realization of work *and* personal relationship.

REFERENCES

Adams, Pauline Gordon, and Emma Shore Thornton. "An Inquiry into the Process of Collaboration." *Language Arts Journal of Michigan* 2 (Spring 1986): 25–28.

Aisenberg, Nadya, and Mona Harrington. *Women of Academe: Outsiders in the Sacred Grove*. Amherst: University of Massachusetts Press, 1988.

Allen, Nancy, et al. "What Experienced Collaborators Say about Collaborative Writing." *Journal of Business and Technical Communication* 1.2 (1987): 70–90.

Ashton-Jones, Evelyn. "Coauthoring for Scholarly Publication: Should You Collaborate?" *Writing and Publishing for Academic Authors*. Ed. Joseph M. Moxley. Lanham, MD: University Press of America, 1992. 269–87.

Ashton-Jones, Evelyn, and Dene Kay Thomas. "Composition, Collaboration, and *Women's Ways of Knowing*: A Conversation with Mary Belenky." *Journal of Advanced Composition* 10.2 (1990): 275–92.

Bate, Barbara. "Themes and Perspectives in Women's Talk." Bate and Taylor 303–14.

Bate, Barbara, and Anita Taylor, eds. *Women Communicating: Studies of Women's Talk*. Norwood, NJ: Ablex, 1988.

Belenky, Mary Field, et al. *Women's Ways of Knowing: The Development of Self, Voice, and Mind*. New York: Basic, 1986.

Borden, Carla M., ed. "Edited Excerpts from a Smithsonian Seminar Series. Part 3: The Humanities and Social Sciences." *Knowledge* 14.1 (1992): 110–32.

Bruffee, Kenneth A. "Collaborative Learning and the 'Conversation of Mankind.'" *College English* 46.7 (1984): 635–52.

Burnett, Rebecca E., and Helen Rothschild Ewald. "Rabbit Trails, Ephemera, and Other Stories: Feminist Methodology and Collaborative Research." *Journal of Advanced Composition* 14.1 (1994): 21–51.

Dillard, Jill, and Karin L. Dahl. "Collaborative Writing as an Option." *Teacher as Writer: Entering the Professional Conversation.* Ed. Karin L. Dahl. Urbana, IL: NCTE, 1992. 272–79.

Ede, Lisa, and Andrea Lunsford. *Singular Texts/Plural Authors: Perspectives on Collaborative Writing.* Carbondale: Southern Illinois University Press, 1990.

———. "Why Write ... Together?" *Rhetoric Review* 1.2 (1983): 150–57.

Ervin, Elizabeth, and Dana L. Fox. "Collaboration as Political Action." *Journal of Advanced Composition* 14.1 (1994): 53–71.

Harding, Sandra. Introduction. *Feminism and Methodology.* By Harding, ed. Bloomington: Indiana University Press, 1987. 1–14.

Hood, Jane C. "The Lone Author Myth." *Scholarly Writing and Publishing.* Ed. Mary Frank Fox. Boulder, CO: Westview, 1985. 111–25.

Kaplan, Carey, and Ellen Cronan Rose. "Strange Bedfellows: Feminist Collaboration." *Signs* 18.3 (1993): 547–61.

Kutz, Eleanor, et al. "Crossing Boundaries, Comedy Teams, and the Rhetoric of Collaboration: How Writing Works." CCCC Convention, NCTE. Nashville, 19 Mar. 1994.

Lunsford, Andrea, and Lisa Ede. "Collaboration and Compromise: The Fine Art of Writing with a Friend." *Writers on Writing.* Vol 2. Ed. Tom Waldrep. New York: Random House, 1988. 2 vols. 1985–88. 121–27.

Nelson, Marie Wilson. "Women's Ways: Interactive Patterns in Predominantly Female Research Teams." Bate and Taylor 199–232.

Plowman, Lydia. "Tracing the Evolution of a Co-Authored Text." *Language and Communication* 13.3 (1993): 149–61.

Qualley, Donna J., and Elizabeth Chiseri-Strater. "Collaboration as Reflexive Dialogue: A Knowing 'Deeper Than Reason.'" *Journal of Advanced Composition* 14.1 (1994): 111–30.

Roen, Duane H., and Robert K. Mittan. "Collaborative Scholarship in Composition: Some Issues." *Methods and Methodology in Composition Research.* Ed. Gesa Kirsch and Patricia A. Sullivan. Carbondale: Southern Illinois University Press, 1992. 287–313.

Sandler, Bernice R. *The Campus Climate Revisited: Chilly for Women Faculty, Administrators, and Graduate Students.* Washington, DC: Project on the Status and Education of Women, Association of American Colleges, 1986.

Spender, Dale. *Man Made Language*. 2nd ed. 1985. London: Pandora-HarperCollins, 1990.

Violanti, Michelle T. "Collaborative Research: Seeking Legitimation in Scholarship." *Women's Studies in Communication* 15.1 (1992): 65–89.

Constance L. Russell, Rachel Plotkin, and Anne C. Bell

— 8 —

Merge/Emerge

Collaboration in Graduate School

Recent feminist scholarship has demonstrated that knowledge is neither objective nor absolute; the manner in which we search for and produce it greatly influences what we inevitably find (Lather, 1991; Haraway, 1991; Harding, 1991). Accordingly, for those of us who understand environmentalism as something other than a rational application of scientific solutions to essentially technical problems and regard it, instead, as a creative, interdisciplinary response to complex social, spiritual, and attitudinal phenomena, collaboration makes utter sense.

As graduate students working in environmental studies and education, we have discovered the collaborative approach to be emotionally, practically, and theoretically nourishing. Through our work together, we have become conscious of possibilities we would otherwise have ignored and have accomplished things we would not have done as lone graduate students. Collaboration gives us the support and hence the courage to engage complex issues in our field and to occasionally take unpopular positions. It has also allowed us to broaden the type and increase the number of learning opportunities and projects in which we participate. And collaboration affirms our commitment to honoring a multiplicity of voices and attending to the importance of relationships both among humans and between humans and the rest of nature.

Since 1993, the three of us have been conducting workshops for elementary and secondary school students on wildlife conservation issues, as well as researching and writing papers on environmental education and environmental philosophy for presentation at conferences and for publication. In many cases, what seemed at first unattainable as individuals became reality as a group. It is from these experiences and places that our discussion of the collaborative process is situated. We make no pretense toward grand theory building in this chapter; as neophytes to academic collaboration, we are still very much in the process of reflecting on how and why we ourselves work together. Nonetheless, we do hope to highlight ways in which collaboration can enhance the graduate school experience and will suggest why this approach is particularly appropriate for those whose work involves environmental studies and education, ecofeminism, and human/nonhuman relationships.

The Graduate School Experience

Both institutional constraints and a shared commitment to environmental and social justice issues brought us together. Frustrated by a lack of advanced courses in our field, two of us initially linked up to create a reading course which later metamorphosed into a thesis support group. Later all three of us were seeking a collaborative project for the field experience component of two separate courses. Given our similar interests in environmental education and activism, we decided to conduct a series of workshops on the phenomenon of extinction. These initial collaborations have since blossomed into a variety of teaching, research, and writing projects.

As graduate students in progressive faculties, we have been extremely fortunate to have encountered little resistance to receiving course credit for collaborative projects. Indeed, for the most part, we have been encouraged in such endeavors. We recognize, however, that such acceptance is hardly the norm and have had, on occasion, what is probably a more typical response: a professor is sympathetic in theory to collaboration but, within the framework of a course, feels that it somehow mutates into a form of cheating. As Abel, Hirsch, and Langland suggest, "collaborative work does not mesh with the academy's conception of the individual mind producing discrete and measurable contributions, [and thus] it frequently encounters opposition" (1983, p. 166).

The key concern for many academics appears to center around

measurement and evaluation. Working within an atomistic paradigm, most institutions simply do not have in place procedures that can accurately (or should we say, quantitatively) assess collaborative work. We are granted acceptance based on our individual abilities and achievements, graded as individuals, and given graduate scholarships to conduct solitary research projects. With this in mind, we are conscious of the need to keep our own individual projects on track, in addition to our collaborative ventures, lest someone "misconstrue a preference to work collaboratively for the inability to write independently" (Chait, 1988, p. 23).

We began working together before we had much awareness of the potential institutional drawbacks. Not long after our first collaborative articles were in review and we had presented our first conference paper together, we began to hear stories of how others before us had found that such work counted for little when it came to tenure and promotion. As graduate students and aspiring academics, we were surprised and disturbed to hear of Richard Chait's findings that "some universities assign numerical values to the scholarly publications of promotion and tenure candidates and then divide the 'points' by the number of co-authors" (1988, p. 23). No wonder, then, that Paula Caplan calls the valuing of cooperative work one of the myths of academia of which young scholars need to be cognizant (1993, p. 53).

Despite our increasing awareness of some of the pitfalls of collaboration, we so greatly benefit from what Carey Kaplan and Ellen Cronan Rose have called "intellectual and emotional synergy" (1993, p. 547) that we feel compelled to continue. Working within the context of an environmental crisis can be at times disheartening and frustrating; collaboration with friends and colleagues helps us maintain our strength and has provided us a security we often feel lacking as young female academics.

For us, friendship is key in fostering these supportive conditions. Not only do we respect each other's goals and theoretical positions, but we also like each other as individuals. The collaborative process for us is therefore not strictly business; we invariably start every meeting together by sharing recent occurrences in our personal lives, late-breaking gossip, lots of laughter, and when we are able, a little wine and food as well. Within this congenial atmosphere, we create a relaxed and safe place to begin our work.

Creating these types of learning places may be particularly

important for female graduate students. Caplan, in her study of women in academia, has demonstrated how difficult negotiating the patriarchal terrain of graduate school can be for women. Based on her interviews with women faculty, she concluded that "the worst mistake we can make on the job is to remain isolated from other people, especially from other women" (1993, p. 85). Hence she devotes a significant portion of her chapter on general survival skills to the importance of networking and collaboration (1993, pp. 85-99).

For us, working together has been invaluable in this regard. Given our determination to bring nonhuman nature and human/nonhuman relationships to the forefront in our research, we are situated in the margins not only of academia and the discipline of education but even within environmental studies. Finding strength in numbers has thus been important to us. For example, the three of us chose to enroll in the same graduate class in critical pedagogy and immediately noticed how empowering kindred spirits can be. This particular class consisted of individuals deeply committed to feminism, antiracism, and other human social justice issues; we thus ought to have had much in common. Yet our concerns with anthropocentrism were often seen by our peers not to enrich but to "take away" from the serious issues at hand; indeed, at one point, we were even accused of "hijacking" a class discussion. (Anthropocentrism refers to the prevailing human-centered worldview characteristic of modern industrial society. It is based on the assumption that humans are different from and superior to the rest of nature and therefore can and ought to dominate.) As individual fledgling scholars, we may not have been able to manage such tension in a pedagogically creative way. With three of us, however, our questions and ideas came together to create a more confident and articulate voice. Instead of the common occurrence of feeling sidelined as the token environmentalist, we were engaged in a more serious way both by the professor and our fellow class members.

Multiplicity of Voices

We bring with us to our collaborations diverse academic backgrounds (animal behavior and psychology, French and English literature, religious studies), work experiences (social work, teaching, animal welfare), and learning and writing styles; and we are at different points in our academic careers (two of us are midway through doctoral programs, one is midway through master's studies). We also bring a variety of contacts from our individual academic and activist involvements. These different levels and types of experiences help us in a very practical way: our strengths are complementary. More than simply a rewording of the cliche that two heads, or in our case three, are better than one, as Mary Midgley maintains:

> The process of properly digesting and absorbing new ideas calls for many collaborators. . . . If the right kind of active, creative helpers are not present, the penalty is that the biases and weaknesses of the original proposer go uncorrected. (1989, p.71)

For us, the challenge of having three writers/editors per paper eventually results in subtler, more sensitive, and more carefully argued works than any of us produces alone.

Nonetheless, we recognize that we have remarkably similar backgrounds and values and thus do not bring vastly different perspectives to our collaborations. As Sandra Harding writes, it is important to consider "the social location of our own research—the place in race, gender, and class relations from which it originates and from which it receives its empirical support—as part of the implicit or explicit evidence for our best claims as well as our worst ones" (1991, p. 12). As white, middle-class Canadians, we are uncomfortably aware of the racist, sexist, and classist roots of Western environmentalism (Guha, 1989); we thus try to be vigilant to the ways in which we may unwittingly reproduce these oppressive relationships. And as three heterosexual women who wish to challenge models of competition, dominance, and aggression in accounts of both human and nonhuman lives, we acknowledge the possible role of our socialization as females and our subsequent rejection of "masculinist" values.

There are doubtless many more ways in which our social location influences our teaching, writing, and approach to research, some of which we are blithely unaware. While we foresee an ongoing need to continue this sort of probing, we also feel that participation in collaborative projects is one way of pushing each of us to be more open to other ideas. Collaboration is thus particularly appropriate for those researchers, writers, and teachers who, like us, are committed to honoring a variety of voices.

Despite our many similarities, the process of merging our perspectives into coherent presentations or papers has not proven to be straightforward. Sometimes it becomes obvious in a simple oversight like one of us writing that we had been feminists since our teenage years and subsequently finding out that that was not true for all of us. At other times, our differences are more substantive. For example, we disagree in our understandings of the relative importance of androcentrism and anthropocentrism in environmental degradation and hence have different comfort levels with explicitly naming ourselves "ecofeminist."

It is thus a struggle to ensure that we each maintain the "I" in our search for a "we." Certainly within educational activities and presentations, each of our voices is quite literally heard. The writing and editing process, however, does not work quite as smoothly. Trying to be supportive while suggesting to another that a dearly cherished sentence may be inappropriate, for example, requires a delicate balancing act. We concur with Janis Birkeland who writes that "Process is as important as goals, simply because how we go about things determines where we go. As the power-based relations and processes that permeate our societies are reflected in our personal relationships, we must enact our values" (1993, p. 20). Hence we each are actively working toward improving our diplomatic skills to ensure that the collaborative process is as open as it can be.

Despite these efforts, we still do manage to silence each other. Certainly one reason is our differential power relations. Two of us, older and further along in our studies, have been known to "railroad" the process, especially when faced with time constraints. Another reason is a hesitancy to be a "cog in the wheel." For example, one of us had been using in workshops a slide of an ex-captive rehabilitant orangutan brushing her teeth with a human toothbrush as both a humourous interlude and as a tool for blurring the boundaries between human and nonhuman primates. Only later did it come up that the other two were somewhat uncomfortable with the anthropomorphism inherent in the slide. While they appreciated that the anthropomorphism emotionally engaged students and allowed for a sense of identification, they were concerned that the slide downplayed the significant differences between the lives of orangutans and the lives of humans. Neither mentioned it immediately because their feelings toward the slide were complex and both felt that to critique a slide that would be on view for thirty seconds would be trivial. Upon further reflection, however, it became apparent that the issues underlying the use of that slide were of philosophical and pedagogical significance.

The issue was first raised in the context of a casual conversation about that particular series of workshops and we settled our differences of opinion with relative ease. Part of our ability to do so reflects our appreciation of ambiguity and contradiction and our willingness to tolerate the unresolvable. Also, since we try to create a safe environment in which to collaborate, we have been able, at least thus far, to deal with contentious issues in a sensitive manner as they arise. Although we did not consciously apply feminist theories of consensus building to this process, our approach in fact mirrors much in that literature.

Another issue requiring our attention was decision making around who ought to be first, second, and third author of our various papers. We must admit that we never even explicitly discussed the issue until we began writing this chapter. Instead, decisions were made more by default: whoever had time to write the first draft was the first author and whoever did the most editing was the second. Although in theory we are committed to rotating first authorship in recognition of the precedence of voice that role gives, in practice, it has not happened that way. It has been the two of us who are further along in our studies, with more experience in writing, who have had the desire and the confidence to assume the responsibility that first authorship entails. Again, once the issue was raised, we were able to critically examine our differential power relations as well as the feelings associated with these relations; explicit discussion of these issues has made subsequent decisions around authorship considerably more straightforward and hence easier.

Despite our growing commitment to collaborative work, we carry the baggage of learning and working within a system that still values the lone expert engaged in objective knowledge production. For example, we have occasionally felt, when in the role of second or third author, that our contributions were insignificant and thus our names not worthy of inclusion on the final article. These feelings are exacerbated in our situation since the three of us differ in writing styles with two of us preferring to write first drafts in isolation; second and third authors can then feel left out even though extensive discussion and planning precede the actual writing.

Part of the problem is the primacy of writing in knowledge production. Accounts of collaboration between teachers and academics working in education also attest to this tension. Marilyn Johnston (1990) points out that researchers tend to be dominant over teachers because it is the researchers who usually initiate projects, structure papers, and craft interpretations. And this is so, Patti Lather notes, even for emancipatory researchers whose work involves resisting and transforming structural inequalities and who thus insist that "we must go beyond the concern for more and better data to a concern for research as praxis" (1991, p. 57). We too have begun to recognize some of our own oversights.

For example, we submitted a paper for publication that was based on a series of workshops given to three different secondary school groups. In presenting accounts of our experiences with these students and teachers, we did not actively ensure that they agreed with our interpretations nor did we get explicit permission to quote the anonymous student evaluations in our paper. In retrospect, we realize how our own understanding of collaboration needed expanding. We now recognize that collaboration can extend beyond fellow researchers and writers to include the teachers and students with whom we are working. In our latest project, two teachers, both feminists and environmental activists, requested our assistance with an educational initiative of their schools' environmental clubs. Our role became that of facilitators and potential sources of information rather than that of visiting experts telling the students what *we* thought was important. In concert with both the students and teachers, we developed a set of mutually acceptable learning objectives for the project based on their prior and desired knowledge and experiences.

We have always been committed to getting student input into the content and process of our environmental education activities. In one of our first endeavors, we consulted students a few weeks prior to a workshop and simply asked them what they would like to know and do. For the most part, the responses were minimal. Initially we attributed this lack of interest and engagement to their having spent years in a system that favored the transmission of knowledge from teacher as expert to student as empty vessel. Upon further reflection, we realized that perhaps we needed to elicit student participation in more creative ways. Consequently, in our most recent project, we devoted an entire workshop to "scoping" out the needs and desires of the students. The results were astounding; the students actively challenged our initial ideas and helped revise and plan the subsequent workshops both in terms of content and process.

We have entered this collaboration, then, with a vision of the students and teachers as active partners in the search for and production of knowledge. And if this project becomes something that we all feel ought to be shared at conferences or in a paper, we hope that the teachers and students can also be actively involved in that process as well. For us, this project incorporates a number of features we consider essential to our understanding of feminist collaboration: a variety of perspectives is not only respected but actively sought out in a nonhierarchical manner sensitive to context and to relationships. Nonetheless, we recognize the need to continually attend to our powerful positions as university researchers throughout the collaborative process.

Relationships

Just as any valued relationship, collaboration can be both challenging and time consuming, yet ultimately satisfying. Indeed, one of the reasons it works for us is precisely because we do conceive of collaboration as another type of relationship that requires work and care. Clandinin, Davies, Hogan and Kennard write:

> For us, collaboration is about caring relationships between people. Caring is an ethical activity. . . . Just as we cannot mandate caring relationships, we cannot mandate collaborative relationships. The work undertaken in collaborative relationships is uncertain and improvisational. We cannot predetermine our inquiries. Certainty is not found in the situations of our work or in the lives that we compose for ourselves. For us, the only certainty in collaboration is the caring that guides our responses. (1993, p. 220)

This emphasis on the importance of relationships affirms our own approach. We believe that knowledge is always produced in relation to others, human and nonhuman. While we could each write singly authored pieces acknowledging the inspiration and assistance of the other two in a footnote, by working collaboratively we explicitly acknowledge that many of our ideas are generated as a group and ensure that there is plenty of room for this process to happen in the future. Collaboration also helps us transgress a variety of boundaries that are often maintained in academia, for example, between doctoral/master's student, teacher/student, academic/school teacher, and expert/activist.

Part of our commitment to collaboration and to environmentalism arises from our understanding of ourselves as "not merely unique individuals all bundled up in our own needs and feelings. Our very selves extend beyond our bodies to the beings, human and non human, to whom we are all connected" (Fawcett, 1989, p. 16). Indeed, we concur with philosopher Neil Evernden who suggests that "whether we refer to it as attachment to the other or as extension of the boundaries of self, the fundamental fact of our existence is our involvement with the world" (1985, p. 46). This approach is central to much environmental thought with its emphasis on interconnectedness, community, and the importance of relationships.

A sensitivity to relationships fuels our work and is not limited to our human relationships. We aim, within our environmental education activities and within our daily lives, to open up the possibility for what Patrick Murphy has called interanimation where "humans and other entities develop, change, and learn through mutually influencing each other day to day, age by age" (1991, p. 149).

Our continued attention to the relationships between humans and nonhumans informs our decisions about both the content and process of our activities. For example, we make concerted efforts to go outside when conducting environmental education workshops, question the ecological impacts of our pedagogy, and feel compelled to challenge anthropocentrism wherever we see it. For us, nature is "one more player in the construction of community" (Cheney, 1989, p. 128), and an active agent in the coconstruction of the narratives of our lives.

Our commitment to the varieties of relationships in which we find ourselves also leads to our commitment to activism and to grounding our knowledge production in practice; as Lather writes, "in our action is our knowing" (1991, p. xv). We are thus each involved in a variety of separate extracurricular projects, which include helping create an environmental education center in a rural school, working to improve standards for captive wildlife, and volunteering for a conservation organization.

Participation in a variety of collaborative projects is not without risk. We often find ourselves engaged in a juggling act trying to honor our "conflicting needs to 'tell the truth,' to justify ourselves, to maintain friendships, and to keep secure our places in the women's [and other] communities in which we live and work" (Keller and Moglen, 1987, p. 495). For example, recognizing that publication is indeed public, we struggle in selecting which critiques we feel comfortable sharing beyond our small groups and those that we should keep to ourselves lest they end up damaging causes to which we are committed or threatening friendships we hold dear.

Lather contends that true collaboration "is characterized by negotiation: negotiation of description, interpretation and the principles used to organize the first draft report" (1991, p. 58). It is far easier to engage in isolated arm-chair theorizing about the way the world is or ought to be. The more we collaborate on work grounded in practice, the more complex, hence messier, it becomes. Theoretically exciting as we may find the results of this process, we do recognize that it too has its pitfalls. As Clandinin maintains:

> The closer one is to practice, the less status there is associated with the work. The highest-status knowledge is located furthest away from practice. The knowledge that is valued is the knowledge of certainty, not the tacit, uncertain knowledge of the practitioner. (1993, p. 178)

Yet it is precisely this type of knowledge we find attractive, especially given our attention to relationships, our recognition of the inevitability of contradictions, and our uneasiness with universal theories.

Caplan suggests that "academic endeavours that involve applied, practical, action-oriented, 'relevant,' 'political,' or community-based work" and interdisciplinary or team research are usually devalued in traditional academic institutions (1993, p. 196). She goes on to suggest that it is no coincidence that it is often women who are engaged in such work.

Is it coincidence that we are three women? That is something on which the three of us have not reached consensus. We each respond differently to the questions Kaplan and Rose ask of themselves and their readers: "Is our collaboration extraordinary, an accidental act of grace? Or has it been, could it be, reproduced? Is collaboration a peculiarly female and/or feminist mode of production?" (1993, p. 557). For two of us, it has been easier to collaborate with women than men and we suspect that women are more likely to engage in this form of knowledge production. One of us, on the other hand, has collaborated extensively with her male partner and thus doubts that the phenomenon is that straightforward. Nonetheless we are all committed to working toward pushing the notion of what gets to count as collaboration and hence wish to be open to potential collaborators beyond academic, female, and feminist circles.

REFERENCES

Abel, E., Hirsch, M. and Langland, E. (1983). "They shared a laboratory together": Feminist collaboration in the academy. *Women's Studies International Forum* 6(2), 165–67.

Birkeland, J. (1993). Ecofeminism: Linking theory and practice. In Greta Gaard (ed.), *Ecofeminism: Women, animals, nature*. Philadelphia: Temple University Press.

Caplan, P. J. (1993). *Lifting a ton of feathers: A woman's guide to surviving in the academic world*. Toronto: University of Toronto Press.

Chait, R. (1988). Providing group rewards for group performance. *Academe* 74(6), 23–24.

Cheney, J. (1989). Postmodern environmental ethics: Ethics as bioregional narrative. *Environmental Ethics* 11, 117–134.

Clandinin, D. J. (1993). Learning to collaborate at the University: Finding our places with each other. In D. J. Clandinin, A. Davies, P. Hogan and B. Kennard (eds.), *Learning to teach, teaching to learn: Stories of collaboration in teacher education*. New York: Teachers College Press.

Clandinin, D. J., Davies, A., Hogan, P. and Kennard, B. (1993). *Learning to teach, teaching to learn: Stories of collaboration in teacher education*. New York: Teachers College Press.

Evernden, N. (1985). *The natural alien: Humankind and environment.* Toronto: University of Toronto Press.

Fawcett, L. (1989). Anthropomorphism: In the web of culture. *UnderCurrents* 1, 14–20.

Guha, R. (1989). Radical American environmentalism and wilderness preservation: A Third World critique. *Environmental Ethics* 11, 71–83.

Haraway, D. J. (1991). Situated knowledges: The science question in feminism and the privilege of partial perspective. In *Simians, cyborgs and women: The reinvention of science* (pp. 183–201). NY: Routledge.

Harding, S. (1991). *Whose science? Whose knowledge? Thinking from women's lives.* Ithaca, New York: Cornell University Press.

Johnston, M. (1990). Experience and reflections on collaborative research. *Qualitative Studies in Education* 3(2), 173–83.

Kaplan, C. and Rose, E. C. (1993). Strange bedfellows: Feminist collaboration. *Signs* 18(3), 547–61.

Keller, E. F. and Moglen. H. (1987). Competition and feminism: Conflicts for academic women. *Signs* 12(3), 493–511.

Lather, P. (1991). *Getting smart: Feminist research and pedagogy with/in the postmodern.* New York: Routledge.

Midgley, M. (1989). *Wisdom, information and wonder: What is knowledge for?* New York: Routledge.

Murphy, P. D. (1991). Ground, pivot, motion: Ecofeminist theory, dialogics, and literary practice. *Hypatia* 6(1), 146–61.

Angela M. Estes and Kathleen Margaret Lant

———— 9 ————

Lesbian Collaboration and the Choreography of Desire

Writer Mary Meigs discusses the problems of identifying herself to her public as a lesbian. While many readers are elated to discover that she is a lesbian, some are disturbed by such avowals. They hope, says Meigs, "that lesbian subject matter will disappear from the work of a lesbian writer. Yet they cannot forget that the lesbian is lurking behind everything she writes, and they comb each book for the reassurance that she is still there and can be judged accordingly" (33). Because of such reactions, Meigs wonders whether such declarations should be made. On the one hand, the lesbian writer who "has chosen not to come out" benefits from her discretion because she is, Meigs says, able "to elude direct charges against her, for she can refuse to fit definitions or to feel responsible for her characters" (30). On the other hand, the writer who does openly acknowledge her lesbianism is liberated from the incessant questioning and probing of her work and her psychology ("Is your work autobiographical?" 30) since she has answered the question for which many of her readers are seeking answers in her works: "Are you a lesbian or not?" Moreover, she enjoys the "euphoria of sisterhood" (32) which her avowal of lesbianism affords her with respect to her lesbian readers. She can even briefly entertain the satisfying "secret hope that her book will dissolve homophobia" (31).

Meigs observes, however, that—having come out as a lesbian writer—she frequently finds herself in a state of *posteuphoria,* in which "the joy has seeped out of avowal" (33). The lesbian writer, Meigs explains, soon becomes aware that she is firmly enclosed by the identity that she has embraced and has sought to celebrate with her readers; she "is forever sealed in her lesbian identity like an insect in plexiglass" (31). From that moment on, her readers search her works for the "lesbian lurking behind everything she writes," and when they find her, they are justified in calling into question the quality of her work. As Meigs puts in, "the intention of the labeler is to cast suspicion on her vision of the world" (34).

As Meigs demonstrates, then, relationships between writer and reader and between writer and work may be turbulently disrupted when the writer asserts a lesbian identity, when she terms herself lesbian. We would like to address an even more troubling issue than the work and identity of the lesbian writer. We want to ask what happens when there are two lesbians lurking behind a work. What happens when lesbians collaborate? What, in fact, constitutes "lesbian collaboration," and how does such collaboration function? Even the phrase itself, "lesbian collaboration," has a sinister and disturbing ring, hinting perhaps that unwholesome and certainly improper things are going on in the province of that collaboration. We want to explore what sorts of things go on in this alarming arrangement, and we want to offer ourselves as individuals engaged in several overt and deliberate acts of lesbian collaboration.

The first two steps have, thus, been taken: we have come out to our readers, and we have termed ourselves "we," thereby admitting to collaboration of an arguably indecent kind. Since we shall use ourselves as our only field of inquiry, it is appropriate that we explain what we mean—in our case—by "lesbian" and what we mean—in our case—by collaboration. We have been friends for fifteen years, and for five of those years we were lovers. We are now colleagues and friends, both tenured faculty members in a state university English department. We are also collaborators, having written and published together four papers, read together six collaboratively written conference papers, chaired conference sessions together, and taught classes together; each of us also reads and critiques everything the other writes alone—including poetry, book reviews, and informal essays. We are currently completing a book together, and we shall probably continue our collaborative efforts—which, in truth, extend far beyond our professional activities.

The term *lesbian* is necessarily problematic. We would like to stress that our view of lesbianism is not an essentialist one; we do not, in other words, hold with the position that there is a consistent, overarching, indwelling, and universal lesbian essence. But we choose to retain this word for strategic reasons. (For considerations of the difficult questions of lesbian identity, lesbian subjectivity, and lesbian positioning, see Anzaldua, Butler, Christian, de Lauretis ["Queer Theory" and "Sexual Indifference"], Fuss, Marcus, Phelan ["(Be)Coming Out"], Rich ["Compulsory Heterosexuality"], Smith, Stimpson, Vicinus, Wittig, and Zimmerman.) Diana Fuss cautions that any consideration of the notion of "homosexuality," the hazards of which word may be likened to the hazards of the word *lesbian*, is complex and difficult; she asserts that "any identity is founded relationally, constituted in reference to an exterior or outside that defines the subject's own interior boundaries and corporeal surfaces." With respect to sexual identities, she goes on to observe that "sexual object choice is not even so 'simple' a matter of psychical identifications and defenses; it is also a result of the complex interaction of social conflicts, historical pressures, and cultural prohibitions" ("Inside/Out" 2). Sexual identities, if we may for a moment render "lesbianism" as sexual identity, is then—in our view—a matter of social construction, not of biological or psychic or emotional essence.

But even accepting Fuss's argument that sexual identity is a social construct, it is difficult to repudiate without struggle such a category as lesbian—especially for those of us for whom this category has served as the major force in the construction of our own sense of self. Adrienne Rich persuasively articulates the necessity of retaining the term *lesbian*: "The word *lesbian* must be affirmed because to discard it is to collaborate with silence and lying about our very existence; with the closet-game, the creation of the *unspeakable*" ("It Is the Lesbian" 202). Fuss, too, offers a reason for retaining these terms; she points out that essentializing terms, such as lesbian, can serve a purpose, that although essentialism may be the root of oppression, it may also be used as a means to change, as a place from which to make oneself heard: "We need both to theorize essentialist spaces from which to speak and, simultaneously, to deconstruct these spaces to keep them from solidifying. Such a double gesture involves once again the responsibility to historicize, to examine each deployment of essence, each appeal to experience, each claim to identity in the complicated contextual frame in which it is made" (*Essentially Speaking* 118).

Shane Phelan concurs with Fuss and provides a workable view of lesbianism when she points out that recent lesbian theorists "have begun to develop theoretical bases for new interpretations of lesbian identity and sexuality." Despite the problematic character of terms such as *lesbian*, Phelan argues that theorists such as Anzaldua, Fuss, Butler, and de Lauretis have foregrounded the disruptive potential of lesbian subjectivity: "While retaining *lesbian* as a meaningful category, they have each worked against reification of lesbians, toward views of lesbianism as a critical site of gender deconstruction rather than as a unitary experience with a singular political meaning" ("(Be)Coming Out" 766). In Phelan's terms, then, lesbianism becomes a *place* where certain things happen, and she asserts that such a place or positioning must also be seen as socially constructed. Lesbianism, according to Phelan, is "not an essence or a thing outside of time and place but . . . a critical space within social structures" (766). In a similar way, Teresa de Lauretis conceives the positioning of feminists of color and lesbian feminists; she asserts a subjectivity which is "eccentric," "at once inside and outside" the structures which shape consciousness. And she argues that "such an eccentric point of view or discursive position is necessary for feminist theory at this time, in order to sustain the subject's capacity for movement and displacement, to sustain the feminist movement itself" ("Eccentric Subjects" 139).

In his work on mass culture, Alexander Doty also locates "queerness"—under which rubric he cautiously and with qualification includes lesbianism—in specific sites or situations, and he associates those sites with certain actions:

> The queerness of mass culture develops in three areas: (1) influences during the production of texts, (2) historically specific cultural readings and uses of texts by self-identified gays, lesbians, bisexuals, queers; and (3) adopting reception positions that can be considered "queer" in some way, regardless of a person's declared sexual and gender allegiances. (xi)

Doty stresses that the "queerness" of the texts of the mass culture is "less an essential, waiting-to-be-discovered property than the result of acts of production or reception" (xi); the "queer" text, then, is either made queerly, put together with some queer aspect, or it is, for whatever reason, consumed queerly, taken in to meet some queer need. Provocatively, Doty goes on to point out that the queerness in mass culture texts frequently exists—or at least is said to exist—connotatively, at a subtextual and therefore deniable level. Queer readings are termed "*sub*-textual, *sub*-cultural, *alternative* . . . or pathetic, delusional attempts to see something that isn't there" (xii).

Most important, however, Doty argues that the queerness of mass culture texts may be "uncloseted" and given equal attention alongside more conventional readings of these texts; when this happens, he asserts, "the queerness in and of mass culture might be used to challenge the politics of denotation and connotation as it is traditionally deployed in discussing texts and representation. In this way the closet of connotation could be dismantled, rejected for the oppressive practice it is." As Doty conceives it, relegation of a concept or issue to the connotative level of a text is a way of establishing a hierarchy of interpretation; one reading—the denotative—is valued over another—the connotative. But as Doty explains, what is easily dismissed as connotative may actually be quite obvious to a different reader of a given text: "I've got news for straight culture: your readings of texts are usually 'alternative' ones for me, and they often seem like desperate attempts to deny the queerness that is so clearly a part of mass culture" (xii). In these terms, "queerness" would be no longer "deniable" (xii). Doty says quite plainly, "queerness has been set up to challenge and break apart conventional categories" (xv).

In our construction of lesbian collaboration, we would like to focus on the two predominant metaphors by means of which these critics grapple with the issue of lesbian and homosexual identity. The theorists we have discussed consistently characterize homosexuality and lesbianism in terms of place and in terms of process. Rather than asserting a lesbian identity, then, we wish to assert that lesbianism, as we have experienced it, is a place from which we view the world, ourselves, our lives, and it is a process by means of which we make meaning from that perspective. Neither the process of lesbian experience nor the place of lesbian desire can be fixed, for each functions upon the other, offering an infinity of acts and situations that could be termed "lesbian." In characterizing both the place and the process of lesbianism, Vicinus asserts that "Lesbian desire is everywhere, even as it may be nowhere. Put bluntly, we lack any general agreement about what constitutes a lesbian" (468). Even as Vicinus hesitates to impose a definition upon the term, she reifies what she calls lesbian desire. While "lesbian desire" may not be fully coded, it can be felt. We, too, believe that lesbian desire moves us, and the shape we give that desire is determined by the lesbian space in which we move and by the lesbian project/process in which we engage.

To conceptualize lesbian collaboration, then, we must answer the questions What is it like? What does it do? How does it work? The best answers, the most satisfying, to such questions are provided by analogy. But Elizabeth Meese points out the uncontrolled nature of figurative language: "Like description, figuration works on the principle of likeness, resemblance of one thing to another" (80). Meese warns that slippages enter the use of metaphor and analogy, and our deployment of analogy will prove no exception to Meese's rule. Given, thus, the revolutionary potential of lesbian space as constructed by the writers we have considered and the slippery nature of figurative language, we will offer an analogy, but it will reshape itself even as we use it. We find our collaboration to be a kind of dance, specifically a dance in the dark which is momentary and finite. The dance does not occur all the time, for it is a ritualized movement which brings us close, gives us strength, and even enlightenment and love. Most important of all, by dancing in the dark—our desire—our lesbian need and compulsion and energy— moves us together in this choreography of our own.

Lesbian collaboration, then, as choreography—a ritualization at once cultural and new—involves both positioning and process, and in our lesbian collaboration, this positioning and this process involve our locating ourselves in language and moving powerfully through that language. In her discussion of lesbian writing and writing as a lesbian, Elizabeth Meese observes: "Writing demands that I bring a 'self' (I could say myself) into existence. A self I create as I write, as I say 'I' and 'lesbian,' searching for the words, syntax, and grammar that can articulate the body, my body, and perhaps yours" (71). But this process is difficult for the lesbian writer because language tends to erase the lesbian, to confine her to the shadows. Patriarchal culture denies or demeans the lesbian; to encode her desire, she frequently finds herself confronted with linguistic structures that negate her subjectivity and preclude her positioning herself as lesbian. It is the task of the lesbian writer, then, to enter, as Meese puts it, into a "complex choreography . . . to make sense" (70).

Language is, thus, the repository of the law, according to Meese, and if the law—as well as "reason, its regulatory agent" and "propriety" (72)—"perpetuates our subjugation," it does so by our entry into language: "In language, as we take on 'selves,' we offer ourselves up for regulation. The sentence awaits us. The paradoxical condition of being 'before' [the law], which we have accepted in order to speak, remains in effect/affect until death" (73). For Meese, the lesbian writer, and for us, the lesbian collaborators, "Our task is to discover ways to challenge and to subvert the law before death, to risk inciting it through unthinkable forms of resistance. What, after all, do I have to lose by breaking the law?" (73). In our attempt to choreograph our desires, we realize as well that "the sentence awaits us," for we have only the traditional structures of our culture with which to begin our effort—the dance and music of our collaboration. Thus, we encounter a barrier in the very medium of our work together, but as our desire compels us, we are strengthened by our dancing, our collaboration.

The first tactic of lesbian collaboration, then, must be to challenge and subvert the law by forming an improper bond. We dance together—two women where a woman and a man "should" be. The bond is improper for two reasons. First, it involves two women engaging in an act that can be seen as an icon for the procreative sexuality which patriarchal culture favors. (We presume here that traditional partnered dancing may be taken as an emblem of heterosexual courtship.) And second, our dance forges an improper bond because it disrupts our culture's most favored view of imaginative creativity—that of the isolated, lonely, creative genius. As Valerie Miner puts it, "Writing has long been glorified as virtuoso performance" (21). As yet, we have not broken "the sentence," but we have rewritten it slightly. As Meese says, "It is as though, through a properly improper writing, the contrast with the father's law, which constitutes the female (subject) as object, can be shattered" (74). Thus, even a minor rewriting of the heterosexual script of creation, both biological and imaginative, is disturbing to the dominant ruling paradigms.

We have discovered that our "dancing" together, though at first glance no threat to patriarchal structures of power, disturbs many. One of us, involved in a personnel action, was criticized for co-authoring scholarly work with the other. On his evaluation, which became a permanent part of her record, a reviewer wrote, "She has collaborated on several articles with a senior colleague. How can we be sure how much of this work she has actually done?" This professor was careful not to insult the member of our collaborative duo who enjoyed the security of a higher rank and tenure, but he was threatened enough by the act of our collaboration to undermine it in his evaluation of the junior faculty member. He called into question the validity of a creative act that was shared, that was not undertaken in the solitary spirit of what he considered genuine intellectual effort.

Although this captious professor made public his distrust of a collaboratively written effort, his real fears probably arose from the other aspect of our work which undoubtedly seemed even more improper to him—the fact that two women, obviously deviant, were working together. Clearly the thought that we could write together, that we dared to "collaborate," was unsettling. And had he known the feminist zeal that fueled our enterprise, had he understood how disruptive our effort to turn language to our purposes could be, he may have been justified in his fear of our work. For by entering language together, we "take back some part of our mouth to speak with" (208), as Luce Irigaray puts it, but we do this only "when our lips speak together" (205), only when we reforge the stories and the selves that patriarchal culture has pulled asunder: "You/I become two, then, for their pleasure" (210). By telling the traditional stories, by speaking the old language, we do not reach each other, we cannot construct selves that encode some essence of our lesbian desire; but by speaking together we begin.

This is what our colleague feared: that we would speak—or worse, write—the unspeakable. For, together, our fears no longer hold us back. What language forbids us to speak, we draw from each other. As Irigaray says to her reader/lover/interlocutor, "If you/I hesitate to speak, isn't it because we are afraid of not speaking well? But what is 'well' or 'badly'?" When our lips speak together, when we are locked in our dance, we "don't worry about the 'right' word," the right movement, the proper, logical, scholarly attitude. All is permitted and all is forgiven. Every movement is allowed as long as the other and the two of us together move in step. And since our dance is self-created, self-generated, there is no misstep. When one of us moves differently, the other responds—touch, glide, twirl. There is, as Irigaray puts it, "No truth between our lips" (213), there is only us—our experience, our desire, our perception—unshaped, unmonitored, and unhidden.

If propriety and reason are the hallmarks of heterosexist patriarchal discourse, if these are the forces that alienate us from ourselves by representing us as object and never allowing us to represent ourselves as subject, we are not inhibited by these forces in our dance. Thus, we dance in the dark, for the "truth" of the light of day—reason, enlightenment—is that which has hidden us from ourselves. Cixous asserts that "Nearly the entire history of writing is cofounded with the history of reason, of which it is at once the effect, the support, and one of the privileged alibis. It has been one with the phallocentric tradition. It is indeed that same self-admiring, self-stimulating, self-congratulatory phallocentrism" (879). Cixous argues that our desire and our unconscious ("that other limitless country") are "repressed" by the traditions of reason and propriety. And woman is, she tells us, negated by the codes of reason and propriety (880).

While our writing must ultimately be brought to conform to certain strictures of patriarchal discourse, our play, our dance in the dark is never constrained by this frigid "enlightenment." Our collaborative sessions are riotous, disorganized, sloppy, and unpredictable. We sit in the study one of us has set up in her home. We are surrounded by books, mismatched and ancient furniture—much of it remains from our life together—and piles of manuscripts, xeroxed articles, notes, and outlines. Our dog—yes, she belongs to both of us—barks and occasionally whines for attention. We set ourselves away and apart from the forces that would constrain us within proper and respectful poses. We are frequently unbathed, always disheveled, and completely accepting of each other. Curiously, we never work together in our offices at the university, for these are clean, well-lighted environments that keep us, our colleagues, and our students "safe." The impropriety of our dancing together liberates us from all the other proprieties that might modulate our voices: Will we offend colleagues? Will we transgress the decorum of scholarship? Will we seem reasonable and well mannered?

Not only does the choreography of our lesbian collaboration liberate us from the patriarchal codes that keep us from finding ourselves as subjects in language and that keep us—with the same strategies—from each other, but it also keeps us working. It fuels us when we flag. When one of us falters, when she misses a step, the other holds her up, pulls her through and leads when necessary. In discussing the effects of women writer's groups and the tendency of such groups to foster "the spirit to continue writing," Valerie Miner attests to the synergistic energy of women committed to common cause: "Working together provides significant feminist testimony. These writing groups can create environments where our voices will be heard and our languages understood. They provide forums for analytical argument and artistic support" (21). When we speak alone, we are inhibited by the proprieties of patriarchal culture; it is dangerous to speak too freely. Together we goad each other, literally and sometimes even physically, into extreme and improper statements. If *lesbian* is a word, as Elizabeth Meese asserts, "written in invisible ink," hidden in the shadows, seeking but infrequently finding that voice which gives it "self," then by writing together, we nurture this word. The lesbian cannot be hidden in our writing, she cannot "lurk" behind our words. The lesbian sits in the room with us and she laughs.

This laughter, lesbian laughter, is probably the most powerful aspect of our collaboration. But in some ways it is the most frightening. Helene Cixous characterizes the joy of the woman writing as the laugh of the Medusa. But woman is constrained from her writing by her fear of patriarchal disapproval: "I was ashamed. I was afraid, and I swallowed my shame and my fear" (876). Cixous asserts that women write in secret, hiding their efforts because they cannot liberate the power within them and at the same time remain the women discourse has molded them to be: "You've written a little, but in secret. And it wasn't good, because it was in secret, and because you punished yourself for writing, because you didn't go all the way; or because you wrote, irresistibly, as when we would masturbate in secret, not to go further, but to attenuate the tension a bit, just enough to take the edge off" (876–77). The Medusa is a monster, a specifically female monster, and Cixous urges her reader to liberate the monstrous: "Write, let no one hold you back" (877); look, she tells us, at the female monster, the Medusa, for she is a source of strength: "You have to look at the Medusa straight on to see her. And she's not deadly. She's beautiful and she's laughing" (885). Together, we engage in and engage our monstrousness—willingly, openly, together. Mary Meigs affirms the monstrousness of lesbian writing: "All these writers are 'inassimilable,' that is, they refuse to conform to patriarchal expectations, and are viewed with the 'embarrassment' that monsters provoke" (36). And she also associates this with humor: "Humor is often overlooked by readers, perhaps because they perceive that its true purpose is to mock covertly their most cherished beliefs. . . . Yet humor is part of the language of defiance that enables feminists to live in a repressive climate" (37).

Our ridiculousness and thus our impropriety seem to know no bounds, but the excesses of our riotous behavior serve to relieve the many frustrations our collaboration generates. Since we write every word together (one of us always types, both talk—often at the same time), we never lose touch with each other, but sometimes the intimacy and intensity become wearing, the partners too close, and we need to distance ourselves from each other and from our work. At other times the lesbian desire our dance tends to liberate cannot be restricted to the scholarly pages we compose; the careful, responsible, and measured pages of our academic writing alienate us so fully that we become dispirited. At such times, the dance must allow for a new figure, a twirl, an arabesque, a dip. Such movements are accomplished in surprising ways. Our dog, for example, frequently aids in attenuating our anxieties. We refer to her—despite the fact that her name is Cassy—as Miss Malone and discuss quite seriously with her how her work in dog studies is coming. We inquire after her social life, asking if she has met any interesting creatures in the neighborhood, if she has attended any conferences lately, and we have—when quite desperate, when exhausted, when the words and ideas would simply not flow—even lent Miss Malone our glasses, found her a scarf, and had her pose for a photograph to accompany her forthcoming book, a revision of her doggy dissertation.

At other times, our frustrations and anxieties make themselves apparent in our use of language. As one of us dictates a particularly mellifluous phrase, the other will type it, adding obscenities or ludicrous peculiarities that make us both laugh. We comb our work for typographical errors, regaling each other with tales of how our work will be misread because of these errors, how we will be made famous by these misreadings, or how we will be seriously maligned for the jokes we have inadvertently left in our texts. Even describing these activities—making them public—makes us cringe because we realize that we are not maintaining the appropriate, socially sanctioned view of academics, especially dignified female academics. We feel, in other words, that our true monstrousness is showing. But what is telling is that every bit of our humor, all of our jokes, have one target. Each undermines, makes ridiculous, mocks the structure in which we struggle to find voice. Each of our jokes makes fun of us as academics, mocks the institutions and the forms in which we, as professors of English, find ourselves mired. Each serves as a moment of uninhibited release by means of which our desire to express and to find a language for the lesbian, the us, the experienced, the lived, is released. With that comes a chance to call into question the rules of both the narrative structures we have chosen (scholarly prose) and the very establishment of the academic environment. The fact that we are reluctant here to reveal some of our more foolish jokes made at the expense of the profession indicates how far our collaboration allows us to go, the risks we can take in our intimate moments of collaboration. When the pressures to encode our thoughts and our desires in appropriate and proper language become immense, these wild, brief moments sustain us. At these times, our dance becomes frenzied and ungovernable.

The wildness of this dance, however, must not be allowed to overshadow the very real work we do as we dance in the dark, in the completely private and safe room of our own. In an essay which has not lost its power to move feminist readers after more than twenty years, "When We Dead Awaken: Writing as Re-Vision," Adrienne Rich comments upon the vigor and excitement of the early moments of the women's movement in the mid-twentieth century: "It's exhilarating to be alive in a time of awakening consciousness." But Rich goes on to observe that such a time can also be difficult and distressing: "It can also be confusing, disorienting, and painful. This awakening of dead or sleeping consciousness has already affected the lives of millions of women, even those who don't know it yet" (34–35). One of the major tasks of this awakening, as Rich sees it, is the act of reassessing our cultures; she calls this act "re-vision": "the act of looking back, of seeing with fresh eyes, of entering an old text from a new critical direction—is for women more than a chapter in cultural history: it is an act of survival" (35). Our writing together has frequently followed Rich's paradigm—we have sought to bring a perspective we would call distinctly lesbian to a text that may have eluded such reading before.

And if we borrow again from the time during which Rich first penned and spoke these words at the Modern Language Association Conference (1971), we can demonstrate how our skills of re-vision are fostered by our collaborative choreography. One of the most important sites of feminist thinking during the seventies was the consciousness-raising group, the relaxed collection of women who discussed, argued, commiserated, and analyzed their ways through that energetic decade. We taught one another during those times to seek, to think, to write, to learn. Most important, we pushed one another beyond our own analyses. Someone always had something more, some further thought that enabled us to think our way beyond the scripts we had inherited. We still have much to accomplish, but it would never have happened without those frequently problematic and myopic sessions we called "consciousness raising."

In some ways, our revision of texts, as we collaborate, is fostered by that same kind of environment. We encourage each other to think, we invite each other to talk, and finally we teach each other to write what has not yet been written. We see newly and write newly. And we do this because we work together. When the vision fails, we talk some more. When the mind falters, one of us gets tea. When we have had too much, we cry. But we are never alone. The importance of our collaboration, then, lies in the fact that it is an effort that we always share. And beyond the fact that we always share this dance is the fact that it always leads us someplace new. Together we can say things, know things, push ourselves to moments we would never have reached alone. Within the boundaries of individual authorship, we may have acquiesced to the prohibitions that constrain our writing and our thoughts. But together we danced through the minefields—to borrow an analogy from feminist writer Annette Kolodny, who characterizes her own experience in the practice of feminist criticism in just these terms.

Having spoken extensively about the process of lesbian collaboration and the choreography of our desire, we should add something more specific about the implications of writing from this site. Teresa de Lauretis is firmly committed to reconceptualizing the notion of homosexuality as an unstable exterior that serves to stabilize the more centered perspectives and subjectivities of heterosexuality. De Lauretis writes that

> homosexuality is no longer to be seen simply as marginal with regard to a dominant, stable form of sexuality (heterosexuality) against which it would be defined either by opposition or by homology. In other words, it is no longer to be seen either as merely transgressive or deviant vis-a-vis a proper, natural sexuality . . . , according to the older, pathological model, or as just another, optional "life-style," according to the model of contemporary North American pluralism. ("Queer Theory" iii)

Homosexuality, thus, is not a site simply of transgression or a positioning of the subject along a spectrum of varied life patterns. Rather, male and female homosexuality may be, de Lauretis writes, "reconceptualized as social and cultural forms in their own right, albeit emergent ones and thus still fuzzily defined, undercoded, and discursively dependent on more established forms." In de Lauretis's terms, then, lesbianism does not mark "the limits of the social space by designating a place at the edge of culture," but in fact, "gay sexuality in its specific female and male cultural (or subcultural) forms acts as an agency of social process whose mode of functioning is both interactive and yet resistant, both participatory and yet distinct, claiming at once equality and difference, demanding political representation while insisting on its material and historical specificity" (iii).

For de Lauretis, then, "lesbian and gay sexualities may be understood and imaged as forms of resistance to cultural homogenization, counteracting dominant discourses with other constructions of the subject in culture" (iii). But although we find lesbianism and the lesbian subject resistant and transgressive, we cannot, as de Lauretis makes clear, reduce lesbianism to simple transgression. If this is true, perhaps our dance in the dark takes place more publicly than we know. De Lauretis encourages us to acknowledge the disruptive nature of queerness; as Doty puts it: "Queerness has been set up to challenge and break apart conventional categories, not to become one itself" (xv). But de Lauretis's refusal to relegate queerness to the margins of the culture is significant. We may dance in the dark, but the results of our dance—our work—does find its way into the light of day, into the journal, the conference, the classroom, the lecture, the book review. As Phelan expresses it:

> Lesbianism challenges heterosexual privilege, . . . it challenges heterosexist gender conceptions, without going so far as to say that it provides us with its own privileged epistemology. Lesbianism provides the vantage point for a negative dialectic, a displacement and critique—what de Lauretis calls "a space of contradictions, in the here and now, that need to be affirmed but not resolved." ("(Be)Coming" 786)

We hope that our work does participate in this important endeavor, but when we are together, when we engage ourselves in the choreography by means of which we make real our lesbian desire, by means of which we find ritual and language that allow us our lesbian subjectivity, we are alone, dancing in the dark. The understandable jealousy of our current partners is an impediment, but we are content to exclude everyone from these moments of writing and thinking together, by means of which we find our voice. It is quite inconceivable to us that this collaboration will ever end. I would, thus, say to you, my partner, my collaborator, my friend, the words Luce Irigaray so eloquently penned: "And only the limiting effect of time can make us stop speaking to each other. Don't worry. I—continue. Under all these artificial constraints of time and space, I embrace you endlessly" (217).

REFERENCES

Anzaldúa, Gloria. *Borderlands/La Frontera: The New Mestiza.* San Francisco: Spinsters/Aunt Lute, 1987.

———. "Bridge, Drawbridge, Sandbar or Island: Lesbians-of-Color *Hacienda Alianzas.*" *Bridges of Power: Women's Multicultural Alliances.* Ed.Lisa Albrecht and Rose M. Brewer. Philadelphia: New Society, 1990. 216–31.

Butler, Judith. *Gender Trouble: Feminism and the Subversion of Identity.* New York: Routledge, 1989.

Christian, Barbara. "Trajectories of Self-Definition: Placing Contemporary Afro-American Women's Fiction." *Black Feminist Criticism: Perspectives on Women Writers.* Elmsford, NY: Pergamon, 1985. 171–86.

Cixous, Helene. "The Laugh of the Medusa." *Signs* 1 (1976): 875–93.

de Lauretis, Teresa. "Eccentric Subjects: Feminist Theory and Historical Consciousness." *Feminist Studies* 16 (1990): 115–50.

———. "Sexual Indifference and Lesbian Representation." *Theatre Journal* 40 (1988): 155–77.

———. "Queer Theory: Lesbian and Gay Sexualities: An Introduction." *differences* 3 (1991): iii–xviii.

Doty, Alexander. *Making Things Perfectly Queer: Interpreting Mass Culture.* Minneapolis: University of Minnesota Press, 1993.

Fuss, Diana. *Essentially Speaking: Feminism, Nature, and Difference.* New York: Routledge, 1989.

———. "Inside/Out." *Inside/Out: Lesbian Theories, Gay Theories.* Ed. Diana Fuss. New York: Routledge, 1991. 1–10.

Irigaray, Luce. *This Sex Which Is Not One.* Trans. Catherine Porter with Carolyn Burke. Ithaca, NY: Cornell University Press, 1985.

Kolodny, Annette. "Dancing through the Minefield: Some Observations on the Theory, Practice, and Politics of a Feminist Literary Criticism." *Feminist Studies* 6 (1980): 1–25.

Marcus, Jane. "Under Review: How to Read a Hot Flash." Afterword. *Sister Gin.* By June Arnold. New York: Feminist, 1989.

Meese, Elizabeth. "Theorizing Lesbian: Writing—A Love Letter." *Lesbian Texts and Contexts: Radical Revisions.* Ed. Karla Jay and Joanne Glasgow. New York: New York University Press, 1990. 70–87.

Meigs, Mary. "Falling between the Cracks." *Lesbian Texts and Contexts: Radical Revisions.* Ed. Karla Jay and Joanne Glasgow. New York: New York University Press, 1990. 28–38.

Miner, Valerie. "An Imaginative Collectivity of Writers and Readers." *Lesbian Texts and Contexts: Radical Revisions.* Ed. Karla Jay and Joanne Glasgow. New York: New York University Press, 1990. 13–27.

Phelan, Shane. "(Be)Coming Out: Lesbian Identity and Politics." *Signs* 18 (1993): 765–90.

———. *Identity Politics: Lesbian Feminism and the Limits of Community.* Philadelphia: Temple University Press, 1989.

Rich, Adrienne. "Compulsory Heterosexuality and Lesbian Existence." *Signs* 5 (1980): 631–60.

———. "It Is the Lesbian in Us . . ." *On Lies, Secrets, and Silence: Selected Prose 1966–1978.* New York: Norton, 1979. 199–202.

———. "When We Dead Awaken: Writing as Re-Vision." *On Lies, Secrets, and Silence: Selected Prose 1966–1978.* New York: Norton, 1979. 33–49.

Smith, Barbara. "The Truth That Never Hurts: Black Lesbians in Fiction in the 1980s." *Wild Women in the Whirlwind: Afra-American Culture and the Contemporary Literary Renaissance.* Ed. Joanne Braxton and Andree Nicola McLaughlin. New Brunswick, NJ: Rutgers University Press, 1990.

Stimpson, Catharine R. "Zero Degree Deviancy: The Lesbian Novel in English." *Where the Meanings Are: Feminism and Cultural Spaces.* New York: Methuen, 1988. 97–110.

Vicinus, Martha. "'They Wonder to Which Sex I Belong': The Historical Roots of the Modern Lesbian Identity." *Feminist Studies* 18 (1992): 467–97.

Wittig, Monique. "The Straight Mind." *Feminist Issues* 1 (1980): 102–10.

Zimmerman, Bonnie. "What Has Never Been: An Overview of Lesbian Feminist Literary Criticism." *The New Feminist Criticism: Women, Literature and Theory.* Ed. Elaine Showalter. New York: Pantheon, 1985. 200–24.

Mary Ann Leiby and Leslie J. Henson

10

Common Ground, Difficult Terrain

Confronting Difference through Feminist Collaboration

> Th[e] interplay of personal and scholarly concerns has always been a distinctive characteristic of feminist inquiry; it is also a distinctive pleasure of feminist collaboration, which erases the boundaries between self and other, private and public, work and play. (Abel et al. 167)
>
> The real power, as you and I well know, is collective. I can't afford to be afraid of you, nor you of me. If it takes head-on collisions, let's do it: this polite timidity is killing us.... As Lorde suggests ... it is in looking to the nightmare that the dream is found. (Moraga 34)

That day was a nightmare. We had been team teaching for two months, walking together to class, taking the same path, covering each day that familiar, "common" ground. We had shared the same experience, been fired with the "pleasure of feminist collaboration": the joy of "eras[ing] boundaries." But something changed that day. Something at first subtle, then explosive. We had been discussing, as usual, the text we would be teaching, each of us highlighting our own concerns, until together we came to a shared vision of our lesson plan for the day.

Leslie: . . . but these sections might reinforce heterosexism and homophobia.

> **Mary Ann:** Wait a minute! That's not heterosexism, let alone *homophobia*. Heterosexism is when. . . .

For Leslie, Mary Ann's voice took on an authoritarian, pedantic tone, droning on so loudly that it silenced her. It was a familiar silence for Leslie. And her silence continued even as we entered the classroom. As usual, we stood on the stage, in front of the eighty students taking our freshman-level, Women's Studies/composition course.

> **Mary Ann:** (breaking off her theoretical monologue on heterosexism) Do you want to start with the quiz?
>
> **Leslie:** (silence).
>
> **Mary Ann:** Leslie! Do you want to start with *the quiz*!
>
> **Leslie:** (silence).
>
> **Mary Ann:** Well, do you at least want to write the assignment on the board? Leslie? Leslie? Look out there; we have to teach in one minute! Obviously you're pissed at me—why, I don't know—but we've got to teach. Leslie! Leslie!
>
> **Leslie:** (in a bitter tone) Yea, whatever. (to the students, in a professional voice) We'll start class today with the quiz.

We managed to get through that class, to separate the nightmare of a very personal issue from our public, professional duties. Despite the pain of stumbling onto the difficult terrain beyond our common ground, we came to understand over the next three years the necessity of such conflict. We learned that even with our shared commitment to a radical feminist ideology, our differences came between us. Leslie had been angered by Mary Ann's effacement of her feelings as a lesbian-identified bisexual, by the audacity with which Mary Ann, a heterosexual woman, had defined Leslie's oppression for her.

Our experience led us to see that the "common ground" of feminist collaboration—with its "distinctive pleasure"—exists simultaneously with feminist collisions; common ground is also difficult terrain. Abel and her colleagues worked together when the "terrain" of the academy was dominated by privileged white males, when women were not as prevalent, and thus were more isolated; their "pleasure" of collaboration came, in part, from the greater sense of security and belonging it afforded them. Moraga, however, wrote during that same period (the early 1980s) about her exclusion as a lesbian of color from such collaboration, and the need for women in the academy to confront difference and thus create even greater collective power. Women's collaboration in the academy can be genuinely comforting—embodying Carol Gilligan's "ethic of care" (74); however, when two or more women of conflicting subjectivities[1] come together, such comfort can be merely an illusion, a "polite timidity" masking the type of nightmare *we* experienced, in which the voice of the privileged silences that of the oppressed.

Thus, we realized we needed a theoretical/practical model for building coalition across our differences, one that valued those "head-on collisions" Moraga argues are necessary. Through our friendship, our collaboration over the next few years, and our work in the areas of critical and feminist pedagogy, language theory, cultural criticism, and radical feminist theory/activism, we constructed a method of feminist collaboration in the academy. This method relies upon examining with ourselves, our students, and other feminists the collisions we have had with each other as a result of our different subjectivities: Mary Ann's as a working-class, heterosexual woman of partial Jewish ancestry, who has at times disabling health problems, vs. Leslie's as an able-bodied, middle-class, lesbian-identified bisexual of Catholic upbringing.

Our model draws upon the work of theorists of critical and liberatory pedagogy and feminist theorists; we also incorporate the work of theorists of feminist pedagogy. Because critical pedagogy, feminist theory, and feminist pedagogy are interrelated and difficult to separate, rather than debating their interrelational tensions, we focus on what they contribute to understanding the role of difference in pedagogy. According to Giroux, critical pedagogy emphasizes "the importance of a multicentric perspective," which allows teachers and students to "analyze how the differences within and between various groups can expand the potential of human life and democratic possibilities" (*Border* 175). Such a pedagogy, however, leads to difficult terrain. As Lorde explains, because "[i]nstitutionalized rejection of difference is an absolute necessity in a profit economy . . . we have *all* been programmed to respond to the human differences . . . in one of three ways": ignore it, copy it, or destroy it (115). We have also been programmed to listen to "that piece of the oppressor which is planted deep within" us (Lorde 123). Feminist pedagogy also devises models for teaching and learning which create alternative ways of dealing with difference.[2] Weiler states that within "feminist pedagogy, we can begin to acknowledge the reality of tensions that result from different histories, from privilege, oppression, and power as they are lived by teachers and students in classrooms" ("Freire" 470). By admitting to our students how we ourselves fall into these oppressive patterns, we can move students toward an understanding of these patterns in themselves.

Here, we examine the "institutionalized rejection of difference" Lorde describes and how this rejection has impacted our collaboration, noting how analyzing and engaging with our own resistance to difference can be useful to developing what Giroux, following Teresa de Lauretis, terms a "pedagogy *of* and *for* difference" ("Schooling" 142). Our analysis of the narrative beginning of this essay explains how the interrelation of privilege and oppression contributes to the "institutionalized rejection of difference." We also show how the academy itself resists difference and collaboration and explain how feminist collaboration can undermine the competition and dominating use of authority encouraged by the academy. We present our theoretical/practical model for dealing with difference and conclude with how our guest speakers and student projects enact a feminist pedagogy *of* and *for* difference, thus expanding the possibilities of the academy.

By examining concrete instances of confronting difference, we create what Lundgren calls a "text *for* pedagogy," which, as Giroux explains, is "both a process and a product" ("Ideology" 32). As a "product" our text is inseparable from the "process" we describe: a long-term engagement with specific differences. The "product" is only useful insomuch as other feminists engage and collaborate with our "process" by examining their own reactions to the confrontations and pedagogical techniques we describe, and by analyzing how these reactions relate to their own subjectivities. As Weiler notes, "feminist teachers, if they are to work to create a counter-hegemonic teaching,[3] must be conscious of their own gendered, classed, . . . raced [and other aspects of their] subjectivities as they confirm or challenge the lived experiences of their students" (*Women* 145) and, we add, the lived experiences of other feminists in the academy.

A text *for* pedagogy, Giroux argues, "promote[s] modes of schooling based on the critical dimensions of an emancipatory ideology" ("Ideology" 32). Citing de Lauretis, Giroux explains that a pedagogy *of* difference addresses how "the representations and practices of difference are actively learned, internalized, challenged, or transformed," while a pedagogy *for* difference "is characterized by 'an ongoing effort to create new spaces of discourse, to rewrite cultural narratives, and to define the terms of another perspective—a view from elsewhere'" ("Schooling" 142). This type of critical pedagogy involves "a critical interrogation of the silences and tensions between the master narratives" of the academy and "the self-representations of subordinate groups as they might appear in 'forgotten' histories, texts, memories, experiences, and community narratives" ("Schooling" 142). Because feminist collaboration is always in danger of replicating the oppressions in the academy (classism, ableism, anti-Semitism, and so forth), it is crucial to examine difference through that collaboration. We need to face, however, that "this kind of pedagogy and exploration of experiences . . . is risky and filled with pain" (Weiler, "Freire" 470).

In the incident described earlier, Mary Ann used the academy's "master narrative" to silence Leslie's self-representation, her response to the text, and more importantly, her memories and experiences of homophobia. Leslie's position was a very painful one; only through a risky exploration of her *own* experience, however, was Mary Ann able to identify the pain that motivated her to wield her heterosexual privilege. As Gail Pheterson notes, "Every human difference [is] a confrontation with self" (152). Mary Ann had to recognize that her need to defend heterosexism stemmed from her experiences of rape and childhood sexual abuse, which taught her to define herself through her (hetero)sexuality. Pheterson explains, "Oppression and domination are experienced as a mutually reinforcing web of insecurities and rigidities"; hence, "the more dependent a heterosexual woman is upon male approval . . . , the more threatened she will be by lesbian autonomy" (152).

This exploration of experience did not come easily for us. Because oppression breeds "a package of psychological processes that distort reality and weaken personal strength" (Pheterson 151–2), Leslie had to work through the internalized oppression which caused her to doubt her own perception of the text, and of her life—oppression dating back to childhood sexual abuse. After a few weeks, Leslie dealt with this oppression enough to voice her anger; and Mary Ann admitted she was being heterosexist and had no right to define heterosexism for Leslie. It took several more semesters of engaging with each other for Mary Ann to discover that sexual abuse was one source of her need to wield her privilege; only in writing this essay did she realize the role her class position played. The "head-on collision" was risky and painful, but through it we came to a more comforting space, within ourselves and with each other, and with other feminists.

We came closer to reaching the "affirming community" Abel, Hirsch, and Langland describe (106) only by traversing difficult terrain and realizing the academy encouraged, indeed sanctioned, Mary Ann's use of heterosexism. Recognizing the academy's resistance to difference as connected to its resistance to collaboration is necessary for achieving a pedagogy *of* and *for* difference, and a feminist collaboration *of* and *for* difference. Despite many academics' commitment to collaborative teaching and learning, the structure of the academy is resistant to collaborative work, with the exception of peer tutoring. For example, Bruffee points out that students have internalized "long-prevailing academic prohibitions against collaboration" because such "collaboration skates dangerously close to the supreme academic sin, plagiarism" (26–27). Feminist pedagogy theorists have documented how the traditional classroom privileges "patterns of competition and argument in discussion," devaluing the collaborative interaction preferred by female students (Maher 495–96). Don Dippo and his colleagues, pointing to the similarities between their work and that of feminist educators, state that the "indeterminateness of more collaborative approaches to teaching and learning often leads to head-on conflicts" with many "institutional imperatives" (89): with the authoritarian structure of the classroom (85), competitive grading (89–90), textbook-centered curricula (90–91), we are enmired in an industry which rewards individual efforts at the expense of collaborative ones (92). As they note, coauthored publications are valued far less than single-authored ones, and a "commitment to emancipatory teaching and collaborative scholarship can lead to marginalization and even unemployment" (92).

Because of these strictures against collaboration, Thomas claims that collaborative teaching is dead: "Team teaching began in the late 1960s with high hopes of success. It has, however, failed. . . . classrooms [seem to] provide an especially uncongenial environment for teamwork" (1). Thus, in the academy, collaborative ground is not merely difficult terrain, but virtually uninhabitable. Why such a hostile environment for collaboration? Does the academy see those who collaborate as "collaborationists," enemies of the academy itself? It is clear to us that this resistance to collaboration is also resistance to a pedagogy *of* and *for* difference. We turn to our own experience to illustrate the academy's resistance.

Where we teach, graduate student teachers and professors are required to undergo an evaluation process to be granted departmental and university-wide teaching awards. We were teaching "Writing about Identity: Issues of Privilege and Oppression"—a coup in itself, given the university's difficulty accommodating a collaboratively taught class. We wanted to be evaluated as a team but were given separate evaluators, which placed us in competition with one another. The two evaluators had vastly different perceptions of the academy's relationship to collaboration and pedagogy *of* and *for* difference. One evaluator rejected the anticollaborative standards, considered us a team and recommended us together for a departmental award. His comments revealed his belief that the academy has a responsibility to address difference in pedagogy: "This is exactly the kind of intellectually rigourous multicultural education that [our university] needs." The second evaluator viewed the academy as virtually uninhabitable ground for collaboration and difference, compared our teaching to an Olympic event, and noted the enormous "difficulty" of "teaching the essay in the context of identity politics." However, when it came to supporting our *feminist* collaboration and our *feminist* pedagogy *of* and *for* difference, and recognizing their relation to our differing subjectivities, he backed off, virtually effacing our differences.

For this course, we primarily used texts representing various marginalized subjectivities and made links to personal examples that highlighted the heterogeneity of each of our own subjectivities. But the second evaluator viewed us as presenting "a unanimity of position," a "united front" that was "oppositional to preferred or dominant ideology." He felt that we should have "disagreed" more often to model "how to argue" and to demonstrate "that the teachers' point of view is not law." He was concerned that we not replicate what Paulo Freire terms "the banking model of education" (58) and wanted to ensure that students could freely and equally present diverse viewpoints. However, his concern turned out not to be for all students, but for "the men." He stated that "only women were responding to the questions" we raised. His critique is useful in connecting the academy's resistance to collaboration and pedagogy *of* and *for* difference to its myopic (privileged) male centeredness. It is also useful in demonstrating why feminism is so necessary to such a pedagogy.

Frances Maher notes that the banking model of education is particularly pernicious for *female* students, in that "men in general have often been described as the 'subject' for which women are the 'object'" (494). Female students have *already* been objectified through sexism and become further objectified through banking model education. Madeleine Arnot observes, because "[w]omen have become colonized within a male-defined world . . . in education [they] have learnt *how* to lose" (64–65); they [and, we add, other oppressed groups] have been encouraged to underachieve and to accept their inferior status as "natural" (66). Our evaluator was not concerned with women's history, however; he assumed we were guilty of reverse sexism. His assumption was that if we simply *competed* with one another (rather than collaboratively presented similar ideologies informed by *differing* subjectivities, and encouraged students to do likewise), men in the class would not perceive us as the "law." They would then feel comfortable enough to emulate our argumentation, competing with us as well as the *other* students—"the women"—to produce meaning. Thus, the classroom would have become a space for common ground—a level playing field.

According to Peter McLaren, this belief in an equitable classroom is informed by "a politics of pluralism which largely ignores the workings of power and privilege"; in the classroom, as in society in general, "knowledges are forged in histories that are riven with differentially constituted relations of power" (201). Because of these "histories," the classroom is difficult terrain; it is also, as Giroux notes, like democracy—"a terrain of struggle" (*Living* 146). As "there will always exist more than one conception of justice and the public good" even among feminists—"it is among and across these differences that one" must "fight the tyranny of master narratives"

(*Living* 146). Our evaluator, relying upon the academy's "master narrative" of competition, could not perceive the difference between this master narrative and the voices of two women collaborating and engaging with the "tyranny" of that narrative. He interpreted us as having one voice which spoke the "law" of feminist ideology, ignoring M. M. Bakhtin's point that even the supposedly "homogenous" language of a dominant group is in fact stratified (289–90).

That day, the privileged white males *were* silenced, but only momentarily, and not by us; most days, we had to check these students from using an aggressive "master narrative" of competition to cut off the voices of women and less privileged men. The presence of the evaluator—a visible embodiment of the academy's hierarchical, competitive power structure—silenced the white male students. This is not to say that teachers from oppressed identity positions can never be dominators, but to point out that the teacher's subject position matters. As Kobena Mercer notes, the "identity of the enunciator inevitably 'makes a difference' to the social construction of meaning and value" (193). In addition to visible gender, race, and age factors, being "out" to our students about our differences in sexual orientation, class, and ablebodiedness made a difference in how our students perceived us. For example, Leslie was accused early in the term of focusing far too much on lesbian issues; not until Mary Ann, who had in fact emphasized these issues, pointed out this discrepancy did student perceptions change. The students learned they had been perceiving Leslie as lacking authority and credibility on lesbian issues because of her subjectivity, when ironically, the opposite was the case.

To view authority, then, as presenting the same static, hegemonic "law," regardless of teachers' subjectivity, is to ignore the insights of feminist and critical pedagogy on the role of the teacher's authority. bell hooks says that "many women have had difficulty asserting power in the feminist classroom for fear that to do so would be to exercise domination" (*Talking* 52). Thus, one goal of feminists is to devise alternative, nondominating methods of exercising authority. hooks recommends: "elect[ing] not to assume the posture of all-knowing professors" (*Talking* 52). We can do this by admitting to students that, like them, we fall into using the three destructive methods of dealing with difference that Lorde describes; as Elizabeth Ellsworth reminds us, "No teacher is free of these learned and internalized oppressions" (99). This is not to say feminist teachers should abjure any use of authority; rather, we need to use authority in Giroux's "emancipatory form"—"as a terrain of struggle . . . [that] reveals rather than hides . . . its interests and possibilities" ("Schooling" 137).

Shrewsbury argues that "empowering pedagogy does not dissolve the authority or power of the instructor," but creates a system in which "the teacher's knowledge and experience" is used "to increase the power of all" ("What" 11). Sharing our head-on collisions, and how we worked through them, enables us to "move from power as domination to power as creative energy" ("What" 11). Because the instructor's power is not the only power in the classroom, feminist teachers must decide whether or not to use their authority to silence oppressive views. Julie Brown asks, "Should a male student be silenced" for remarking that women who were raped and killed "'got exactly what they deserved'" (57)? If we are open in the classroom about our own subjectivities and the ways in which we have been both oppressor and oppressed, we may be able to use our own knowledge and experience to address such dilemmas.

Revealing information about ourselves enables students to face the reality of oppression and demonstrates the validity of complex feminist theoretical points. When students such as the one Brown mentions make oppressive remarks, it is possible for us to embody the very differences they attempt to efface (or to bring in guest speakers for the same purpose). This model also demonstrates that through such a collaborative engagement with difference, we can meet upon common ground; we can actively expand the boundaries of our own subjectivities, which as Giroux says are "undergo[ing] constant transformations" (*Living* 74), and create for ourselves "insurgent subjectivit[ies]" (*Living* 77). We can become "border-crossers" (Giroux, *Border* 170).

Revealing certain experiences to our students and other feminists is often difficult and painful, and teachers should only collaborate in this way when we are ready. As JoAnne Jones explains, we are "forced to constantly decide how safe it is to self-disclose," and we must remember that what we *do* share depends on whether or not "it will be helpful" (104). For example, we use the "head-on collision" described in our narrative, as well as Mary Ann's experiences with sexual abuse, to help students grasp Adrienne Rich's points about compulsory heterosexuality. Rich argues, "The enforcement of heterosexuality for women [is] a means of assuring male right of physical, economic, and emotional access" to women (167). By separating women from one another, rendering them objects of exchange for men, "compulsory heterosexuality simplifies the task" of men who exploit women by leading women to "accept" such exploitation (166). This acceptance stems from women being forced to find self-worth in heterosexuality.

While we emphasize the connections between sexism and heterosexism, we also point out the dangers in not acknowledging "the specificity of the oppression" and in "attempting to deal with [it] purely from a theoretical base" (Moraga 29). To clarify how to avoid these dangers, we make use of our personal experience. For example, we share with our students an incident that helped us recognize that "specificity," emotionally and materially, rather than simply theorize it. One night a group of drunken fraternity men verbally harassed us outside the post office. They began with the usual "Hey babies" and "What are you girls doing tonight?" We ignored their remarks, but we could not ignore what they were doing to their semiconscious friend: dragging him from their car and screaming, "Come on, you sissy! What are you, a queer boy?" As they held him up against the car, one of them said, "What about those girls?" "They're just a couple of fucking dykes," another yelled as he punched his "friend" into unconsciousness. As we raced to the car and tore out of there, Mary Ann realized, for the first time, how heterosexism and homophobia multiply the fear and violence in sexism; even though these "men" assumed Mary Ann was a lesbian, *she* knew the truth, and whether justified or not, felt a degree of safety in her heterosexuality. But Leslie, petrified that they *did* somehow know about her lesbianism, screamed in the car, "How did they know? How the fuck did they know?"

Thus, Leslie realized what heterosexual privilege was: her fear that they *knew* was in direct proportion to her lack of that privilege; and, Mary Ann realized what heterosexual privilege was, because she felt the intense fear of losing that privilege. She knew that she could never again attempt to define heterosexism for a nonheterosexual woman, because she had glimpsed the "specificity" of Leslie's oppression. She also realized on an emotional level that her need to maintain her heterosexual privilege was linked to the specificity of her own oppressions of poverty and sexual abuse; she had been clinging to the illusion that her heterosexuality could make her safe from those oppressions.

Mary Ann shared another experience with our class to demonstrate how she had learned as a poor, sexually abused woman that such safety did not exist. Often students believe in this safety, and blame the victims of battering and sexual violence, even when they understand intellectually that such blame is not warranted. Women must be safe somewhere, they want to believe. To explode this dangerous myth of compulsory heterosexuality, Mary Ann tells what happened to her when she was sixteen. She tells how poverty and abuse at home led her to quit high school and move into an apartment with her boyfriend in the city, working sixty or seventy hours a week in a nursing home kitchen to pay the rent; how he was laid off from his job and began to sell drugs, then to drink and take drugs, and finally to batter Mary Ann. And how, one night, when the violence and screams were so loud that the downstairs neighbors called the police, how those police came and knocked her boyfriend out, then raped her repeatedly, anally and vaginally, as she slipped into a coma to be left for dead. She could not consider "pressing charges" (as most students would suggest), because the cops *knew* where she lived, that she was poor and underage, that her boyfriend sold drugs, and that they could, if they wanted, come back and kill her.

When Mary Ann shares this experience, most of our (predominately white middle-class) students respond with stunned silence, then begin to struggle with their disbelief. A "head-on collision" occurs between the students' belief system and Mary Ann's experiences. At this point, Mary Ann explains that, while police can and do rape white, middle-class women, it is much easier for them to rape poor women and women of color, and go unpunished. As Barbara Smith argues, "Somebody who is already dealing with multiple oppression is already more vulnerable to another kind of attack upon her identity" (125). Leslie then discusses how her class privilege initially made it difficult for her to imagine what Mary Ann had endured, and how by recognizing this privilege she could see that she had lived in a much safer neighborhood, with parents who could provide for her medical care and legal representation. By giving this explanation, Leslie demonstrates how dealing with class difference by ignoring it is a denial of privilege: seeing it as a "given" to which all have equal access. The strength of our feminist collaboration occurs when students, witnessing Leslie's initial "ignorance" of difference, see it transformed into acknowledgment. They can then move from defensiveness and guilt toward "common ground" with Leslie: they too have just been "ignorant." Now they can understand what Judit Moschkovich says—that we are all "responsible for the *transformation* of [our] ignorance" (79)—and they can begin to hear Mary Ann's experience differently.

We thus embody Weiler's point that "privilege and oppression are *lived*," that exploring our differences "is risky and filled with pain" ("Freire" 470, our emphasis). Mary Ann can finish her story, but now the students are less likely to resist it; they know that it is a *lived* experience, which results from classism and not failure to use resources accessible to everyone. They can then replace their version of what should have happened after the rape—Mary Ann's pressing charges against the police—with what actually happened. When she came out of the coma, she was given no VD tests, gynecological exam, or rape counseling; instead, the financial "counselor," having discovered that Mary Ann's parents were on welfare but that she had a full-time job, shoved a pen in Mary Ann's hand and forced her to sign a legal document, which in her barely conscious state she could not even see. This document declared Mary Ann an emancipated minor, making her financially responsible for herself. She left the hospital weeks before she was ready, returning to work while still on a liquid diet. Mary Ann explains that she was lucky: she had a job.

We discuss how, as in Mary Ann's case, child abuse and class oppression reinforce each other. We also explain how other forms of oppression are linked: the fourteen-year-old gay male from a wealthy family is kicked out of the house by his homophobic parents; he ends up a prostitute. Many women of color are forced into prostitution because of racism and poverty. And then there is our friend, a twenty-five-year-old, black, lesbian Ph.D. candidate in engineering, who says she is harassed each time she goes out with other engineering students to a college bar: some white male always offers her money, assuming she must be a prostitute. We explain how, while we have been sexually harassed at bars, because of our white privilege we have never been assumed to be prostitutes. Such connections help students to relate their own experiences of oppression and privilege to ours.

Students make such connections during class discussions when and only when they feel comfortable revealing their experiences. We point out early in the semester that whenever we share aspects of ourselves, we do so by choice, and that there is a process involved in our choice. Leslie explains that she only recently began discussing publicly her experiences of date rape, first in therapy groups, then at community workshops she and Mary Ann organized, then later in the classroom. We agree with bell hooks that "teachers must be actively committed to a process of self-actualization that promotes their own well-being if they are to teach in a manner that empowers students" (*Teaching* 15). It is important that we have worked through our pain before using these examples so that we do not, out of internalized oppression, damage our students and ourselves. Because of the process involved in dealing with difference—our own and others'—we have made anonymity and choice crucial aspects of our feminist pedagogy *of* and *for* difference. Our writing assignments, class projects, group work, and guest speakers never force students to deal with their own oppression or with others who are privileged in relation to them. But we do make privileged students accountable when they ignore, copy, or destroy difference. Like Laurie Crumpacker and Eleanor Vander Haegen, we let students know "we oppose all forms of discrimination . . . and will not allow the belittling of any group" (95); after all, these "groups" are human beings sitting together in a classroom.

The freshman writing sequence in our Women's Studies/composition course encourages students to confront difference as it is embodied by other students in the class. The first part of this two-part sequence is adapted from David Hoehner's composition assignment based on N. Scott Momaday's *The Way to Rainy Mountain*. For this essay, students must explore an aspect or aspects of their own subjectivity by writing in three "voices": mythical/fictional, historical, and personal; such writing moves them toward an understanding of the "heteroglossia" of their own subjectivities. We require research of these "voices" through not only standard library methods, but also through interviews with people who share their subjectivity or have experiences relevant to it. For example, a rape survivor who chooses to write about this experience is encouraged to speak with rape counselors, rape-victim advocates, feminist activists, and other survivors. Thus, collaboration is a requirement, but students *choose their collaborative partners based on what will be most empowering for them.* We also encourage students, particularly those of marginalized groups, to collaborate with one another. A group of Jewish women shared their personal experiences, historical research, interviews with relatives and rabbis, and a book on Jewish folktales. One such student concluded her essay by stating that she learned the value of her Jewish culture and was inspired to pass it on to her children and grandchildren. For her, collaboration was indeed empowering: she resolved to join a Jewish women's group on campus and to become an activist fighting anti-Semitism.

For the second essay, students engage with the "identity paper" of another student (all of which is done anonymously). Students choose whether to include their anonymous paper in a file from which they all choose an "identity paper." Each semester we have had only one African American male student in a class of eighty, so one such student chose not to have his paper included; since he wrote about his race and gender he obviously could not remain anonymous. Another semester, the only African American male chose to include his paper and allowed other students to interview him. He had been belittled throughout his education for wanting to explore the history of African Americans. With the first essay of our sequence, however, he was encouraged to do so. He read over forty books and included his own artwork in the essay, artwork he had not done for years due to a racist teacher's discouragement. Through engaging with his paper—the extreme racism it recounted, as well as the incredible strength and creativity which that racism could not kill—white students were forced to acknowledge their own privilege and racism. The white students were more open to this process because, after all, they chose to begin it.

In "Interdisciplinary Perspectives of Women"—the introductory, core course for the Women's Studies major—we use an advanced form of the two-part writing project described above. Students focus on a problem affecting women; one that affects them personally, or one with which, due to their privilege, they have had no previous experience. Students go through the same process our freshmen do, without writing about it; they are required to do the same type of collaborative research, in particular, interviews with women affected by the problem and activists working to solve it. From this, they produce a final essay project that details the causes of the problem, and, more importantly, a concrete, practical solution, which can be implemented at a personal, local, state, or national level.

Along with guest lecturers, we, as political activists, provide our students with multiple examples of such solutions and how they might be implemented: for example, our own community workshops on the intersections of classism and homophobia; collaborative projects completed by former students, which have the potential to effect positive changes for women at the national, state, and local levels; as well as the achievements of our guest lecturers. We and our guest lecturers also discuss how the common ground of these collaborative solutions came about through "head-on collisions," and the risky, painful exploration of privilege and oppression required to work through these collisions. Through our feminist collaboration in the academy—our friendship, collaborative teaching, political activism, cooperative research, and ultimately our theoretical/practical model of a feminist pedagogy *of* and *for* difference—we have tried to provide students, other feminist teachers, and ourselves with hope. We ourselves must embody what bell hooks calls for: "models for radical change in everyday life that would have meaning and significance to masses of women" (*Talking* 34).

We see those role models in our guest lecturers: Betty Campbell, an African American woman who lobbied the Florida state legislature and received over one million dollars for campus rape awareness programs; Maria Masque, a Latina lesbian who braved the white-male dominated urban planning department at our university, and despite its opposition, produced an oral herstory of inner-city lesbians; and Cynthia White, an African American woman who is struggling against poverty to produce a new literary magazine on our campus, one which represents voices like her own that have been excluded from current campus magazines. We see those role models in our students: the medical student who organized a group of other medical students to educate children about sexual abuse; the African American student who was gang raped and returned to her high school to give a presentation warning other young women about rape at fraternities and athletic dorms; the sorority students who researched eating disorders and developed a local education and prevention program, which will be implemented nationally; the working-class, white student who wrote about her marginalization in the academy; the Muslim student who wrote on the racism faced by Muslim women in the United States and who made us face our own racism in not including anything positive about Muslim women in our course. (We now include her essay in our course readings). And finally, we see those role models in ourselves, in our courage to brave the difficult terrain of difference and to meet one another on the common ground of feminist collaboration. The purpose of crossing that difficult terrain is to reach that empowering solidarity, in order to improve the lives of not just some women, but all women, indeed, all people, to heal the "split that originates in the very foundation of our lives, our culture, our languages, our thoughts" (Anzaldúa 80).

NOTES

1. We prefer the term *subjectivity* versus *identity* because, as Henry Giroux and Peter McLaren point out, "identity" implies a unitary, fixed subject, whereas "subjectivity" acknowledges the role of self-understanding—the ways "individuals make sense of their experiences"—as well as the role of cultural forms that enable or constrain such understandings (14). "Subjectivity" also addresses the heterogeneity of identity, and "the fact that individuals consist of a decentered flux of subject positions" dependent upon "discourse, social structure, repetition, memory, and affective investment" (14–15).

2. For an excellent bibliography of feminist pedagogy, one which includes a section on theorizing difference, see Carolyn M. Shrewsbury's "Feminist Pedagogy: An Updated Bibliography."

3. Weiler is drawing from Patti Lather, who argues that Women's Studies is "counter-hegemonic work" (54). Lather uses Antonio Gramsci's concepts of hegemony and counterhegemony to discuss the potential of such work, particularly curricular transformation. Defining "hegemony" as "the terrain upon which groups struggle for power" (55), she argues that Women's Studies mobilizes "counter-hegemonic forces" which "stymie consensus ..., present alternative conceptions of reality, ... [and] develop" the subjective conditions necessary for "struggle toward a more equitable social order" (55–56). Our model focuses on the "head-on collisions" between differing subjectivities, which are necessary for this counterhegemonic work.

REFERENCES

Abel, Elizabeth, Marianne Hirsch, and Elizabeth Langland. "'They Shared A Laboratory Together': Feminist Collaboration in the Academy." *Women's Studies International Forum* 6.2 (1983): 165–67.

Anzaldúa, Gloria. *Borderlands / La Frontera: The New Mestiza*. San Francisco: Aunt Lute, 1987.

Arnot, Madeleine. "Male Hegemony, Social Class, and Women's Education." *Journal of Education* 164.1 (1982): 64–89.

Bakhtin, M. M. *The Dialogic Imagination: Four Essays*. Ed. Michael Holquist. Trans. Carl Emerson and Michael Holquist. Austin: University of Texas Press, 1981.

Brown, Julie. "Theory or Practice—What Exactly Is Feminist Pedagogy?" *The Journal of General Education* 41 (1992): 51–63.

Bruffee, Kenneth. *Collaborative Learning: Higher Education, Interdependence, and the Authority of Knowledge*. Baltimore: Johns Hopkins University Press, 1993.

Crumpacker, Laurie, and Eleanor M. Vander Haegen. "Pedagogy and Prejudice: Strategies for Confronting Homophobia in the Classroom." *Women's Studies Quarterly* 3 & 4 (1993): 94–113.

Dippo, Don, et al. "Making the Political Personal: Problems of Privilege and Power in Post-Secondary Teaching." *Journal of Education* 173.3 (1991): 81–95.

Ellsworth, Elizabeth. "Why Doesn't This Feel Empowering? Working through the Repressive Myths of Critical Pedagogy." *Feminisms and Critical Pedagogy*. Ed. Carmen Luke and Jennifer Gore. New York: Routledge, 1992. 90–119.

Freire, Paulo. *Pedagogy of the Oppressed*. Trans. Myra Bergman Ramos. New York: Seabury, 1973.

Gilligan, Carol. *In a Different Voice: Psychological Theory and Women's Development*. Cambridge: Harvard University Press, 1982.

Giroux, Henry A. *Border Crossings: Cultural Workers and the Politics of Education*. New York: Routledge, 1992.

——. "Ideology and Agency in the Process of Schooling." *Journal of Education* 165.1 (1983): 12–34.

——. *Living Dangerously: Multiculturalism and the Politics of Difference*. New York: Peter Lang, 1993.

——. "Schooling as a Form of Cultural Politics: Toward a Pedagogy of and for Difference." *Critical Pedagogy, the State, and Cultural Struggle*. Ed. Henry A. Giroux and Peter McLaren. Albany: State University of New York Press, 1989. 125–51.

Giroux, Henry A., and Peter McLaren. "Writing from the Margins:

Geographies of Identity, Pedagogy, and Power." *Journal of Education* 174.1 (1992): 7–30.

Hoehner, David. "From Israel to Oklahoma: *The Way to Rainy Mountain*, Composition, and Cross-Cultural Awareness." *Approaches to Teaching Momaday's* The Way to Rainy Mountain. Ed. Kenneth M. Roemer. New York: MLA, 1988.

hooks, bell. *Talking Back: Thinking Feminist, Thinking Black*. Boston: South End, 1989.

――――. *Teaching to Transgress: Education as the Practice of Freedom*. New York: Routledge, 1994.

Jones, JoAnne, Patricia Romney, and Beverly Tatum. "Feminist Strategies for Teaching about Oppression: The Importance of Process." *Women's Studies Quarterly* 1 & 2 (1992): 95–110.

Lather, Patti. "Critical Theory, Curricular Transformation and Feminist Mainstreaming." *Journal of Education* 166.1 (1984): 49–62.

Lorde, Audre. *Sister Outsider*. Trumansburg, NY: Crossing, 1984.

Maher, Frances. "Women Students in the Classroom." *Rereading America: Cultural Contexts for Critical Thinking and Writing*. First ed. Ed. Gary Colombo, Robert Cullen, and Bonnie Lisle. New York: St. Martin's, 1989. 493–502.

McLaren, Peter. "Multiculturalism and the Postmodern Critique: Toward a Pedagogy of Resistance and Transformation." *Between Borders: Pedagogy and the Politics of Cultural Studies*. Ed. Henry A. Giroux and Peter McLaren. New York: Routledge, 1994. 192–222.

Mercer, Kobena. "Skin Head Sex Thing: Racial Difference and the Homoerotic Imaginary." *How Do I Look? Queer Film and Video*. Ed. Bad Object–Choices. Seattle: Bay Press, 1991. 169–222.

Moschkovich, Judit. "—But I Know You, American Woman." Moraga and Anzaldúa 79–84.

Moraga, Cherríe. "La Güera." Moraga and Anzaldúa 27–34.

Moraga, Cherríe, and Gloria Anzaldúa, eds. *This Bridge Called My Back: Writings By Radical Women of Color*. 2d ed. New York: Kitchen Table, 1983.

Pheterson, Gail. "Alliances between Women: Overcoming Internalized Oppression and Internalized Domination." *Reconstructing the Academy: Women's Education and Women's Studies*. Ed. Elizabeth Minnich, Jean O'Barr, and Rachel Rosenfeld. Chicago: University of Chicago Press, 1988. 139–53.

Rich, Adrienne. "Compulsory Heterosexuality and Lesbian Existence." *Feminist Frontiers III*. Ed. Laurel Richardson and Verta Taylor. New York: McGraw-Hill, 1993. 158–79.

Shrewsbury, Carolyn M. "Feminist Pedagogy: An Updated Bibliography." *Women's Studies Quarterly* 20.3 & 4 (1993): 148–60.

———. "What Is Feminist Pedagogy?" *Women's Studies Quarterly* 20.3 & 4 (1993): 8–16.

Smith, Barbara, and Beverly Smith. "Across the Kitchen Table: A Sister-to-Sister Dialogue." Moraga and Anzaldúa 113–27.

Thomas, Gary. *Effective Classroom Teamwork: Support or Intrusion?* New York: Routledge, 1992.

Weiler, Kathleen. "Freire and a Feminist Pedagogy of Difference." *Harvard Educational Review* 61.4 (1991): 449–74.

———. *Women Teaching for Change: Gender, Class and Power*. New York: Bergin and Garvey, 1988.

Diane Lichtenstein and Virginia Powell

11

Collaborative Leadership

Feminist Possibility, Feminist Oxymoron

"Can there be a coherent theory of feminist collaboration?" ask Carey Kaplan and Ellen Cronan Rose in the conclusion of their "Strange Bedfellows: Feminist Collaboration" (559). If by coherent, Kaplan and Rose mean a single explanation that neatly accounts for all interactions labeled "collaboration" and also provides a flexible and useful definition of feminist, then the answer is no. If, on the other hand, they mean a process by which those who are collaborating and who self-consciously attempt to integrate feminist practices can reflect on and share their experiences, then we would answer yes. Except for Kaplan and Rose's essay, little has been written on feminist collaboration and virtually nothing on collaborative leadership. At the present time, the great majority of discussions about collaboration in academia focuses on teaching and research. In 1991, for example, the Association for the Study of Higher Education, George Washington University's Clearinghouse on Higher Education, and GWU's School of Education and Human Development published a report titled *Faculty Collaboration: Enhancing the Quality of Scholarship and Teaching*, by Ann E. Austin and Roger G. Baldwin. Mary Frank Fox and Catherine A. Faver have also written about collaborative research in "The Process of Collaboration in Scholarly Research" and "Independence and Cooperation in Research: The Motivations and Costs of Collaboration." And in her Presidential Address to the Western Social Science Association (1990), Marilyn Stember urged her listeners to collaborate through interdisciplinary enterprise.

We hope that this discussion of our collaboration as co-chairs of a Women's Studies program contributes to such a constructive and dynamic theory. Collaborative leadership, especially feminist leadership, differs from collaborative research and teaching in its implications for power relations, as well as in the number of people and institutions affected. In our experience, collaborative/feminist leadership directly involved not just the two of us but the dozen students and faculty who comprised the Women's Studies Committee. That is, even as we shared administrative tasks as collaborators, we worked with, provided leadership to, and had institutional power over the governing body of that Program.

The Context within Which We Collaborated

Beloit College is a small, private, undergraduate institution in southern Wisconsin. Its traditional liberal arts curriculum is complemented by an emphasis on interdisciplinary, international, and experiential studies. Students are encouraged to study abroad or in domestic off-campus programs (such as Urban Studies in Chicago), and are required to build breadth into their course plans by supplementing a major with an interdisciplinary minor, a second major, or teacher certification. The Beloit College Women's Studies Program, which was established in 1985, offers a minor. All faculty who teach in the program, except one, have appointments in other departments; the single faculty member in Women's Studies is part-time and temporary. In any given semester, the program offers six to eight courses such as Introduction to Women's Studies, Women and Politics, Psychology of Women, Women and Literature, Sociology of Sex and Gender, and Feminist Theory. Officially, the Program is managed by a committee of three: the chair (in our case, co-chairs) and two (one) additional faculty appointed by the dean. Unofficially, most of the faculty who teach in the program, as well as four or five of the twenty-five students who are minors, attend and vote at committee meetings.

Between 1985 and 1987, Beloit's Women's Studies Program struggled to survive. Three key faculty members left the college, no students were declared minors, the program had no budget, and course offerings were sporadic. Then, with the help of a new dean and several new faculty members with interests in Women's

Studies, the woman who became chair in 1987 strengthened a young and fragile program by pressuring for institutional resources for it. These resources extended from the more mundane—a bulletin board and a separate alphanumeric listing for Women's Studies courses in registration materials—to the more substantive—a budget, a student work study position, office space, and development money to run a Women's Studies faculty seminar. Committed to building respect for the program and for the questions asked by scholars in Women's Studies, our predecessor labored to establish a constituency among both students and faculty.

In the spring of 1990, the two of us negotiated the possibility of serving as co-chairs. Each of us was reluctant to chair alone, because we were relatively new to the college (Ginny had been at Beloit for two years and Diane for three) and because we feared additional pressures on our already limited time. Hesitant or not, we felt we had little choice since the current chair was stepping down and Beloit had no senior faculty interested enough in Women's Studies to chair the program. Although we will be discussing our collaboration in terms of feminist process and practice in this chapter, we want to make it clear here that we first decided to co-chair for practical and expedient reasons. In other words, we collaborated in order to share the administrative workload rather than as an attempt to act on our commitments to feminist processes of shared power and leadership.

An identity as co-chairs was not new for us. During 1989–90, we were serving as co-coordinators of the Associated Colleges of the Midwest's Committee on Women's Concerns. Through this work, we had discovered that we had similar work patterns and rhythms, that neither of us dominates a conversation but both are willing to say what needs to be said, that our ideas about feminist process were compatible, that we communicated openly with one another, and that we were developing a friendship. Even before our term as co-coordinators, we had worked productively together as members of Beloit's Women's Studies Committee. While on that committee, we had attended meetings regularly and had helped with two large projects: the construction of a general syllabus for the Introduction to Women's Studies course and the organization and running of a faculty seminar in Women's Studies.

In the fall of 1990, we inherited a program that was vital to Beloit College. And because of its "health," defined by resources and visibility, we were able to focus more on the internal dynamics and identity of the program. The Women's Studies Committee met weekly and spent time debating questions such as: What does Women's Studies mean within the context of a liberal arts college and curriculum? What shall constitute a course in Women's Studies? How shall we define membership on our Program Committee? How can we address questions of diversity and difference, particularly with respect to race, ethnicity, social class, sexuality, and national identity, in our curriculum? What would an ideal curriculum in Women's Studies at Beloit look like? How shall we balance curricular concerns with larger political concerns, on the campus and in our society?

As both cause and effect of these discussions, members of the Women's Studies Committee accomplished the following during our two years as co-chairs: planned and hosted an external review; undertook an internal, college-mandated review of our curriculum in terms of its multicultural content and possibilities; applied and won approval (but not funding) for a full-time tenure track position for the program; began discussions with the college's development office about the possibility of an endowed chair or lecture series in Women's Studies; revised our curriculum, a process which involved discussions of mainstreaming and of the Advanced Seminar in Women's Studies; and began to implement our curricular goals through the development of a set of guidelines that sketched our current understandings of "Women's Studies." Several of these projects had been in process when we assumed responsibility for co-chairing the program.

Our Collaboration as Co-Chairs

As co-chairs, we truly co-labored. Through daily telephone calls or short meetings, we discussed and divided up the work that needed to be done. That work took the form of preparing the next academic year's budget, lobbying the dean for more money, advising the committee about how to spend that budget, writing memos, opening and filing the mail, corresponding with the registrar about enrollments, and supervising a work-study student. In addition, we ran a search for the faculty member in Women's Studies, set the agenda for meetings, advised the committee about priorities for future meetings, and raised questions with the committee about the direction of, as well as tensions within, the program. A crucial benefit of co-laboring was the opportunity to consult each other on issues facing the program, and to share the responsibility for and consequences of those decisions. Co-laboring also enabled us to bring different perspectives to bear both on immediate questions and on the management of the program. We complemented each other's strengths in supportive and productive ways.

Our collaboration became personally and politically meaningful to us because we worked with rather than against our differences (we will discuss these differences later). We provided leadership to each other in the sense that we taught each other how to administer a program, and we supported each other in our attempts to use feminist processes in that administration. In a fundamental way, our differences strengthened our collaboration because we trusted each other to do the work of the program and to divide that work equally. This seems like such a simple and basic feature of collaborative work, feminist or otherwise. But we had had experiences with others where the work was not fully shared, and we therefore treasured this reliability.

On another level, we trusted, or respected, our partner's visions of Women's Studies and feminism. It would be a mistake to say that we came to feminism via the same route, or that feminism has similar meanings in our lives. But we do share an understanding of and commitment to Women's Studies, in part because we had had parallel experiences. Women's Studies had been a crucial part of our training in graduate school, each of us had written a dissertation on women and/or gender, we had mentors who were path breakers in Women's Studies, we came to Beloit fully engaged in and dedicated to Women's Studies, we had been involved in Women's Studies programs before, we taught regularly in Women's Studies, we belonged to the National Women's Studies Association, and we subscribed to Women's Studies journals.

Our common experiences and shared goals certainly made our collaborative work more efficient, but we do want to stress that we **are** very different, particularly in regard to personal history and disciplinary experiences. Ginny is an aspiring ex-Catholic; white; heterosexual; German and Irish; first-generation college graduate, first ever of her nuclear and extended kin group to get a doctorate; from a family that values self-sufficiency through hard physical labor rather than mental work or education; struggling with the ideologies and practices of individualism which characterize the upper-middle-class and professional life she leads; married and childless; of mixed class parentage; irreverent to authority (this is somehow related to the litany of requirements that characterized her upbringing as a Catholic); the daughter of hard-working and heavy-drinking parents, sister to three brothers and four sisters.

Diane describes her identity differently. She is also white and heterosexual. But she is Jewish and celebrates that identity; she is a mother and is married; her parents both went to college and graduate school; her one sibling, a sister, also has a Ph.D.; many of her relatives are educators; although her parents grew up poor, as the children of Eastern European immigrants, they provided their children with upper-middle-class opportunities (these opportunities took educational forms—music lessons, summer enrichment programs—rather than expensive vacations or fancy cars); while she is comfortable with many of academia's rules and its complex boundaries between self and community, she resists its insistence that work should dominate family.

Our autobiographies mapped out the paths we took to feminism. Ginny grew up in a family where gender rules were rigid and conventional, where the most appropriate work for a woman was in the home as a wife and mother. She therefore had to react against her family and find her own way to a professional life. Diane did not have to do that—her parents expected her to attend college, and they supported her decision to pursue a Ph.D. And her mother—a strong, capable, smart woman—was a model who provided her daughters with feminist-oriented compasses.

Of course, our families were not the only influences on our definitions and understanding of feminism. We went to graduate school in the early 1980s, at a time when feminist questions were being posed anew and when Women's Studies courses were appearing with regularity. We were interested in and energized by Women's Studies' effects on the academy. Because we had studied feminist scholarship at the same time and as it was developing, we found many similarities in our approach to Women's Studies when we began to collaborate at Beloit. We had comparable sensibilities with respect to feminist ideologies. We thought about our lives in terms of feminist values of equity and equality, we came to appreciate feminist processes that emphasized inclusion and democracy, and we recognized and prized the characteristics of connection, sharing, and caring that have been attributed to women.

We believe that this mix of similarities and differences fostered our collaboration. While they could have generated conflicts between us, or made it difficult to work together, they did not. We used our similarities to forge a vision of Women's Studies at Beloit, and we worked to engage our differences so that they functioned as complementary strengths while we provided leadership to each other and to the Women's Studies program. Why were we able to engage those differences? Because they fell within a workable range of disparity. Since we were thinking and working within a shared ideological plane, we were able to notice, value, and work with our differences.

We don't want to suggest that we always agreed on what needed to be done, or even on what the issues were. Indeed, the fact that we did not agree suggests another kind of trust that was important to our collaborations. We felt comfortable testing our ideas and proposals with each other, knowing that they would be heard by a loving critic who would provide honest and useful feedback. Being all too familiar with the internal fighting that can plague Women's Studies committees, we saw this ability to collaborate on ideas and visions as unique and precious. With the energy we created for ourselves, we compelled each other forward. We felt that we were not alone, that we were listening to and challenging each other to evaluate and analyze our responses and suggestions.

We believe that the differences in our analytical skills fostered by our disciplinary backgrounds also contributed to our success as collaborators. Ginny, trained as a sociologist in a graduate program that emphasized radical theory and practice (e.g., Marxism, psychoanalysis, feminism), was taught to see and to analyze power dynamics and to link such analyses with programs for social change. Diane, trained in literary studies, learned to "read" the ways in which words and texts replicate as well as produce cultural power relationships. So, Ginny could assess the dynamics of the college's reluctance to act on a difficult decision, while Diane could read the coded anger or frustration concealed in a colleague's memo. Without forcing it to be so, or even being aware of it, we made the collaboration interdisciplinary.

Never irreconcilable, our differences did not threaten us. In fact, we rarely felt competitive. Might this have been the result of our intellectual division of labor? Or could it be because of our differences that we did not measure ourselves against each other? Being trained in sociology and literature, respectively, we have developed different skills. Pursuing scholarship in different areas, we don't compete for the same prizes. And having different family configurations, we don't compete through our children. Our differences, then, actually helped produce the trust which in turn contributed to our successful collaboration.

That collaboration enabled us to accomplish much more than simple administrative tasks. Although we still cannot name it, we believe that something in the quality of our shared and communal enterprise enabled us to initiate and complete projects and that we accomplished more together than either one of us would have alone. Perhaps this can be explained by feminist theories that suggest that women define themselves in and through their relationships and connections with others. It seems to us that such a personality structure was at work to facilitate our collaboration. The fact that we were sharing a position and its responsibilities nourished our confidence, which in turn strengthened our leadership of the program.

Our ability to work together paralleled the deepening of our friendship so that each dimension of our relationship nourished the development of the other. As we discussed issues facing the program, we exchanged information about our personal lives and histories, and we shared our concerns about work, friendships, and families. We moved back and forth between these two kinds of talk, between administrative work and self-disclosure, listening to each other with the kind of intensity and interest that new relationships bring. Through these "simple" yet intimate exchanges of biography and daily life, we became close friends.

We felt involved, committed, and even vulnerable in our collaboration. Because we shared more than just memo writing and agenda setting, the work felt interesting and energizing. While we believe that we could each work with someone whom we trust to complete program-related tasks but whom we do not entrust with our personal concerns, we would have less to lose, or to gain, from such a relationship. Our collaboration succeeded so dramatically in part because of this chance to feel something valuable on a personal level.

We want to make explicit the implication that through our collaboration, we clarified and transformed our individual approaches to Women's Studies. We learned from each other and taught each other, often simultaneously. We grew, together, to understand more deeply the complexities of Women's Studies, of administering a Program, and of collaborative leadership itself.

Collaborations with Committee Members

At the same time that we were negotiating our own relationship, we were interacting with other members of the Women's Studies Committee. As a result, our collaboration was being influenced by others' reactions even as we brought decisions, arrived at through collaboration between us, to the group.

We began our term expecting that our collaborations with Program Committee members would amplify and complement our own collaboration. We thought that theories of feminist leadership and collaboration would mean the practice of sharing decision making so that power differences—between co-chairs and group members, between part-time and full-time faculty members, between students and faculty—would be minimized and responsibility for the program would be held collectively by all committee members. In essence, we wanted to extend our collaboration to group members by bringing all issues and concerns to the group, by running meetings through consensus, and by acting as resource persons for students and faculty in the program. This model for administering a program is not at all common at our institution.

Despite our goals and expectations regarding our leadership, we often experienced the group "collaboration" as difficult and even painful. Meetings themselves were often uneasy. On occasion, a group member exploded with anger, at us or at other group members. One source of tension at those meetings, and for Beloit's Women's Studies Program generally, is the question, How much of our time should be devoted to concerns that are feminist in nature but not directly linked to Women's Studies at the college? For those of us who teach at small colleges, where those involved in Women's Studies are likely to be the same individuals concerned about women's experiences, the question is complicated. Committee members vary in their opinions on this issue. When we co-chaired, we attempted to focus attention on academic matters, in large part because we felt challenged enough by them. We know our decision frustrated some committee members. With hindsight, we think that we should have spent more group time discussing connections between "activist" and academic feminism, individuals' relationships to each other, and the reasons we all were active in Women's Studies.

Contributing to the tension within the Women's Studies Committee were two other structural facts: we had more control over the agenda and direction of the program than did committee members; we were not always fully inclusive, because we thought it unwise to be. As part of our duties as co-chairs of an academic program, we had access to information that other committee members did not. Specifically, we received directives from the dean, opened the mail, and read our colleague's course evaluations. We also controlled other components of the program. We handled correspondence, kept the program's files, ran the weekly meetings, brought items to those meetings, and oversaw the plans for a semester's course offerings. We assumed that these administrative tasks were part of our responsibilities as co-chairs. As it turned out, control over these seemingly mechanical details actually provided us with a larger view of the program—where it fit within the institution, and a sense of its future possibilities. This control also conferred unexpected powers: to request a meeting with the dean and then to speak on behalf of the program, to ask for more money for part-time instructors, to evaluate faculty members' performance, and so on.

On occasion, an administrator provided us with information that we hesitated to share with a group of fifteen, because we thought it might intrude upon a person's privacy (personnel matters), because it would violate confidentiality (again, personnel and evaluation matters), or because our own instincts cautioned us against making public what had been confided to us in private.

What seemed to us fairly routine (routine as defined by the institutions in which we had been living and learning) sometimes produced confusion, frustration, and even anger on the part of committee members. Also problematic was the fact that certain committee members perceived our collaboration as collusion; because we talked about difficult matters before meetings, we might have appeared to have a set position. That we consulted each other "privately" (in one of our offices or on the telephone) and "rehearsed" our views before we arrived at a committee meeting may have created the appearance of a single point of view. So, while we were aware of the differences between us, others may not have been. The dynamic between committee members and us sometimes felt like a them/us split.

We were conflicted by the ideal of inclusivity. Committed to that ideal in the abstract, we often bumped up against our institution's implicit and explicit policies and our own misgivings about making all information public. Knowing that we had been endowed with the responsibility of managing the Women's Studies Program, we sought ways to reconcile the demands of the Women's Studies Committee, the expectations of the college, and our own goals.

Questions and Reflections

We have assumed that a feminist organizational model reaches for inclusivity, consensus, and equality. But what does this really mean? Complete involvement of all interested individuals? Open discussion of all program concerns, including personnel questions? Or might it mean open discussion of only some matters? If this is the case, who chooses the topics for group consideration? A committee? An individual? A team of managers? Is feminist process simply the right to challenge the ways in which a group is functioning? Within the context of feminist process, what can leadership mean?

We would like feminist leadership to mean creating a space in which others may test possibilities. On a practical level, the leaders can create that space by deciding what are and are not committee issues and by taking care of the non-committee issues themselves. This would allow more time for creative discussion among committee members. As for the concern about leaders deciding what are and are not committee matters: we believe that the very fact of having two people, rather than one, making these decisions functions as a check to the feared autocrat/dictator. For our part, we always tried to do what we thought was best for the program.

During the two years we co-chaired, we often felt inadequate and even guilty, because we imagined that we were falling short of our goals of feminist leadership. As we reflect back, we realize that perhaps those goals were untenable. And because they were, we were doomed to feel as if we had failed, to feel like "bad feminists." We believed that collaborative leadership should foster feminist processes. We also believed that those processes should include groups in decision making and would automatically create inclusivity. When we discovered that we had to balance a hierarchical model of leadership against our image of an inclusive model, we found ourselves compromising both with the Women's Studies Committee and with the institution of Beloit College.

The title of this chapter suggests that feminist leadership is an oxymoron. In our experience, it is. When we made feminist processes a priority, leadership as we thought we understood it receded. For example, when we opened up the agenda at a group meeting, we heard everyone's opinions but our own. Then, when we carried out our duties as leaders (as Beloit College defines them), feminist processes seemed to fade. Here, we think of "bureaucratic" decisions we made without group consultation—about staffing of Women's Studies courses, for example.

What we just said might imply that the root of the oxymoron grows out of the dilemma of attempting to make feminist principles and processes conform to the male institution of academia in general and Beloit College in particular. Indeed, this was part of the problem. We felt blocked in our attempts to carry those processes outside the Women's Studies Program. When we discussed our program with non-Women's Studies colleagues, for example, it was not unusual for them to criticize our "tedious and cumbersome" group process. In the end, committee members were left to resolve program concerns by working against the grain of the institution and the conventional leadership practices of our colleagues. We must confess, however, that we also discovered how conventional institutional models provide frameworks for efficiency, a not insignificant item for those of us who teach at small colleges. While we still honor the ideal of inclusivity, we now know that asking a group of fifteen people to take care of every detail involved in running an academic program quickly becomes burdensome, boring, and counterproductive to the good of that program.

At the same time that we acknowledge the utility of certain traditional practices, we recognize how institutional pressures contributed to tensions within the Women's Studies Committee. As we experienced it, our attempts at feminist leadership were hampered by the institution's structures forcing us into a power relationship *over* rather than shared leadership *with* other committee members. Personnel matters are a case in point. Simply by having access to a colleague's teaching evaluations, we had power over that individual. We could use those evaluations to ask the dean for a salary increase, or for rebuke. Either way, we were assigned the duty of evaluating faculty and making recommendations about those faculty to the dean, and therefore had power that was not shared equally.

Tensions within the Women's Studies Committee also stemmed from a gap between theory and practice as well as from our inability to recognize, and therefore acknowledge and close, that gap. That is, we valued the goals of feminist process and conceptualized these goals in abstract terms. Yet when it came time to complete a project or finally resolve a dilemma (should all Women's Studies course books be ordered through the women's bookstore in Beloit rather than the College bookstore?), we experienced frustration at the amount of time and personal emotion and energy we were spending. Commitment to theoretical ideals did not mitigate our negative responses, but if we had been more conscious of our dilemma, we might have found ways to build practice from theory and theory from practice.

Did our collaborative model, imperfect as it was, shape the future direction of the program? At the very least, co-leadership does seem to have become an accepted model for the Women's Studies Program. The president, the dean, the registrar, and many others have had to accept this. But what about direct effects on the program? Do two people running a program affect that program differently than a single person does? Was the dynamic of our interaction communicated to the working of the program, or was our "will" felt as a single will, although we felt it as collective?

We believe that two people do create unique questions and goals that differ from those that would have been devised by each person working alone. For us, a question which immediately follows is, Are there features of collaborative work that strengthen feminist processes of democratic inclusion? Ironically, the fact that we *were* a "we" might have facilitated the committee's challenges; an angry committee member might have been less likely to point a finger at an individual. Perhaps our co-leadership did actually foster openness because committee members knew they could raise difficult questions about the processes of the group and because they trusted us to get our work done. And maybe we successfully projected a model of collaboration, of co-chairs who actually shared the responsibility for the program.

As difficult as it is to admit, we are also beginning to see how collaborative leadership might actually discourage feminist processes even as it promotes them. In our experience, co-chairs are perceived as being a united front who not only take care of everything and who need neither guidance nor help from the committee, but who have more power as a consequence of having more information, a title, and the benefit of extensive discussion.

And what was the effect of our collaboration on the college? Instead of the dean sending one memo to the chair of Women's Studies, he had to send two. Instead of having one chair present at chairs' meetings, we had two. Instead of having one signature at the bottom of all-college mailings, there were two. Perhaps we caused some of our colleagues to think about what we were doing, despite their impatience for and their jokes about our group process. And maybe, by making part-time faculty voting members of a committee, we gave them a voice. But it is hard to say with great confidence that our collaboration affected the college, except in one tangible way. Apparently, co-chairs have become a model for leadership of Interdisciplinary Minor Programs. While this phenomenon might stem from the interdisciplinary nature of minors as well as from the problems of work load, it might also be a deliberate and self-consciously chosen model of leadership given visibility, legitimacy, and a "trial run" by Women's Studies.

The collaboration between the two of us seemed easy and relatively uncomplicated when compared to our collaborations with other members of the Women's Studies Committee. Why? In part because we were more or less equal to each other, having the same access to power and information, while others in the group had less access to that power/information. Our collaboration with a group of fifteen was also difficult because the ideological/epistemological/political/disciplinary differences among group members were sometimes vast, and our desire to focus attention on academic matters left us little time to bridge or work on these differences.

We can only echo what others before us have said about difference. Our collaboration as co-chairs suggests that as feminists we can engage and enjoy differences; our wider collaborations with members of our Women's Studies Committee suggest that difference continues to divide us. However, despite the tensions we and committee members experienced, we do believe that Beloit College's Women's Studies Program has grown stronger, and we believe that our collaborative leadership contributed to that strength.

Postscript

The process by which we wrote this chapter stymied, frustrated, and involved us in ways we had never experienced before when writing our own individual papers. We discovered something very important about our interaction: we converse with each other dynamically. We tried to include an example of a conversation in order to provide a blueprint of how we work together. But every time we read through what we had written, it sounded mechanical. So we decided to delete any and all staged dialogues and to speak in a collective voice throughout.

We collaborated on this chapter for more than a year and a half. In that time, we took turns drafting, revising, posing questions, supporting and guiding each other. As was true of our co-chairing, when one of us became frustrated or lost sight of the larger goals, the other would relieve her, not only by taking a turn with the chapter, but by talking to her. We wrote together infrequently, but every sentence reflects the activity of two people.

REFERENCES

Austin, Ann E., and Roger G. Baldwin. *Faculty Collaboration: Enhancing the Quality of Scholarship and Teaching.* ASHE-ERIC Higher Education Report No. 7. Washington, DC: George Washington University, School of Education and Human Development, 1991.

Fox, Mary Frank, and Catherine A. Faver. "Independence and Cooperation in Research: The Motivations and Costs of Collaboration." *Journal of Higher Education* 55 (1984): 347–59.

———. "The Process of Collaboration in Scholarly Research." *Scholarly Writing and Publishing*. Ed. Mary Frank Fox. Boulder, CO: Westview, 1985. 126–38.

Kaplan, Carey, and Ellen Cronan Rose. "Strange Bedfellows: Feminist Collaboration." *Signs* 18 (1993): 547–61.

Stember, Marilyn. "Presidential Address: Advancing the Social Sciences through the Interdisciplinary Enterprise." *The Social Science Journal* 28 (1991): 1–14.

Anne O'Meara and Nancy R. MacKenzie

12

Reflections on Scholarly Collaboration

The most comprehensive study of collaborative writing to date is work done by Andrea Lunsford and Lisa Ede in 1984–85. In surveys and interviews, Ede and Lunsford asked experienced collaborators in business and academic settings to describe the texts they produced collaboratively; the processes they used as they planned, wrote, and revised; the decision-making processes that led to the assignment of duties; and their attitudes toward collaborative projects (see *Singular Texts* 149–250).

In the course of their studies, Ede and Lunsford came to distinguish between two collaborative modes—the hierarchical and the dialogic. They identify the hierarchical mode as the dominant one in our culture. Hierarchical collaboration is highly structured with well-defined goals and clear roles assigned to the participants. In these collaborative contexts, productivity and efficiency are highly valued, and differences among participants are seen as problems to be overcome. The dialogic mode, in contrast, is loosely structured, with participants shifting roles and valuing the process of goal articulation as much as goal attainment. In this mode, multiple voices and differences are regarded as a strength (*Singular Texts* 132–33).

While it might be tempting to associate the hierarchical mode with men and the dialogic with women, Ede and Lunsford caution against a false binary opposition that is "harmfully reductive" and fails to represent fully their own experience (*Singular Texts* 134). In fact, when they focused on the two organizations in their study that were predominantly female—the Society for Technical Communications (STC) and the Modern Language Association (MLA)—they found that neither group reported a preference for the dialogic method. Women in the STC most often used the hierarchical mode, and women in the MLA did not favor any collaborative mode, doing most of their research and writing individually (Lunsford and Ede 236–7).

In *Faculty Collaboration: Enhancing the Quality of Scholarship and Teaching*, Ann E. Austin and Roger C. Baldwin note that collaboration rates and styles vary considerably depending on the nature of the discipline. Drawing on Martin J. Finkelstein's work in *The American Academic Profession*, Austin and Baldwin report: "Collaboration is not widespread in the humanities. It is more common in the social sciences, and it is almost the norm in the physical sciences" (25). One reason for these differences is that strong paradigms and highly specialized methods and equipment make division of tasks easier in "data disciplines" like physics and chemistry, whereas in "word disciplines" like English literature or history, there is "less theoretical justification for any particular arrangement of tasks or priority of concerns" (25).

In addition to describing differences in collaborative styles and practices, Austin and Baldwin investigate factors necessary for successful collaboration—effective communication skills, conflict management strategies, and group role assignment procedures (53–66). Other scholars have studied experienced collaborators to identify specific interpersonal characteristics of effective collaborators (Allen et al.). Scholars have also applied insights from other disciplines, for instance gender studies (Lay). Whereas researchers have studied the effects of institutional hierarchies on business writing in general and occasionally on collaborative writing (for instance, Odell and Goswami), Austin and Baldwin provide the best description of the barriers to collaboration posed by academic institutions—including review practices as well as promotion and tenure procedures (67–74; 83–89).

One of the barriers that Austin and Baldwin mention is lack of designated time and travel money for collaborative work, especially for researchers who do not live or work near their collaborating colleagues (87). Recent research on collaboration has begun to highlight how these seemingly "extraneous" features influence collaborative processes. For instance, in an interview discussing the collaborative project that became *Women's Ways of Knowing,* Mary Field Belenky describes how she and her three collaborators—Blythe

McVicker Clinchy, Nancy Rule Goldberger, and Jill Mattuck Tarule—maintained a continuing conversation by meeting together periodically over three years at a central location:

> Very regularly, then, every five or six weeks, we were able to sit down together and work around the clock for three or four days at a time. I can't tell you how important it is to have this kind of time for working, sleeping on your thoughts, and returning to the conversation—without distractions from children and telephones. We all had raised families as well as having careers, and the luxury of that kind of sustained conversation was just terrific. The pajama party was very important to the process. (qtd. in Ashton-Jones and Thomas 278)

This explicit discussion of conflicting responsibilities, geographic separation, and other factors common in academic collaborative situations is also seen in an interview with Lunsford and Ede (Calderonello, Nelson, and Simmons) and in the papers presented at a Midwest/Modern Language Association panel on "Feminists in/and Collaboration" (papers and presenters are listed in MMLA 24 [1991]: 70). A description of the collaborative processes of these women would be inaccurate and incomplete without reference to these "extraneous" factors.

Although Lunsford and Ede do not identify the dialogic mode as the woman's mode of collaboration, they remark that they first caught glimpses of the dialogic mode—the mode that more accurately described the bulk of their experiences than does the hierarchical mode—in comments by women scholars ("Rhetoric" 236; Ede and Lunsford, *Singular Texts* 133). Similarly, we notice that it is in reports by experienced women collaborators that we catch glimpses of features that are central to our own scholarly collaboration. We notice, for instance, the mention of the prevalence of talk during coauthoring (Ede and Lunsford "Why Write . . . Together? 152), of melding as a drafting method (Allen et al. 79), and of the necessity of establishing drafting procedures that help one maintain one's own voice, particularly at the beginning of collaborating (Belenky in Ashton-Jones and Thomas 279–80). We add to these discussions by examining in detail how talk, drafting processes, and context shaped our own collaborative processes. We also explore the importance of two areas that have gone relatively unexamined in the literature: choosing research methods that encourage dual/multiple perspectives and using "resonators" (outside readers and other supportive noncollaborators).

Our reflections have grown out of four years of talking, thinking, researching, and writing collaboratively. Our collaboration began with a grant to experiment with methods of incorporating critical thinking instruction into collaborative writing projects. In the course of this initial study, we collaborated on the grant proposal itself and on syllabi and exercises for the affected classes; we observed each other's classes and read the process logs kept by each other's students as well as their collaboratively written texts. Later, we found ourselves collaborating on conference proposals, conference presentations, and articles. Our collaborative writing has ranged from one-page abstracts to our thirty-page grant report, and our oral presentations have ranged from twenty minutes to two hours.

Collaborative Talk

Even though social interactions are recognized as a central and continuous feature of collaborative research and writing, the function of talk in forwarding collaboration deserves more sustained examination. In most cases, the negotiations required in collaborative writing tasks—agreeing on content, language, schedules, and working methods—are accomplished through conversation. When we reviewed our collaborative practices, we discovered that we had spent much more time talking than writing and realized that talking played a much more central role in our processes than we had at first expected. We found it useful to describe our talk in terms of the four categories of group talk outlined by VanPelt and Gillam (194): procedural, substantive, writing, and social talk.

Procedural talk is discussion that establishes working methods and deadlines. Particularly at the beginning of our project, procedural talk helped us familiarize ourselves with each other's preferences in terms of work habits and priorities for scheduling. Preparing for our meetings kept our momentum going by requiring us each to accomplish certain tasks so that we would have something to report to the other. Geraldine McNenny and Duane H.

Roen observe that one of the benefits of collaboration is that they work longer and harder as part of a team: "We feel we owe it to [our teammates] to work hard; singly, we would never have felt the same obligation to ourselves" (304). Since we didn't know each other very well when we began collaborating, procedural talk helped establish a bond that would later be maintained through social talk.

We believe that agreement on procedures was essential to our successful collaboration. While observing our students, we have noticed that a breakdown in procedural talk can quickly stall a project. We've also noted that when experienced academic collaborators are asked about conflicts they've experienced, their specific examples are more often procedural than substantive. Ede and Lunsford report on the difficulties of deciding where to continue writing after motel checkout time had elapsed during one of their writing project weekends (Calderonello, Nelson, and Simmons 10–11); three coeditors cite procedural conflicts resulting from different working styles and efforts to keep family and professional obligations at bay during working sessions (Freedman, Frey, and Zauhar 5). Other researchers have pointed out that, unlike procedural conflicts, disagreements about content can stimulate the collaborators and result in creative and satisfying solutions (Lay 5–6); for us, these kinds of substantive disagreements didn't seem like conflicts. But disagreements about who should do what by when can threaten the project. Therefore, procedural talk, which works out compromises, becomes the lifeline of the collaborative relationship.

Substantive talk is conversation that centers on the content of written products. Our substantive talk included such topics as the purpose of our texts, their scope and audience, the meaning of our data, and the conclusions we could reach. Substantive talk changed significantly over the course of our project. As we wrote our initial grant proposal, we talked in global terms—about the purpose and focus of the project, research methods, and anticipated outcomes. During the research phase, we made tentative connections by talking about the sources we had read, the progress of our students in the classes included in the study, and our observations as we visited each other's classes. Once the data were accumulated and we began our analysis, substantive talk became the link between our research and our emerging text. Substantive talk in collaborative writing is analogous to trying out sentences in one's head when one is writing alone. Collaborative writing is in fact defined by this social invention, this oscillating back and forth between talking and writing. As we work on offshoot projects, such as this one, we find that substantive talk on the newer projects enriches, and at times modifies, the conclusions we reached on our earlier projects.

Writing talk includes discussions of such elements as approaches to drafting a paper, style and editing, format and headings. Writing talk is a rather broad category, ranging from discussion of surface-level concerns to more substantive issues. On whole-text matters like format and headings, we generally talked it over with each other. But on editing and style concerns, we were more likely to reach consensus by combining our editing annotations from the manuscript margins. Because we both have taught technical writing and share similar approaches to format, headings, and readability, we didn't have trouble adopting a common style. Therefore, editing didn't require extended discussion.

In possessing similar levels of competence and attitudes in terms of writing style, we differ from some other collaborating writers, students in particular. We noted that some of the most heated and detailed student discussions in class revolved around such things as punctuation. In fact, a disagreement over use of the semicolon caused the most conflict in any of the collaborative work sessions we observed. Although it was not the case for us, writing talk could well be the focus of some conflict for other collaborating researchers.

Social talk is chatting about personal and professional lives, making jokes, and the like. It is often regarded as a deviation from task or is grudgingly tolerated as a way to build group cohesiveness, but it is not generally regarded as being integral to the collaborative process. In fact, as teachers, we had in the past been somewhat displeased with student groups who seemed to socialize too extensively. However, we have come to agree with other researchers on collaboration who testify to the importance of social talk even when it vies with more substantive talk for limited collaborating time (Freedman, Frey, and Zauhar 6). Scholars studying collaboration have also pointed out the integral importance of the personal relationships that this kind of talk sustains. Lisa Ede, in commenting on choosing a collaborator, says:

> I could imagine, for example, a situation where I would choose to work with someone primarily because of what she knew or

because that person and I have been investigating the same subject. . . . On the other hand, I don't think anyone would embark on the kind of sustained collaboration that Andrea and I have had over the years without there being other reasons to work together. (qtd. in Calderonello, Nelson, and Simmons 12)

Because our relationship was more professional than personal when we began our collaboration, our social talk was at first minimal. Social talk increased in amount and importance as we became more immersed in the project, approached our deadline for submitting the grant report, and spent long blocks of time working together. We found social talk enhanced our productivity by giving us the motivation and commitment we needed to continue working through the demanding process of planning, organizing, and formulating our lengthy grant report. In addition, then, to the potential for enhanced understanding offered by substantive talk, emotional support is provided through social talk. Such support can go a long way toward combatting the drain on one's physical and emotional energy that occurs when one is involved in a long-term, extensive research project while in the midst of the daily demands of teaching and service that make up academic life. In the end, both of us rated social talk as the most personally satisfying of the four kinds of talk.

Collaborative Research

Research on collaborative writing processes often describes drafting methods in some detail, leaving invention procedures relatively unspecified. This focus on drafting ignores not only the part that talk plays in invention but also the part that research procedures play in fostering and contributing to the collaborative relationship. Most discussions of research treat it mechanically—that is, describing how the research tasks are divided among the group members; this "division of labor" is often seen as one of the chief advantages of doing collaborative projects because individual contributions will add up to more information than an individual could amass alone.

In self-reflexive articles written by collaborating women scholars, we have noticed that the authors do not discuss their collaboration during research in the same analytical way that they describe their collaboration during drafting. By convention, the emphasis in methodology sections of research articles is on describing the methodology itself for such purposes as establishing its validity or providing guidelines for scholars who wish to replicate the study. By conforming to these conventions, studies of collaborative writing have overlooked the relevance of analyzing the methods used in collaborative collection and interpretation of data. Consequently the distinctive nature of collaborative research has not been highlighted. Because collaborative writers ultimately produce a single text, accounts of collaborative writing processes often seek to describe how that singleness was achieved. In so doing, the multiplicity that preceded that singleness gets slighted.

The existence of dual (or multiple) perspectives in collaborative projects is usually assumed simply as a consequence of there being two or more participants; more attention should be given to the advantages of deliberately structuring the research and drafting processes so as to exploit the potential richness of these perspectives. In our retrospective analysis of one of our primary research methods—observation of each other's classes—we realized that the research method itself can encourage the dual perspectives that distinguish collaboration from single authorship.

First of all, in our different roles as teacher versus observer of the same class, we generated different data (see figure 12.1, A_1 and A_2). The observer's notes constituted data that were affected not only by her different physical placement in the room but also by her fresh perspective on the students themselves. Although as teachers both of us regard ourselves as excellent eavesdroppers from behind the front desk, we found that the back-of-the-room observer had a surprisingly different sense of what was going on in the groups. Not only did we have different data on the same groups, but we also had different perspectives on the same data—such as the student texts that resulted from the group work we observed.

Furthermore, because each of us took on the role of teacher in one class and observer in another, each of our internal perspectives was continually shifting as we collected and interpreted the data together (see figure 12.1, B). Because we were engaged in collaborative research writing just as our students were, there was another layer of dual perspective (see figure 12.1, C). Our insights into our students' collaborative processes and texts were influenced by our own

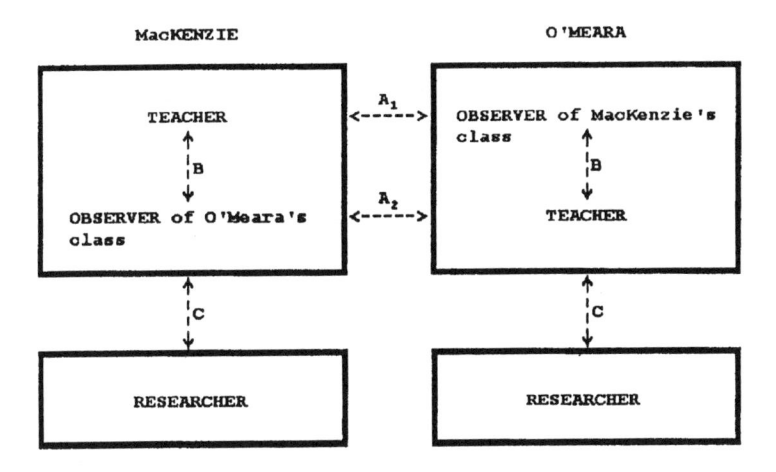

```
     MacKENZIE                              O'MEARA
┌─────────────────────────┐   A₁    ┌─────────────────────────┐
│      TEACHER            │<------->│  OBSERVER of MacKenzie's│
│         ↑               │         │  class       ↑          │
│         │B              │         │              │B         │
│         ↓         A₂    │         │              ↓          │
│  OBSERVER of O'Meara's  │<------->│      TEACHER            │
│  class                  │         │                         │
└─────────────────────────┘         └─────────────────────────┘
           ↑                                     ↑
           │C                                    │C
           ↓                                     ↓
┌─────────────────────────┐         ┌─────────────────────────┐
│      RESEARCHER         │         │      RESEARCHER         │
└─────────────────────────┘         └─────────────────────────┘
```

Figure 12.1

research and writing efforts, and simultaneously their processes gave us a new perspective on our own. These various perspectives (A, B, C) no doubt enriched the dual perspectives we had simply because we were different people.

We believe that analyzing our research processes, particularly that part of our research based on our observations of each other's classes, accentuated differences in perspective, the importance of which we might otherwise have underestimated. In addition to the increased quantity of work that can be produced by a group as compared to a solitary writer, another distinct advantage of collaborative work is that more than one perspective is present throughout the project. Much of the scholarship about the ill effects of reaching consensus too early during collaborative writing (for example, Trimbur) supports our belief in the advantages of fostering dual perspectives in the data collection phase as well. Although the type of cross observation we used as a research method has limited applicability, we favor exploring other research methodologies with built-in mechanisms for developing and prolonging different individual viewpoints as a prelude to negotiating meaning during collaborative writing.

Collaborative Drafting

One of our most striking discoveries while attempting to describe our own collaborative research and writing process was that because of its dynamic nature, it tended to defy description. That is to say, by the time we had a description of our processes written, our drafting process itself had changed in response to the difficulties of trying to describe it. Our experience is not unique. Published research documents a variety of collaborative drafting procedures; long-term collaborators, such as Lunsford and Ede, have pointed out that their processes vary, depending on the project or circumstances (in Calderonello, Nelson, and Simmons 9).

An additional difficulty, which many have noted, is finding terminology that accurately describes complex collaborative writing processes. In their search for descriptive terminology, Allen et al. found it helpful to narrow the focus by distinguishing collaboration involving actual group authorship of a single document from other types of collaborative writing activities—such as group work, consultation, or division-of-labor projects in which each writer contributes a section. Shared-document authors discuss all aspects of the document—from the global to the stylistic—and share responsibility for decision making about it; even within this smaller subgroup, Allen et al. reported a tremendous range of actual drafting processes (84-5).

These distinctions highlighted some features of our collaborative processes and working relationship. We wrote primarily shared documents in the dialogic mode, but we still needed additional terminology to talk more specifically about our writing processes and variety of our texts. In the course of our collaboration, our drafting processes covered a spectrum from what could be called "single authorship" to various kinds of "dual authorship." For instance, on two conference abstracts and one newsletter article, one of us wrote the text without extensive discussion of it with the other beforehand. The other then commented and the author revised; the comments were mostly editorial rather than suggestions for wholesale revisions. But the term *single authored* is misleading at the same time that it does signify one person actually putting the words on the page. The conference abstracts went out under both our names; we felt that we shared authorship for them because they arose out of our collaboration on the larger grant project.

We also had difficulties describing our drafting processes on texts that were more obviously shared documents, where our interaction was more intensive and continuous. Our drafting processes took three forms, which we would describe as melding (in which we independently wrote drafts and then one of us drafted a further version, combining ideas, sections, and even phrases from each within a single sentence); compilation (a division of labor in which we each wrote sections that remained relatively untouched in the final version); and jointly written (in which both of us sat down together at the computer and wrote a version together on the basis of independent drafts, a draft by one person, or our conversation at the time). Drafting was preceded, accompanied, and followed by the kinds of talk we have described above; as we have noted, the majority of our revising and editing was done individually and sequentially as we traded drafts back and forth.

Our first text, the grant proposal, was melded from independent individual drafts. Because it was reasonably short (two single-spaced pages), writing separate drafts of the entire text was feasible. It also seemed desirable. At the start of our collaboration, we didn't know each other very well and at the same time we were mapping out a research project, which would have been difficult enough even if we had known how each other worked and thought. Writing individual drafts after talking allowed us to get our ideas down and deferred the problems of reaching consensus and negotiating our roles until later when we could devote the necessary attention to it. This was especially useful in the proposal sections on project purpose, background, methodology, and expected outcomes, all complex sections; our budget and timetable sections survived virtually unchanged from one person's draft.

In retrospect, it seems that this method had an advantage similar to that which we noted in our section on research. Because making meaning out of our data was difficult, one of us might have deferred to the other's interpretation rather than struggle with her own ill-defined sense of it, but our parallel drafting method enabled us to postpone consensus rather than reach premature closure. One of our students remarked on this problem by saying that "The common middle ground might just be what could be agreed upon and not what was necessarily true." Writing independent drafts preserved two viewpoints that fostered further conversation. Writing parallel drafts is neither more efficient nor easier. The duplication of initial effort and later melding of the versions supports (almost literally) Mary Belenky's observation that "[i]n the academy, collaborative work is demoted, but it should count *double*" (qtd. in Ashton-Jones and Thomas 281). We argue that this duplication is advantageous precisely because it is a double consideration of ideas. Our parallel drafts rarely resulted in oppositions; they were simply not the same. The meaning got made somewhere in the middle as we talked, wrote, revised, reworded, and edited drafts. In the end, it was hard to say on some parts who had written what.

Our parallel drafts were usually written after we had talked about substantive and procedural issues at length. The more clearly we initially defined our audience, purpose, and scope, the easier it was later to meld our parallel drafts. The one occasion when we threw out one writer's draft entirely, rather than attempt to meld even parts of it, was an occasion when we had not agreed upon an audience for an article about critical thinking pedagogy. We could have worked on either draft, but we couldn't have melded both of them into one.

Although the melding method generally worked very well for us, it wasn't our only method. On our long grant report for the project, when it would have been impractical for each of us to write full drafts, we each wrote different sections and compiled them. Although these sections remained relatively unchanged during revision, there are instances of one of us inserting paragraphs or citations in the other's text. On problematic sections, we returned to our earlier method of melding something out of parallel individual drafts.

Our experiments with jointly written drafts came after we had much experience with the melding and compilation methods. We resisted writing jointly for some time. In fact, a year into our collaboration, each of us included comments on parallel drafts for a joint conference presentation indicating that we really preferred not to write jointly. However, shortly thereafter, external circumstances forced us to write jointly, and we were surprised that it wasn't as excruciating as we had feared. As yet, we have still not attempted to compose jointly without substantial parallel drafts to work from.

Collaborative Resonance

Collaborating scholars not only share the research, writing, and meaning-making processes but also serve as an audience for each other; when one is collaborating there is always at least one other person who is willing and interested in reading and talking about one's work. Collaborating on an article doesn't make outside readers unnecessary, however. We found that after producing a text we sometimes lacked the necessary distance and objectivity to evaluate its clarity and emphasis, in much the same way as we did when we wrote single-authored texts. We still needed a reader to respond to our writing.

We also found that as collaborating writers our reaction to feedback from readers was complicated and enriched because, as in our research and writing, we had two perspectives on it. That is, we each read and interpreted the responder's comments, but then we discussed with each other our individual reactions and ultimately incorporated yet another layer of dual perspective. We found this collaborative interpretation of a reader's reactions and the subsequent rethinking that it initiated to be another distinct advantage of collaborating.

Our collaborative invention, research, and writing processes were enhanced not only by our interaction with each other and with readers who were generous with their time and advice but also by our interaction with additional members of the larger academic community. Karen Burke LeFevre's discussion of "resonance" (a term she borrows from Harold Lasswell) emphasizes the invention and collaborative role played by people who serve as resonators: "Resonance comes about when an individual act—a 'vibration'—is intensified and prolonged by sympathetic vibrations" (65). While readers clearly act as resonators, others often assist indirectly by providing various kinds of support: emotional, financial, or political. It is important to realize that while such resonators can play a crucial role in encouraging and facilitating the work of individual scholars, the need for such support can be just as great for researchers who are collaborating. During our retrospective tracing of our collaborative process we became increasingly aware of our own resonators, including colleagues, administrators, and our students who willingly cooperated in their role as research subjects and discussed with us their responses to our work. The contribution of such facilitators often seems to be taken for granted and acknowledged only indirectly, if at all. In thinking about other people's roles in our research project we came to expand our concept of collaboration—what it entails and who participates.

Collaborative Processes in Context

As we have collaborated and reflected on our collaboration, we have frequently noted the variety of collaborative processes that we and other collaborators employ. The question inevitably arises: Why all this variety? Is it a function of the writing context? the text to be produced? the predilections of the collaborating writers? This variety probably stems from a combination of factors, but one factor in particular deserves more attention: the writing context.

Considering the writing context broadly, academic collaborative writing in the arts and humanities differs from collaborative writing in the workplace (and, to some extent, from writing in the sciences). As we mentioned, both of us have taught technical writing and both of us have worked in industry (one as a technical editor at IBM and the other as a technical writing instructor at 3M) and thus have some shared knowledge about writing in business settings. We feel that academic and workplace collaboration differ substantially on issues of authority in both senses of the term—who establishes the purposes and goals of the project and who has control of the final text (authority).

In our experience at least, external control of the text was not the same kind of issue it seems to be in business settings. As academic writers, we are certainly members of a discourse community that privileges specific notions of what constitutes valuable research questions, what form a research article should take, and what conclusions will be acceptable. And, as associate professors (one tenured, one not) in need of publications, we are hardly in a position to flout the conventions of that discourse community. Nonetheless, purpose, audience, content, and even format are much more ill defined in academic contexts than in business ones. Scholarly authors have much more latitude and thus many more decisions to make than do business writers.

These institutional features of academic writing contexts thus favor Ede and Lunsford's dialogic mode of collaboration rather than the hierarchical mode. It may also be that the goals of academic writing in the arts and humanities favor the dialogic approach in collaborative projects. Because in our field we are trying to understand abstract concepts, ideas, and processes, the approach to literature, language, and composition scholarship that seems most appropriate is more a blending of perspectives than a compilation of findings.

On the other hand, collaboration is much more accepted in business contexts and in academic science writing than in arts and humanities. Although academic promotion and tenure committees have been known to ask for a collaborator's individual word count on jointly written documents, corporate managers would probably find it bizarre for an individual to offer this kind of evidence when corporate promotion decisions were being made. In a business context, time, workspace, money, and technological support all follow much more readily from this valuing of collaborative work because it serves the immediate needs of the corporation. All of these features—from the power structure of the organization and its reward system to the specifics of time, space, and computers—influence collaborative processes.

As we reflected on our collaborative processes, we realized that our processes were shaped by contextual factors as much as they were shaped by the more immediate and obvious features of our writing situation, factors such as how long we had been collaborating at the time, the length and kind of text we were producing, and personal preferences. While conducting this research, we both carried our full twelve-credit-per-quarter teaching loads along with our advising and service obligations; both of us are single parents; and one of us commutes eighty miles one way to work. Our circumstances are similar to those of other women reporting on their scholarly collaborative writing. Academic research in the arts and humanities is very likely to be conducted by scholars on their own time; furthermore, these collaborators are quite likely not to live or even teach in the same location. Collaborating women scholars on a Midwest Modern Language Association panel on "Feminists In/And Collaboration" reported planning, writing, and editing in kitchens, motel rooms at conferences, restaurants, and parking lots.

These factors have a pronounced effect on the collaborative processes that are used. Thus, it would be inaccurate to describe our processes without reference to these "extraneous" factors. For instance, we produced our first jointly written text in response to these kinds of factors. In order to meet a deadline, we had to work on a given weekend, and in order for one of us to take care of her children, we had to work at her house. If we had worked at the university where there were two computers rather than at one of our houses—the one eighty miles from campus—where there was one computer, we would probably have composed the draft using our usual composition method—melding. Although many anecdotal references to the contextual features can be found in the literature and in conference presentations, we would like to see more systematic investigation of the ways in which contextual features shape academic collaborative processes. In studies of workplace collaboration, descriptions of a rich interplay among context, processes, and texts are emerging; a heightened awareness of academic context might move us toward similarly rich descriptions of the interplay that is unique to academic collaboration.

Conclusion

Our reflections have highlighted for us the importance of contextualizing collaboration when describing it and of studying collaboration in a variety of contexts. The collaborative processes of writers differ not only because of personal preferences but also—and perhaps primarily—because the processes are a response to key features of the writing situation, such as the distribution of authority among collaborators and between collaborators and their superiors, the expectations and conventions of their discourse communities, the kinds and lengths of texts they are producing, and the kinds of resources and support that are available to them. It would be interesting to explore more fully the contributions of "resonators" to collaborative work in both workplace and academic settings.

We also think it is important to devote more attention to the distinctive nature of collaborative research and drafting methods, particularly to the ways in which they can be structured to encourage and prolong productive differences in perspective. Finally, we have come to realize that collaborative writing thrives on collaborative talk. While substantive and writing talk are clearly integral to collaborative projects, it may be that the quality of this talk is dependent upon procedural and social talk, particularly in academic collaborative contexts where collaborative partnerships and working methods are more a matter of choice than they are in business settings. It would be worthwhile to investigate more systematically the interrelationships of these kinds of collaborative talk in various writing contexts. Our reflections on our own scholarly collaboration have led us to a deeper understanding of these distinctive features and benefits of collaboration.

REFERENCES

Allen, Nancy, Diane Atkinson, Meg Morgan, Teresa Moore, and Doug Snow. "What Experienced Collaborators Say about Collaborative Writing." *JBTC* 1.2 (1987): 70–90.

Ashton-Jones, Evelyn, and Dene Kay Thomas. "Composition, Collaboration, and Women's Ways of Knowing: A Conversation with Mary Belenky." *Journal of Advanced Composition* 10 (1990): 275–92.

Austin, Ann E., and Roger G. Baldwin. *Faculty Collaboration: Enhancing the Quality of Scholarship and Teaching.* ASHE-ERIC Higher Education Report No. 7, 1991.

Calderonello, Alice Helm, Donna Beth Nelson, and Sue Carter Simmons. "An Interview with Andrea Lunsford and Lisa Ede: Collaboration as a Subversive Activity." *Writing on the Edge* 2.2 (1991): 7–18.

Ede, Lisa, and Andrea Lunsford. *Singular Texts/Plural Authors: Perspectives on Collaborative Writing.* Carbondale: Southern Illinois University Press, 1990.

———. "Why Write . . . Together?" *Rhetoric Review* 1 (1983): 150–57.

Freedman, Diane P., Olivia Frey, and Francis Murphy Zauhar. "In Our Own Voices, At Our Own Paces: Editing as a Threesome." Annual Conference of Midwest Modern Language Association. Chicago, 15 Nov. 1991.

Lay, Mary M. "Interpersonal Conflict in Collaborative Writing: What We Can Learn from Gender Studies." *JBTC* 3.2 (1989): 6–28.

LeFevre, Karen Burke. *Invention as a Social Act.* Carbondale: Southern Illinois University Press, 1987.

Lunsford, Andrea, and Lisa Ede. "Rhetoric in a New Key: Women and Collaboration." *Rhetoric Review* 8 (1990): 234–41.

McNenny, Geraldine, and Duane H. Roen. "The Case for Collaborative Scholarship in Rhetoric and Composition." *Rhetoric Review* 10 (1992): 291–310.

Odell, Lee, and Dixie Goswami, eds. *Writing in Nonacademic Settings.* New York: Guilford, 1985.

Trimbur, John. "Consensus and Difference in Collaborative Learning." *College English* 51 (1989): 602–16.

VanPelt, William, and Alice Gillam. "Peer Collaboration and the Computer-Assisted Classroom: Bridging the Gap between Academia and the Workplace." *Collaborative Writing in Industry: Investigations in Theory and Practice.* Ed. Mary M. Lay and William M. Karis. Amityville, NY: Baywood, 1991. 170–215.

Sally Barr Ebest

13

Going against Nature?

Women's Resistance to Collaborative Learning

In their ground-breaking studies of women's moral and intellectual development, Carol Gilligan and Mary Belenky, Blythe Clinchy, Nancy Goldberger, and Jill Tarule suggest that women students would be particularly receptive to collaborative learning. Gilligan notes that whereas men are socialized to work individually and competitively, women learn to build relationships; they tend to be sensitive to others, to listen to their opinions, and "to include in their judgment other points of view" (16). According to Belenky et al., mutual relationships involving verbal interactions "provide women with experiences of mutuality, equality, and reciprocity that are most helpful in eventually enabling them to disentangle their own voices from voices of others" (30). They conclude, "Educators can help women develop their own authentic voices if they emphasize connection over separation, understanding and acceptance over assessment, and collaboration over debate" (229).

These beliefs have been underscored in research conducted by Frances Maher, Lisa Ede and Andrea Lunsford, Elizabeth Flynn, Henry Giroux, and others. All suggest that female students would welcome collaborative learning, while male students would resist it. Anne Gere notes that "theories of collaborative learning build ... on an opposition to alienation and to the highly individualistic view inherent in traditional concepts of authorship and emphasize the communal aspect of intellectual life" (75). Within groups, this view is evident in language based on "negotiation, rather than application of absolute standards" (73). All of these traits are counter to those inculcated in males. According to research reported by Belenky et al., Gilligan, and William Perry, males have been socialized to favor individualism, while females are more comfortable in groups. Males are raised to identify with authority, while females are raised to obey it. Michael Foucault maintains that "children are socialized to use gendered speech styles, vocabularies, and topics" (qtd. in Gannett 68). Male conversational models are hierarchical and competitive, rule bound and determined by status—those in authority determine who speaks and who is listened to (Gannett 72). This research suggests that not only would male students resist collaborative learning as an abdication of the teacher's authority, but that males might also assume authority within a group setting, dominate conversation, and ignore the contributions of their female group members. Yet none of this research has actually examined the effects of collaborative learning on students.

In 1991, I began an ethnographic study designed to do just that. The ethnographic methodology allowed me to move away from the scientific experimental paradigm with its pre-tests and statistical studies. The problem with the experimental approach, as Michael Apple points out, is that when we look at students as "subjects," we ignore the role of context and personal history. "[People] are not simply objects of study, but agents of change, of social forces they create beyond themselves. It is the recognition of these social dynamics, the fundamentally socio-political characteristics of educational policy, practice, and outcomes, that seems to be missing in such research" (6). The ethnographic approach allowed me to conduct indepth research that could examine not only the educational context, but also the role of the students' class, race, and gender, as well as my own role as researcher in constructing my questions, interpretations, and results.

The individuals in this study were thirty-five graduate students pursuing a Master of Arts in English who were enrolled in at least one of three graduate courses between 1991 and 1993. All of these courses were a combination of writing theory and pedagogy; consequently, all involved reading about and participating in collaborative learning, i.e., peer review, reader response, and small group discussion. At the beginning of each course, I informed the students that I was conducting an action research project and invited them to participate. At the end of each semester, I asked the students to sign a consent form allowing me to analyze and quote from their classroom material. In three years, only one refused.

Between 1991 and 1993, I collected a total of thirty-five case studies—thirteen males and twenty-two females. When divided by gender, the men and women were similar in their ages, backgrounds, and graduate hours, and differed only slightly in teaching experience. Both males and females ranged in age from twenty-three to forty-eight and had completed an average of 2.25 semesters of graduate school. The men had taught for an average of one year, the women for 1.5 years.

There were also similarities in their reactions to and acceptance of collaborative learning. Of the thirteen men involved in this study, two immediately accepted collaborative learning and two opposed it; the remaining nine exhibited active resistance. Of the twenty-two women, fourteen accepted and benefited from collaborative learning and three opposed it. The other six resisted, three actively and three passively. Because this latter group comprises 27 percent of the women subjects, and because their behavior contradicts traditional research on gender differences, this chapter focuses on their resistance.

Active Resistance

My definitions of resistance are based on those developed by Henry Giroux and Geoff Chase. Giroux maintains that students' responses to learning fall into one of three categories: accommodation, opposition, or resistance. As Chase explains, students who "accommodate" accept what they are taught. Students who "resist" refuse to learn because they see the classroom ideology as infringing upon their personal beliefs. Thus, although resistance is "movement against the dominant ideology, it is also a movement toward emancipation." Students who are oppositional fail to learn. Although they also move against the ideology of the classroom, they do not move toward anything else (Chase 15).

Giroux warns that theories of resistance have too often been oversimplified and over-generalized (103). He cites previous studies that viewed resistance as apolitical and failed to account for differences in race, gender, and individual personality structure. This study attempts to avoid those pitfalls. By analyzing students' writing processes, their reflective response journals and their teaching logs, I was able to ascertain the reasons for their resistance. By comparing males' and females' attitudes and behaviors, as observed in class and during group work, I could determine if gender accounted for different types of resistance. Overall, by comparing students' learning styles, I was able to categorize their resistance, to describe its manifestations, and to explain its possible sources. The categories of resistance are drawn from those listed by Ruth Ray in *The Practice of Theory:* "epistemological, political, rhetorical, and pedagogical" (155). In my research, I found that students who displayed active resistance did so for rhetorical, pedagogical, or epistemological reasons, whereas those who exhibited passive resistance did so for political reasons.

Resistance for rhetorical reasons was characteristic of inexperienced teachers and writers. People in this category were new graduate students and new T.A.s unsure of their status and therefore unwilling to take any risks with their writing. Students who resisted for pedagogical reasons were novice teachers and semiexperienced but superstitious writers. These people tended to be perfectionists in their teaching and their writing, afraid to lose control in either area. Those students who resisted for epistemological reasons were new at teaching, but old hands at writing. They were skeptical of theories of writing and learning at odds with how they wrote. Across genders, I found similar reasons for active resistance. The students who exhibited passive resistance did not, however, cross gender lines. They were all women.

I first became aware of resistance to collaborative learning in 1991 while studying the responses of students in a graduate seminar on Reading-Writing Theory. Of all my female students, Gail's resistance was most obviously active. When Gail enrolled, she was twenty-four years old. She had just finished her first year of graduate studies in English and her first semester as a graduate Teaching Assistant (T.A.) in our English department. When I observed her classes during the semester, Gail was using a variety of collaborative learning activities. Consequently, I assumed she understood the value of group work. However, I was disabused of this notion when she became my student. The first night of class, Gail told me she did not feel comfortable with collaborative learning as a teaching strategy and she did not want to participate in group work. She had used collaborative learning in her classroom only because of expediency—that's what her fellow T.A.s did—but she felt hypocritical because she found these methods personally distasteful. I discovered some explanation for Gail's discomfort in her journals, where she explained that "for a natural introvert basing class discussion on her own freewrites is hell . . . and introducing a new cure-all theory of education [collaborative learning] is like sending an earthquake through a place that was always home." "Home" was a comfortable style of writing: find out what the teacher wanted, write the paper, and turn it in. Gail "didn't like any feedback on [her] writing." She knew what worked for her and she didn't want to risk anything different.

After reading the theory behind collaborative learning and participating (reluctantly) in some group work, Gail's resistance began to lessen. At midterm, she admitted: "halfway through a theory class, I can honestly say that I would still teach the same way, that now I understand and even accept, some of the reasons why we do the things we do. But one thing hasn't changed. I still don't like it." Gail continued her resistance until the night the students had to exchange first drafts of their midterm essay. At the end of the peer response session, I asked the class to comment on their experience of sharing their writing. Gail admitted that she had never shown her writing to anyone outside of a family member and that, needless to say, she had been skeptical. "Up until this point," she said, "I felt this was just like any other writing course. But I have never gone through anything like this with my writing." She was both pleased and relieved that the feedback from her group had helped her decide what direction to take in her revision. This participation marked the turning point in Gail's resistance. Since she had already taught for one semester, she could see how collaborative learning worked when teaching. It was not until she participated in group work, however, that she came to see its value for her.

Experience also played a role in lessening Susan's resistance. I met Susan in 1992, when she enrolled in Teaching College Composition. When the semester began, Susan was twenty-four years old. She had received her B.A. in English two years before and was beginning a Master's degree. To support herself, she was teaching two sections of Basic Writing at a community college. Like many part-timers, Susan had no training and no experience—she was simply given her books and thrown into the classroom.

Susan was anxious to learn more about teaching. She was also somewhat sympathetic with her students' writing apprehension and willing to try some "new" teaching techniques, such as short reflective writings. At the same time, however, she attributed their writing problems to ignorance or sloth, referring to her students as "neanderthals." This attitude led her to reject collaborative learning as too advanced. "They need the structure of some lecturing," she wrote, "as they seem to either fail to read or fail to understand the assigned material otherwise." Not surprisingly, Susan also rejected peer editing as "premature," a matter of "the blind leading the blind." Week after week, she resisted the theory and practice of collaborative learning; one after another, her teaching logs began "I spent most of today lecturing."

This attitude may have stemmed from Susan's attitude about her own writing process. She admitted that she had "always been a little confused about the idea of rewriting. . . . For me, rewriting has always been an inconvenience." Like Gail, Susan resisted this notion and the peer editing that accompanied it. But her resistance also stemmed from her superstition about the writing process; collaborative learning seemed to interfere with the creative "muse." In her journal, she notes:

> I do feel there is some magic in the writing process. I enjoy that moment of inspiration and the process of discovering my own thoughts and feelings through writing. Collaboration diminishes that. Maybe I have bought into the romantic notion of the isolated writer, but I feel it must be this way for the work to truly be my own. Somehow, the idea of letting others guide my writing during the process disturbed me. I rarely discuss a work in progress and don't like to let others see an unfinished piece. . . . The writer who is too aware of audience loses him or herself.

This entry was written during the fourth week of the semester, while the students were working on drafts of their first essay.

As the semester went on, and the students were introduced to more theory, I could see Susan's resistance begin to lessen. After reading about the relationship between reading experience and writing ability, she wrote:

> I am learning understanding through this class and through my teaching. I am learning that just because something works for me that does not mean it works for everyone. Whenever something is second nature, like reading is for me, it is difficult to imagine why everyone can't do it. By the same token, people who can cook and sew are baffled at my complete incompetence. This class is providing explanations and methods for removing the obstacles. I hope to be able to put them into practice and overcome my own form of tunnel vision.

Soon after this entry, Susan put theory into practice. She tried small group work again in her class, and this time it was more successful. In her teaching log, she explained the difference: "You're right about modeling and narrowing down the focus of what they were looking for. The first time I tried this, I just told them to exchange papers and give each other responses. What did I expect? This was way too unfocused."

Susan's Basic Writing classes ended in the middle of the semester. By then, she had accepted collaborative learning as a useful teaching technique. But, like Gail, she still was not wholly convinced of its application to her as a writer. This was probably due in large part to her educational background. As Susan notes in her journal of November 9, "Nearly all of my learning has been teacher centered or self-taught." Throughout high school and college, classes were lecture based; discussion, if allowed, was teacher centered; and any type of collaboration was regarded as cheating. For both students, their graduate seminars in composition theory and pedagogy were their first collaborative learning experiences.

In this same journal entry, Susan notes that the group work we had done in class had "been really good. I have learned how to teach using groups as well as how to better participate in them." However, when I examined the drafts of her first two essays, there was no evidence of any influence on Susan's writing and revision. For the first essay, between drafts one and three, Susan deleted one paragraph and added two more. Revisions were similar for essay two. Although this paper was much longer and more cohesive, she only added one sentence and deleted another. For both papers, though, Susan led me to believe that she was benefiting from her group work. In her evaluation of Essay 1, she wrote that "the peer editing was helpful" and that she "got some new directions to take to help fix the problems." About Essay 2, she said, "the peer responses were more helpful this time" and that she "got a lot of response. Some of the suggestions contradicted each other, though, so I just went with what I liked in the end."

By the time Susan began her third and final essay, both her attitude and her process had begun to change. In her November 23rd process journal entry, she says "I'm . . . not quite sure what I want to say in this paper, and I don't think I found out in the first draft. I'm eager to see how the others in my group respond to it." Her next two drafts showed only subtle changes. However, she expanded her final paper by six pages of quotations, explanations, and examples in the body, and three pages of solutions to teaching problems in the conclusion. She included these because her group members suggested them; she even pulled comments and examples from her teaching logs to further illustrate what and how she learned.

Susan explains the reasons for these changes in the introduction to her final portfolio, in which she had to submit everything she had written that semester, prefaced by an analysis of her writing process and explanations of all final revisions. She concludes her analysis by admitting her resistance: "The other area that I have become very aware of through this class is the necessity of revision and rewriting. Since I had never really revised papers for a class, I was not proficient in making these changes. When writing the final draft for the first essay, I was aware of some problems it had, but I was unwilling to rewrite it."

Reading, writing about, and engaging in collaborative learning helped Susan to overcome this resistance. In her final journal entry, she writes,

> The group work has been really good. . . . I often feel wrapped up in a paper and am unable to separate myself enough to analyze it well; the group helped me step back and think about it more objectively. Early on, I saw group work as detracting from the originality of the individual. I now see how wrong that was. Merely receiving feedback from others does not mean

that it is necessary to follow their suggestions, but most often the suggestions are right. The peers are not trying to change what the authors write but are instead trying to help them clarify and refine their work.

To recognize and overcome their resistance, students need to understand what they are resisting and why. Collaborative learning can facilitate this process, but I think students must also be willing (and able) to spend some time in introspection and self-analysis. As Susan wrote in the introduction to her portfolio:

> Re-examining the process of writing has allowed me to change my ideas of how to write. . . . This has been beneficial to me in this class and will be beneficial to my writing in the future. More importantly, though, it has changed my thinking and my criteria. The true beneficiaries of these changes in philosophy will be the students I teach.

Passive Resistance

As the name implies, passive resistance is much more difficult to detect and define. When I had Angie and Mary Jo in class, they showed no signs of resistance. I did not become aware of their passive resistance until I analyzed their writing at the end of the semester. In both cases, the students' beliefs about themselves affected their acceptance of collaborative learning.

Angie was one of Gail's peers in the 1991 Reading-Writing seminar. Compared to Gail, Angie seemed enthusiastic about collaborative learning. She respected the concept as a teaching strategy and she was anxious to try it in her ninth-grade literature class. Not surprisingly, Angie evinced the same enthusiasm for group work. She carefully read and responded to her partner's papers, taking care to couch her responses positively, and in turn, listened attentively to her partner's suggestions for revision. When these ideas reinforced her own intuition about problem areas, Angie nodded in agreement. However, when presented with a suggestion that involved a degree of risk, which meant breaking out of academic prose and conventional patterns of organization, she was skeptical.

Prior to their first peer response session, the students had completed a series of exercises to help them further develop their essays. In one, Angie had written a story describing "Jeremy," a typical uninterested student. Her partner thought Angie should use it because it exemplified the students and the problems she would be dealing with. Although she was pleased with her partner's positive response, Angie was also surprised. And so she turned to me for confirmation. Only when I agreed, suggesting she use it as an introduction, was she convinced. "I never would have had the nerve to try anything like this otherwise," she said.

When it came to teaching, Angie exhibited no resistance whatsoever. In fact, her midterm essay focused on how she would integrate collaborative learning into her classroom. But when it came to her own writing, Angie was afraid to take risks. She didn't trust the advice of her peer group, refusing to act on it without the teacher's approval. Angie preferred to take the safe route, writing a traditional comparison/contrast paper and focusing on teaching strategies. It wasn't until I read her final journal entry that the reasons for this passive resistance began to make sense: "I must start with a confession: I was on the verge of giving up teaching English. The kids just didn't seem interested in learning. I would read my favorite poem and they would yawn—kind of a pattern we developed. Their favorite and most frequent question was 'How many points is this worth?' To complicate matters, I had this feeling in the pit of my stomach: I couldn't really blame them."

Angie's confession suggests that she had poured everything into her teaching, only to be met with indifference. The problem may have been a result of outdated teaching strategies, but Angie, like many teachers, took it personally—more personally than she realized. Her feelings of inadequacy were manifested in her behavior as a writer. Collaboration with her peer group and with me helped to change Angie's attitude and rebuild her self-confidence. When her partner indicated places where her writing could be strengthened, she was often supporting Angie's intuitive feelings about necessary revision. When I praised her ideas and seconded her partner's suggestions, I helped give her the confidence to take risks with her writing.

Angie's behavior exemplifies a relatively minor case of passive resistance, but a real one nonetheless. Graduate students often lack self-confidence about their writing, but female graduate students may have even less confidence than their male peers. As Belenky, Clinchy, Goldberger, and Tarule point out, throughout their academic careers, women are taught that the personal voice is inappropriate. Yet outside the academy, that is the voice women have been raised to use. Consequently, mastery of impersonal, academic prose style is an accomplishment. When we ask women students to trust their peer groups' advice, especially when that advice contradicts the way they have been traditionally taught, we may encounter resistance on a variety of levels.

Although Angie's resistance was not immediately evident, it was fairly easy to overcome—she needed to gain confidence in herself, in her writing, and in her group members. Through participation in collaborative learning, she was able to make these changes. But the situation was different with Mary Jo. Like Angie, she understood the pedagogical value and the rhetorical effect of collaborative learning in the classroom; she also knew how and why to use group work. But she had a much harder time recognizing, respecting, and responding to what her group members told her about herself and her writing.

I first met Mary Jo in winter 1991, two semesters before she became a teaching assistant. At that time, she was forty years old, beginning a master's degree after having taught briefly at the secondary level. Although she majored in political science as an undergraduate, as a result of her teaching experience, Mary Jo had decided to focus on English. When she enrolled in Teaching College Composition, Mary Jo initially exhibited a fairly low level of resistance to the theories she was encountering. In her first response journal, she noted that after reading about decentered classrooms and collaborative learning, her first reaction was "No, I totally disagree!" She said she found these theories "unsettling" because they contradicted how she had been taught. Nonetheless, she ended that first entry on a contemplative rather than a rebellious note, signing off with "Interesting."

In subsequent entries, Mary Jo, like Angie, appeared to accept collaborative learning as a teaching strategy. Mary Jo wrote that "having students share their writing with someone other than the teacher was probably the most noticeable success in that writing class I mentioned earlier. . . . Another significant success was sharing myself as a writer with them." A few weeks later, she commented positively about the instruction her son was receiving at his private school, where the English courses linked reading and writing instruction, integrated grammar with the students' writing, and used peer workshops.

Like many of her peers, however, Mary Jo was not wholly comfortable when she participated in collaborative learning. She believed she was an overly slow writer, an "inadequate" reader, and an inexperienced teacher; she felt "somewhat intimidated" when collaborating with one of her peers who was a T.A. and "humbled" after working with a secondary teacher who seemed "much more confident in her writing." These experiences left Mary Jo wondering why she was so timid, but subsequent entries helped to explain these feelings.

Mary Jo felt at a disadvantage because she did not have an undergraduate English major (a recurring lament in her journal responses). These feelings appeared to color her view of herself and her abilities; they also affected her work. Everything had to be done perfectly and, like Angie, carefully. Mary Jo ignored her peer group's suggestions for revision and resisted seeking their advice on subsequent drafts. As she said, "A big part of writing for me is having a particularly strong handle on where I'm going with the writing."

This resistance was reflected to a certain degree when she became a T.A. the following year. Mary Jo believed in collaborative learning as a teaching strategy and she used it in her classes; nevertheless, her classrooms were never wholly decentered. Rather than allowing her students to work out problems in groups, she told them what to do and how to do it. Although she used small groups to read and respond to drafts, she undercut their authority by taking up the drafts and marking them herself.

This behavior continued when Mary Jo enrolled in Reader Response Theory in spring semester of 1992. In this class, the students were assigned to permanent groups of three. Each week, they read, analyzed, responded to, and discussed their group members' freewritten responses. During the first half of the semester, the students responded to theoretical texts; during the second half, they wrote personal responses to short stories. The purpose of the group work was to practice a method of reader response while simultaneously learning to understand one's own language use. To model this method of response, I also read the students' weekly work and responded in kind.

As with the journals and teaching logs used in other seminars, this type of response allowed me to follow my students' progress and respond to any questions they might raise. But it also gave me the opportunity to analyze the students' language traits, such as recurring topics, expressions of feeling, essay structure and length, and technical proficiency—the same traits they looked for in their peers' papers and analyzed in their own writing. In other words, the students were receiving response to their writing from me and from their peer group. This response would in turn enable them to analyze their own language use in midterm and final essays.

It was in this context that Mary Jo's resistance to collaborative learning emerged. She did not appear to resist the collaborative format; in fact, she complained that her group did not give her indepth responses. But their responses were very similar to mine: they noted that even though the weekly journals were supposed to be informal freewrites, Mary Jo's were always formal—clear introduction and conclusion, well-developed body paragraphs, clear transitions, consistent use of formal, "academic" words and phrases, and few if any expressions of feeling. While her peer group scrawled their two- or three-page responses in longhand, Mary Jo submitted almost perfect, well-edited, double-spaced, laser-printed, four-page essays. Whereas some students were writing "I hated this book," Mary Jo wrote, "This text is cursed for me.... I found the reading to be laborious.... I am in basic disagreement with a major feature of [the author's] position." Such indirect statements of feeling were not limited to discussions of academic texts. In writing about continuing disagreements with her son, she was equally distant: "It is indeed unfortunate that I must now move on to the second part of this assignment because I realize the person I currently argue the most with is Scott, my fifteen-year-old son." The group noted that Mary Jo's recurring topics were a need for organization and control, both in her life and in her writing. She seemed to resent pompous, abtruse writing and the authors who produced it, relating their attitudes and verbosity to the male professors she had encountered in graduate school. One of her few direct expressions of feeling referred to these situations: "I don't like feeling intimidated," she wrote. But as a rule, her writing was fairly detached, even when the topic was personal.

As the semester progressed, Mary Jo's writing became slightly less formal and her complaints about her group members tapered off. Consequently, I was taken aback when she came to my office in tears during the last week of the semester. "I can't write this paper," she said. "I've tried and tried, but nothing will come out. I've never had writer's block before, but I just cannot write this paper." We talked about different approaches and touched on the various reasons for her difficulties, but nothing seemed to help. Knowing her penchant for perfection, I assured her that she didn't have to have all the answers; she only needed to attempt an analysis. That didn't help. Finally, I told her that if she couldn't finish the paper in time, she could take a delayed grade. Perhaps the paper would be easier to write during the summer, when the pressures of graduate school had lessened. At the end of our discussion, Mary Jo left the office somewhat relieved, yet determined to try again to produce a draft. But she just couldn't do it. The semester ended with Mary Jo in tears, still unable to overcome her writer's block.

That summer, I read Belenky, Clinchy, Goldberger and Tarule's *Women's Ways of Knowing*, which explains the five stages of women's acquisition of knowledge: silence, received knowledge, procedural knowledge, subjective knowledge, and constructed knowledge. As I read, I began to find some explanations for Mary Jo's writing, and subsequent inability to write. Mary Jo seemed to fall into the definition of a "separate knower," a subdivision of constructed knowledge. The writing of separate knowers tends not to have a personal voice. These women have learned to write the "correct" paper—they can express ideas but not their feelings and opinions. While these papers may earn high grades, the women are not comfortable with their writing. They feel they have fooled the professor; they know this is not their own voice (110).

These women may have gone through most of their lives unaware of this disparity, or at least discounting it because, as Belenky et al. point out, in most colleges and universities, "the subjective voice was largely ignored. . . . It was the public, rational, analytical voice that received the institutions' tutelage, respect, and rewards" (124). When these women realize that their voice is unnatural, or untrue to themselves, they panic. Because this situation seemed to parallel Mary Jo's, I sent her copies of these chapters and asked her to let me know if they helped. Her first response acknowledged their use, but also pointed out the dangers of overgeneralizing. As Mary Jo put it, "First of all let me say that it is my personal view that individuals are not nice, neat packages to be categorized. I see myself as exhibiting characteristics of both separate and connected learners. Similarly, I see myself as moving back and forth among the third, fourth, and fifth stages of constructing knowledge." From there, she went on to explain how she fit into the various categories. Clearly, she was back on track.

At the end of the summer, Mary Jo handed me her final paper, wryly entitled "How I Spent My Summer Vacation." In it, she explained why she resisted her group's feedback and how she overcame her resistance. She began by reminding me of the goal she had set for herself at the end of her midterm essay: "growing up and believing myself to be a competent individual—and giving myself and my writing a chance to be free of manic obsessiveness." However, she continues, "I did not realize how difficult and painful the process of growing up and believing in myself would be. I did not realize how much I would resist." This resistance was manifested in Mary Jo's response to her group's feedback. Throughout the semester, her group members and I had continually pointed out language traits which exemplified her need for perfection and control. But Mary Jo didn't want to see it and she certainly did not want to analyze it. Her passive resistance took the form of writer's block.

In the students' midterm and final essays, they were to analyze and explain the source of recurring language traits found in their weekly responses and discussed by their group members. At midterm, the analyses were based on responses to academic texts, but the final paper included academic as well as personal responses to language stories and literature. Mary Jo's midterm essay had begun to address some of these traits; nevertheless, as she says in her final paper, this was only "the tip of an iceberg."

> At that point, I had not seen a desire for control growing out of [my] insecurity or the anger I experienced when denied control. Issues of control and anger that arise out of my family and socio-economic backgrounds are present in most, if not all, of the language features of my writing. This rock bottom perception has come through an incredibly difficult and painful process of introspection and discovery initiated by the assignments of this class.

Weekly responses from me and her group, especially one member, Karen, facilitated this introspection. Throughout her final essay, Mary Jo cites different instances where her group had pointed out language features, only to be ignored. She concludes:

> Karen really forced my hand . . . when she pointed out that for her the main difference between my writing the first half and the second half [of the semester] is that of "a cool, somewhat argumentative, scholarly writer and a writer who reveals herself to be more of a 'traditional' woman caught between her traditional roles and her raised consciousness."
>
> Karen apparently felt that intellectually I knew some things that on a personal basis I was unable to apply. She is right, of course. What I have learned from this writer's block that grew out of looking closely at the language features of my writing through the responses of my peers and under [my professor's] enabling tutelage is that life, success, intelligence, whatever, do not have to be defined as elements of control. What is important is the realization that the journey, the process of knowing and learning, [is] unpredictable and not easily controlled. The process is messy and illogical. Out of all of this chaos, though, I have grown and changed—matured. Even the anger and frustration of not being able to write because it hurt too much to acknowledge my inability to manage my life perfectly and the anger I felt . . . has been worth the pain.

Discussion

Each of the case studies in this chapter illustrates a different degree of resistance to collaborative learning. Gail did not understand the theories and feared any changes in her writing process; Susan's superstitions about the sanctity of the individual writer led her to reject collaborative learning for herself and her students; Angie was afraid to trust her group, while Mary Jo didn't want to accept her group's findings. None of these women is an anomaly. In fact, their behavior is paralleled by some of the other men and women in these classes. Out of a total of thirty-five students studied, nine men and six women exhibited resistance—almost forty-three percent of all my students over a three-year period. These numbers suggest that resistance to collaborative learning may be typical of a proportion of all students, regardless of gender.

These findings contradict earlier studies of gender and collaborative learning. Kramarae and Treichler found that women "report more ease and more discovery in settings where learning is a communal activity shared equally by students and teacher. Men seem more satisified with authoritarian educational settings" (56). My research found, however, that while 70 percent of the men initially resisted collaborative learning, so did 27 percent of the women; moreover, despite their initial resistance, both male and female students eventually accepted and benefited from collaborative learning. These findings suggest that collaborative learning can be effective for both men and women. They also suggest that feminist researchers should guard against making the same methodological error that flawed earlier work by males: just as men should not generalize about women's learning styles, we should not stereotype those of men. Rather than continue the recent focus on gender differences, perhaps we should begin to look also at similarities.

Across genders, I found similar reasons for active resistance. Gail's reason paralleled Paul's, whom I met the following semester in Teaching College Writing. Neither of these students had ever been asked to examine their composing processes or to share those insights with their peers. Add to that the fact that they were new, insecure graduate students, and one can see how collaborative learning contradicted their rhetorical construct of the composing process. John, Jeff, Charles, Dale, and Dan paralleled Susan in type and level of resistance. None of them had prior teaching experience, but all had writing experience outside the academy. Their approach to writing influenced their approach to teaching. They all believed that writing stemmed from inspiration; consequently, they resisted the concept of writing as a process and rejected the notion that peers could further that process. In other words, these students resisted collaborative learning for pedagogical reasons.

Both males and females played what Peter Elbow calls the "doubting game": "doubting reflects the trial-by-fire foundation of knowledge whereby we feel no position should be accepted until it has witnessed the battering of our best skeptics" (266). Such behavior once again crosses traditional gender lines, for, as Elbow explains, "doubting invites behaviors which our culture associates with masculinity: refusing, saying No, pushing away, competing, being aggressive" (266). For students of both genders, the "trial by fire" involved sharing their writing with their group and using collaborative learning in their own classrooms. Active resistance was overcome by actively engaging in collaborative learning.

The students who exhibited passive resistance did not, however, cross gender lines. In each case, the resistance was initially difficult to recognize because these students played Elbow's "believing game": "Believing reflects the consensus foundation of knowledge whereby we feel no position should be accepted until a respected group of authorities positively endorses it through participation in it. . . . Believing invites behaviors associated with femininity: accepting, saying Yes, being complaisant, listening, absorbing, and swallowing . . . being mute or silent" (266).

These women were passive for political reasons: they did not actively resist because they had been raised not to. Because of their personal background and/or their educational experiences, they had learned to keep silent, to go along. Their resistance became evident only when their group's responses shook their personal beliefs about their writing and themselves. These students appeared to accept collaborative learning because they had been raised to be "good girls." The only evidence of passive resistance was in their writing, characterized by a rigid adherence to formal, academic prose; a refusal to accept the group's advice or to take risks with their writing; or, as in Mary Jo's case, emotional trauma as evidenced in writer's block.

In *Educating the Reflective Practitioner,* Donald Schon points out that when we present students with new theories of learning, we are asking them to "let go of earlier understandings and know-how, along with the sense of control and confidence that accompanies them" (120). Depending upon their prior experiences, the students will either accommodate, resist, or oppose learning. While there is little we can do to overcome opposition, introspection can help students to recognize and deal with their resistance. Response journals and self reflective papers can facilitate the learning process, for they allow students to do what they are asked, yet reflect on what they're doing.

As we saw in Mary Jo's case, this type of writing and response can also help to empower women. This is a side of collaborative learning that is seldom developed outside the composition classroom. Elizabeth Flynn notes that "feminist inquiry and composition studies have much in common," and praises the feminist classroom that includes the teaching of writing and uses writing to teach. "But for the most part," she continues, "the fields of feminist studies and composition studies have not engaged each other in a serious or systematic way" (113–14). This failing may be what Annette Kolodny means when she "worries about the tendency of feminist critics to focus less and less on concrete specifics of classroom power and pedagogy and more and more on esoteric theorizing" (qtd. in Ede and Lunsford 122).

Classroom research, such as that on which these studies were based, can help to bridge this gap. Indeed, as Ruth Ray points out, the goals of classroom research are quite similar to those of feminist criticism (33). Both are concerned with addressing differences in gender, class, and sexual orientation. Both "have been motivated by a desire to bring the marginal to the center, and both attempt to give voice and status to diverse groups in minority positions" (Ray 29). The primary tools of current composition studies—collaborative learning and reflective writing—can provide the data to study these issues. Elaine Showalter underscores the value of this methodology when she argues that "no theory . . . can be a substitute for the close and extensive knowledge of women's texts which constitutes our essential subject. . . . [F]eminist critics must use this concept in relation to what women actually write, not in relation to a theoretical, political, metaphorical, or visionary ideal of what women ought to write" (266).

If we take this approach, we will study not only "le differance," but also the similarities between men's and women's writing. Just as women writers may display traits traditionally attributed to men, male writers may possess traits often associated with females. We need more classroom research that examines men's and women's writing together, within a natural context, to provide a fuller understanding of how both genders construct knowledge. Under the rubric of "collaboration," these studies could focus on the influence of collaborative learning on students' voices, on their writing, on their comprehension, on their teaching, on their attitudes toward learning, on their gendered behaviors, and on their self-knowledge.

While various studies have been conducted at the elementary and secondary levels, very little has been done at the post-secondary level, and virtually nothing is known about the effects of collaboration on graduate students. Yet students in these latter areas are our future teachers and professors. If they do not understand and benefit from collaborative learning, they will certainly not use it in their own classrooms. Those of us who believe in collaboration must demonstrate its value through our research. We can do so by moving beyond decontextualized theory to look at classrooms, teachers, and students so that others may begin to understand how to change the way they teach—and why it's time to change.

REFERENCES

Apple, Michael. *Teachers and Texts*. New York and London: Routledge and Kegan Paul, 1986.

Belenky, Mary F., et al. *Women's Ways of Knowing*. New York: HarperCollins, 1986.

Chase, Geoffrey. "Accommodation, Resistance and the Politics of Student Writing." *College Composition and Communication* 39 (1988): 13–22.

Ede, Lisa, and Andrea Lunsford. *Singular Texts/Plural Authors: Perspectives on Collaborative Writing*. Carbondale: Southern Illinois University Press, 1990.

Elbow, Peter. *Embracing Contraries*. New York: Oxford University Press, 1986.

Flynn, Elizabeth. "Composing as a Woman." In Gabriel and Smithson. 112–26.

Gabriel, Susan, and Isaiah Smithson, eds. *Gender in the Classroom*. Urbana and Chicago: University of Illinois Press, 1990.

Gannett, Cinthia. *Gender and the Journal*. Albany: State University of New York Press, 1992.

Gere, Anne. *Writing Groups*. Urbana: NCTE, 1987.

Gilligan, Carol. *In a Different Voice*. Cambridge: Harvard University Press, 1982.

Giroux, Henry A. *Theory and Resistance in Education: A Pedagogy for the Opposition*. South Hadley, MA: Bergin Garvey, 1983.

Kramarae, Cheris, and Paula A. Treichler. "Power Relationships in the Classroom." In Gabriel and Smithson. 41–59.

Maher, Frances. "Classroom Pedagogy and the New Scholarship on Women." *Gendered Subjects: The Dynamics of Feminist Teaching*. Ed. Margo Culley and Catherine Portuges. Boston: Routledge and Kegan Paul, 1985. 29–48.

Perry, William. *Forms of Intellectual and Ethical Development in the College Years.* New York: Holt, 1970.
Ray, Ruth E. *The Practice of Theory.* Urbana: NCTE, 1993.
Schon, Donald. *Educating the Reflective Practitioner.* San Francisco: Jossey, 1987.
Showalter, Elaine. "Feminist Criticism in the Wilderness." *The New Feminist Criticism: Essays on Women, Literature, and Theory.* Ed. Elaine Showalter. New York: Pantheon, 1985. 243–70.
Trimbur, John. "Collaborative Learning and Teaching Writing." *Perspectives on Research and Scholarship in Composition.* Ed. Ben McClelland and Timothy Donovan. New York: MLA, 1990. 87–110.

Elaine Allen Karls and Roslyn Z. Weedman

14

Revisioning Space

From Territoriality to Collaboration

We share an office smaller than most federal prison cells, and with less light, located in the basement—excuse us—the "lower level" of the Fine Arts Building on our campus. Three years ago, when we were hired, Roz's husband visited our digs (she was anxious to show off this new space) and he was hard put to feign enthusiasm. But his office serves an important function of impressing clients, while tradition holds that our office need only serve as a repository for our stuff and a place to talk to students.

The initial joint decision of how to conceptualize this space changed our lives forever, for the better. There we were—Elaine and Roz—new nontenured hires with a tenuous toehold in the door of the academy that does not admit so many these days. Total strangers, we were informed that space being at a premium, for now, we'd share. We had choices to make at this juncture. We could each, ever so politely of course, stake out our territory, protect it by hauling in tasteful decorations, and preserve it by being ourselves models of nontransgression. We could work out schedules affording each of us maximum solitude and privacy. We like to think of this as the masculine territorial mode, the default mode of office space protocol. Or we could reimagine this space as the nexus of a symbiotic, synergistic partnership, testing the old notion of a whole being greater than the sum of its parts.

Our previous experience with office space didn't help too much. Roz had half an office as a teaching assistant previously, but this was like sharing space with a ghost; neither really set up shop and worked there. Both Elaine and Roz had experiences in a large pool of part-time instructors consisting of 90 percent women whose space ratio was about thirty instructors to one office. This situation is, of course, basically hopeless and useless as any kind of model.

A graphic example of the particular marginalization of women was Elaine's experience while working as a student teacher supervisor in the College of Education at a major university. She was required on many occasions to accompany her professor supervisor in his red sports car, which bore a plate on the front of the car reading, "I'm a Male Chauvinist Pig." From Elaine's perspective, it was nearly impossible not to feel one's professionalism compromised to arrive at area schools in this car. This placard also clarified the hierarchical position of Elaine vis-a-vis her supervisor, not only on a professional level but apparently in life.

Less blatant but even more common, Roz experienced the prejudice heaped on those in higher education who choose to specialize in composition when her graduate chair asked her incredulously if she really wanted to spend (read "waste") a whole 25 percent of her reading-list time on composition. The composition faculty at this particular institution occupied quarters segregated from the rest of the more highly esteemed English department. Separate but equal did not apply here either. The literature faculty was in excess of 90 percent men who clearly enjoyed their superior status. The composition ranks were staffed mostly by women, most of whom were in nontenured positions, often sharing space next to graduate students. Although the head of the composition program was a tenured man, all degreed instructors on continuing one-year appointments were women. In Roz's particular program, women outnumbered men six to one, enjoying, of course, the lowly teaching-assistant status.

All these previous space experiences within the academic community confirmed Gail Griffin's observations that "to be a woman is fundamentally not to belong to most institutions, and if feminism is a kind of conscious womanhood, then to be feminist is to be perpetually aware of that marginality, indeed, it means on some level to choose it, to resist belonging" (26).

We both recall being consciously aware of the significance of finally having a real, physical space that we would own and share as we both claimed and occupied the margin. Our conclusion to our observations and experiences was that in the academy, space does indeed become masculine or feminine—whether it's a car or an office building—and that feminized space is marginalized space.

Roz, Personal Musings, August 1990: My new office mate, Elaine, has so much stuff—I wonder if I do—and she plops it everywhere. But there's some new freedom to that idea. I can plop mine everywhere, too. This is a very interesting woman and if this arrangement is going to work, I've got to get over my notion of office space (see figure 14.1).

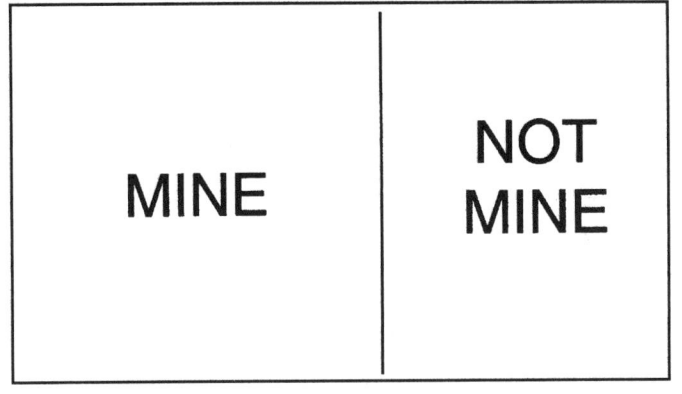

Figure 14.1

I think it's really going to be more like . . . (see figure 14.2).

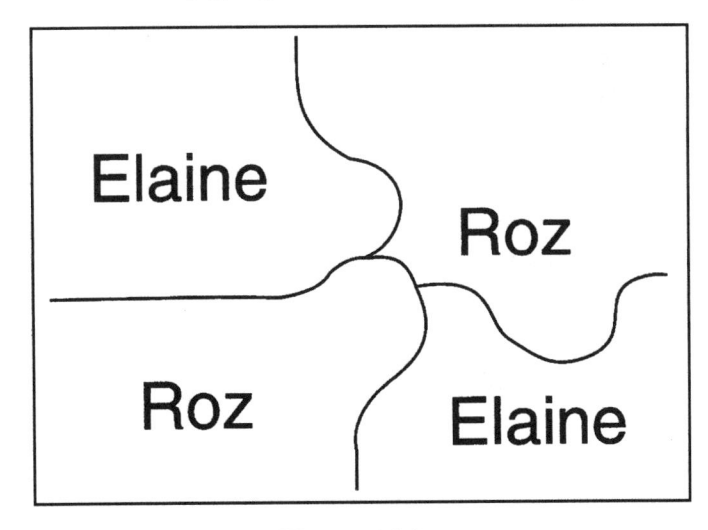

Figure 14.2

Elaine, Personal Musings, August 1990: After years of part time, temporary, jury-rigged college and university appointments, I am hired! (Ok, ok, no tenure stream, no unqualified promises, but one full year ahead in which to teach English among full-time faculty.) Roz and I, newly introduced, each possesses a key to an office we will share. An office! I hear myself casually tossing references to the office in future conversations: "Oh, by the way, would you like my *office* number?" I am, on my first day in that peach-colored cell, overwhelmed by its cavernous eight-by-ten dimensions.

As I drag in the first boxes, I look for Roz—not here! Already I feel concern for not overstepping "her" side. Compared with my car (my previous office), there seems room here almost to install a hot tub or sauna. I want the place to feel like Roz's, not just mine. And I want her, when she arrives, to feel like someone has been making the place more habitable, more homey. I feel a little like I felt on the first day of camp as a girl: let the other girl pick top or bottom, window or center-aisle bed. Be nice. And having met Roz only briefly, I am hopeful for this professional relationship to work out.

Roz, Personal Musings, September 1990: I'm sure I've known Elaine forever. It's unbelievable. Our experiences, our attitudes, our readings of people and situations, our families, our complementary professional backgrounds, our senses of humor—I haven't had this feeling since living in a dorm at the age of 17. I'm not sure I had it then. When I walk into our office and close the door and talk to Elaine, anything goes. It's safe space and I can say exactly what I'm thinking.

Elaine, Personal Musings, September 1990: The semester unfolds in the lower level halls which some here call "the catacombs." Roz is as remarkable a gift to me as this job. I am aware of two pleasing realities. The first is that, as I walk down the hallway, I am always hoping (just before reaching the office door) that the telltale light around the doorjamb will signal Roz's presence. I never wish she weren't there or that the office belonged to me alone. And the second is that, with these paper-thin walls, colleagues can hear Roz and me in the office. Comments in meetings and around the coffee urn sometimes take this turn: "What's so funny? You guys are always laughing." Sharing the office has begun to feel like a conscious political act, inasmuch as our laughter has sometimes been interpreted as conspiratorial. In this work environment defined by individual offices (which signal at least minimal status), I suspect some colleagues have a secret longing for an office mate.

To understand the development of this professional and personal liaison, we can think in terms of Deborah Tannen's book, *You Just Don't Understand*. (Although Tannen's studies have been criticized, we believe correctly, for ignoring differences along race and class lines, her conclusions regarding hierarchy and symmetry make sense when considering the systems at work in higher education, which also tend to exclude considerations of race and class.) Tannen's sociolinguistic studies have shown that women tend to mix personal and public language in a professional setting. Although many men would consider this inappropriate, women, on the whole, arrive at their conversational goals in a more symmetrical way that allows this blending of private and public speech, which Tannen calls "rapport talk in public" (91). The reason for this, according to Tannen, is that women define relationships symmetrically—meaning to establish some common ground with the other person. Men, on the whole, define relationships hierarchically—meaning value placed on the ability to be one-up on the other person. (See Tannen's chapter 2 on asymmetries.) This is not meant as an essentialist argument, but rather an acknowledgment that many women's experience and social formation result in a different communication style. The ability to find common ground, then, contributes to conversations that are personally revealing. Certainly, the style in which this chapter is written is an example of this personal and public mixture of language.

If we go one small step further, we can think of space itself in terms of public and private. An office, for the most part, is a private space with an occasional public function which still retains a sense of ownership. A student in one's office for a conference has a clear sense of who really owns this space. Looking back on Roz's original drawing for space conceptualization of the shared office, we can see that the model is decidedly masculine: the line dividing the space is slightly off center. The somewhat larger space being labeled "mine" allows the office partner to establish a slight hierarchical edge by taking a few extra inches—not enough to squabble over. But once we give up the notion of individually owning space, a number of opportunities arises. The office space moves beyond the first two configurations from Roz's notes to something more like figure 14.3.

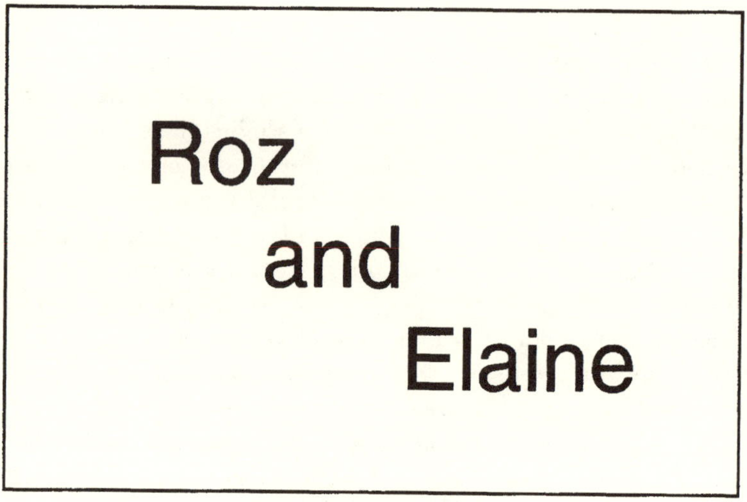

Roz and Elaine

Figure 14.3

When this reconceptualization occurs, the primary purpose of the space shifts. Rather than some private retreat or power base, the space becomes synergistically charged with whatever energy the two of us bring to the space on any occasion. There is some kind of jointly created reservoir to draw on to replenish this individual energy level. In this rather different way, the office becomes a power base in terms of energy rather than asymmetrical maintenance of relationships.

Roz, Personal Musings, October 1990: I sure hope Elaine likes the pink flamingo grabber I got her at Fishtown. I know it will spruce up the office. I wonder if I shouldn't have bought the whole flock of them as they were on sale? I know we could find a million uses.

Elaine Personal Musings, sometime around Thanksgiving, 1990: "Gal Wills Best Friend Her Breast Implants." Who put that headline up on the bulletin board, anyway? And which one of us got the idea for the group project assignment we are each using now? Colleagues are beginning to peek in at our kitsch collection. And it is growing faster than the list of Elvis sightings.

And indeed an otherworldly atmosphere developed in our office space. Now, pictures of Glenda the Good Witch and the Wicked Witch of the West grace our door, with moveable "Roz" and "Elaine" signs to indicate what moods we are in each day. Party lights for every occasion glow from our bulletin board, along with shared texts of new developments in our field. Simpson dolls and magic wands that glow in the dark and a life-size inflatable reindeer live alongside stacks of student journals, newly created lesson plans, piles of shared handouts, and Catherine MacKinnon's *A Feminist Theory of the State*. All these items clearly go together to us, and every day brings new opportunities to see connections that alone we might miss. Colleagues and students regularly add to the collection, both in terms of kitsch art and professional ideas.

This eccentric, energy-charged, shared space developed so quickly that when an opportunity came to attend a learning community retreat one November weekend during the first year, Roz insisted that a reluctant Elaine should go. The whole concept of learning communities was precisely an extension of our reconceptualized office space since a learning community is designed to break down artificial disciplinary walls, or even intradisciplinary walls, that have long been institutionalized. Ideally, a learning community also is taught in a student-centered way, stressing community building, interactive learning, and student control of the learning environment. The learning communities retreat helped us connect with a fascinating collection of synergistically charged colleagues. That weekend, we became part of several different planning teams for perfectly wonderful potential learning communities. It was, however, an academic exercise at that point; the whole learning communities program was just in the planning stages.

Roz, Personal Musings, February 1991: Elaine slammed into

the office holding a memo from our boss regarding teaching choices for Spring semester. This, for our status, included a wide choice of Composition I or the ever-popular Composition II. "Have you seen this?" she asked, obviously in a snit.

I had my feet up and was in a foul mood wondering what had happened to my English 100 thematic structure this semester and when, exactly, it had happened. "Yeah, it's here on my desk somewhere. So what? Are you going to teach Spring?"

"Look, Roz, these choices don't mean us. We'll make our own choices. Let's propose teaching a learning community. We've been talking about it for months. Let's just ask Don and go ahead with it." She threw the memo across the room in disdain, where it landed on the 1950s ceramic poodle figurines and slopped over onto the Pez dispensers. I observed the papered poodles for a moment and felt lots better.

Elaine had again seen a different space that we could both create and occupy. We started planning immediately and were readily approved to teach "Race, Class, and Gender in Popular Culture," a learning community for basic readers and writers. The course combined a college reading and vocabulary development course and Composition I, for a total of nine credit hours. We are convinced that not only did a reconceptualization of noncompetitive space enable us to find the psychic space to step beyond the margins of the memo, but it enabled us to transfer these notions of the learning community to create a positive environment for learning, critical thinking, and intellectual enrichment of our students as well as ourselves.

In planning the first of several intradisciplinary courses, "Race, Class, and Gender in Popular Culture," we initiated a practice we intend to continue forever: instructional planning at the Big Boy Restaurant. The light is good, the food is sustaining and predictable, and the back of a Big Boy placemat can contain almost exactly enough writing to sketch out fifteen weeks of class. It was at the local Big Boy, which is located near the off-campus center where "Race, Class, and Gender . . . " would be taught, that we began to explore our basic shared assumptions for this pilot community. A booth at the Big Boy became as much our collegial territory as our office. We assumed the space as a planning and work space in a way a table in our own college library did not invite. There was no quiet to hush us into quiet. Escaping the academic spaces had a way of reminding us that the curriculum was for students living in a real, noisy, interactive world.

Though we were not and are not clones of one another in our teaching methodology, certain essentials of pedagogy were consistent in the two of us. Because the course goal was to unite a reading and a composing course for basic or developmental learners, our students' fluency in literate tasks had to be assessed, developed, and refined. We were in perfect agreement that this would not best be accomplished through workbooks and reductive sentence exercises. A whole potential classroom environment began to take shape in our conversation in the Big Boy that day. As we laid out our pedagogical concerns, we continually returned to an elemental need we felt to shape the teaching and learning environment around students' own texts, own conceptualizations of readings, and own ability to intellectually stretch into a space we wanted to make available to them.

Both of us had spent that year experimenting with principles we had learned from a provocative text about teaching developmental English. *Facts, Artifacts, and Counterfacts,* by David Bartholomae and Anthony Petrosky, outlined a model in use at the University of Pittsburgh that set up the developmental English classroom more like a graduate school seminar. Students read whole texts, responded to them in original writings, and vigorously engaged in reading-informed debate on the issues presented in their readings. Bartholomae and Petrosky's students literally engaged in acts of translation as they moved from the words of the text into language of their own (beyond plot summary and fact-for-fact synopses). Perhaps, as we had spent the year happily relinquishing our need for personal territory and space, we were in a preparatory mode to relinquish classroom physical and intellectual territory to our students—even students, we guessed, whose prior classroom experiences likely had prepared them to be passive, to listen, to digest what they could, to own little more space than their student desks would occupy.

In the planning phases, we had to ask ourselves what the consequences of surrendering the classroom territory to more active student interplay might be. Could it result in students gaining a more authoritative voice in speaking about, writing about, and interpreting texts? If we surrendered more territory (intellectual, physical, pedagogical) than would be typical in a traditional college classroom—particularly a developmental classroom—would the experiment result in a reduced level of learning?

"Is there a life more riddled with self-doubt than that of a woman professor, I wonder?" articulates a character in May Sarton's novel of women in academic life, *The Small Room* (29). We have often, in the quiet space of our office, discussed how frequently we do feel like impostors in the isolated (and traditionally masculinized) classroom territory. The concept of joint classroom territory freed each of us of some individual insecurities about our teaching performance. One would urge the other on, validate the other in attempting risky new pedagogy. This seems to have freed us to allow students to share territory previously marked as the teacher's province. As a student panelist at a workshop following this course confirmed, "In the learning community, it wasn't their [the teachers'] time; it was our time."

Following are some observations about our own growth and our students' growth in the atmosphere of redefined space. Perhaps we should note here that one discrete incident is not a unique experience. Many fine classroom instructors have always worked toward the most effective ways to facilitate student learning, some by team teaching.

What we do set forth as a contribution from this experience is a matrix of connections from feminist and feminized symmetrical physical and intellectual office space to an ability to facilitate others on the margin of the academic community to own academic space in a similarly symmetrical way. Rather than learning to value and masculinize space, we can consciously take a previously masculine space and make it suit us—and our marginalized students. Here are some moments in the progress of this community.

> Roz, Personal Musings, May 1, 1991: (first day of the learning community): Well, I'm all set to go meet Elaine for our first day. It's been a long time since I've felt so keyed up over a first day. I don't want to look like a dud in front of Elaine—I just know she's fabulous. Working with Elaine in our little office this past year has really been quite an experience. At_____ I felt stagnated in my teaching, but now I feel I'm moving forward again—in fits and starts some days, but in a forward direction.

> Elaine, Personal Musings, May 2, 1991: I really am aware that these touchy topics (which are central to the theme, "Race, Class, and Gender . . .") would be harder to broach if I were the lone teacher. I wouldn't try the theme at all if it weren't for Roz or another supportive person. Today I blithely addressed my class: "I am a white, middle-class woman. Based on that, what do you think you know about my life?" Would I say that alone in a room? Probably (?) not.

The class met for four full days per week for the seven-and-one-half-week spring term. With just an hour off for lunch, the work day was long and warm. We viewed the day in two halves, the morning session commencing with a writing warm-up "Question of the Day" on the board for quiet reflective writing. Every day this activity culminated in a few students (and sometimes Roz or Elaine) sharing their impromptu writing, which was generated from the previous night's reading. A coffee pot was installed the first day to acknowledge that adults working in a confined space for hours at a time require some amenities, which home (or almost any work place other than a classroom) would include. A bulletin board was given over to the students' cartoon and article contributions, and began to look a great deal like our own office door. Students signed in on a clipboard, which allowed us to keep track of attendance without taking roll.

> Roz, excerpt from freewrite response to "Question of the Day": When you think of yourself, do you first identify yourself by race, class, or gender? I'm sure I think of women first. Because this always meant the difference—the difference, when I was very young, of who got to be the doctor and who got to be the nurse; who was expected to go to college and who was allowed, sort of as an exception; who got to be an auctioneer (a third-grade ambition of mine stifled by the masculine definition of the occupation); who got to travel on the debate trips in high school and who couldn't because there were no female accommodations; who had to be locked into the dorm and who had no curfew; who wanted to get married and who wanted to escape. So these differences make me always aware of women.

> Elaine, excerpt from freewrite on same question, May 1, 1991: When I went away to college in 1970, there was a girl in my

dorm named Bea. She didn't shave her legs or her armpits, and she called herself a Women's Liberationist. I don't recall hearing the word *feminist* until some time after that. I was fascinated and intimidated by Bea, who was vocal, full of views I had never considered. She mocked some of our professors and found ways to counter their control with her divergent thinking. Bea introduced me to Ms. magazine and to the idea that the Women's Movement was deeper and more substantial than the bra burnings seen as central to the movement in that time.

Knowing Bea changed me in terms of how I would marry, who I would marry, and how I would conduct my married life. It changed my career aspirations. It changed the way I would mother, daughter, and be a member of our society.

Our students accepted our freewrites as members of the community and not as authorities on these questions. Their voices were as strong and respected as ours.

The first week, we demonstrated our sense of how a class discussion should be structured. We sat with our students in a circle, threw out a tennis ball, and waited for a student to catch it. We asked: "In a regular classroom conversation, if a teacher poses a question (in other words, 'throws out the ball'), what should the student do?" Our students immediately responded "return the ball." Of course, students traditionally learn to throw back the ball in the form of a correct (that is, succinct, uncluttered, uncontentious) answer. We explained that in this class, the conversational ball—and the knowledge—didn't always reside in the teacher. The metaphorical ball was to make its way around the community, was to be passed student to student to student, not teacher to student and back again. They were so taken with the ball analogy that they insisted on keeping the real tennis ball handy for every classroom seminar. A few times, a student became so eager to speak that she walked across the room and took it from another student. Once or twice, the ball was stolen overnight. We like to imagine that a student, eager to fill some private space with uninterrupted talk, spoke loud and long while holding that ball. It was always returned to its place.

We envisioned the traditional classroom space as a territory configured something like figure 14.4.

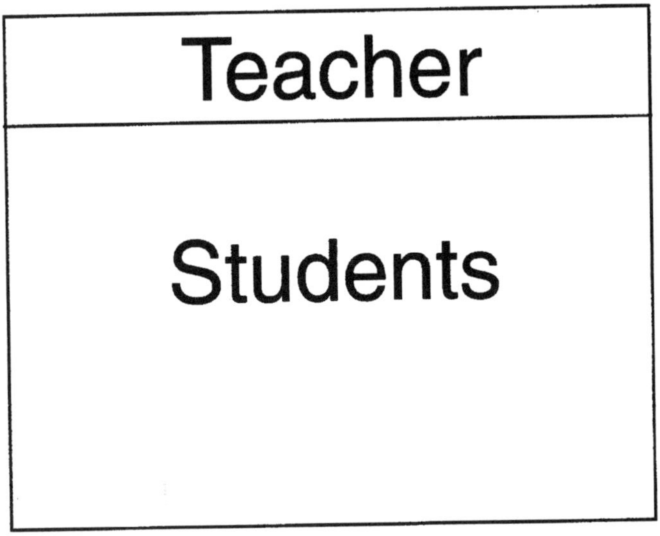
Teacher
Students

Figure 14.4

Our classroom, we hoped, could achieve something more nearly like figure 14.5

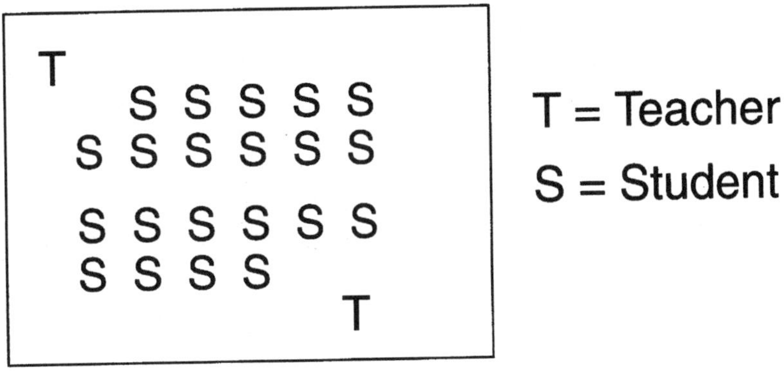
T
S S S S S
S S S S S S
S S S S S S
S S S S
T
T = Teacher
S = Student

Figure 14.5

or figure 14.6.

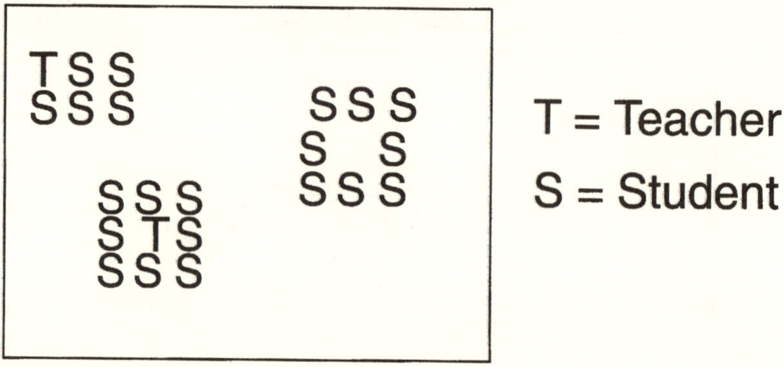

```
TSS
SSS         SSS
            S  S      T = Teacher
     SSS    SSS
     STS              S = Student
     SSS
```

Figure 14.6

    Photographs taken at various times during one day in the community attest to the ways in which students felt free to sculpt the classroom physical space. At one point in the day, students are grouped in threes and fours in circles, poring over each other's writings. At another time, the chairs are lined up in rows in the familiar schoolroom pattern. One photo shows students lounging along the radiator with coffee cups and books in their hands. Yet another picture shows most of the central floor space bare, with chairs all pushed up along one side of the room. This configuration may have made a dramatization or debate possible. Certainly, whatever happened in the community that day, Roz and Elaine were not the ones who moved all the chairs into place or assumed responsibility for the kaleidoscopic patterns of change in that learning space.

    As the students gained autonomy within the walls of the classroom, we noticed that they more readily moved beyond the classroom, defining areas of the Delta College Ricker Center as spaces for continuing the classroom conversation or extending the classroom work. Time in the canteen became time to look over one another's papers. Some dilapidated sofas in a hallway became a gathering place for a loyal handful who met before class each morning so they could pounce on us with new questions and pronouncements about last night's reading. For these adult nontraditional learners, who had never known the ivied alcove of a university library or the mellow atmosphere of a campus pub, they were claiming spaces in the Delta College Ricker Center and defining them as hospitable environments for intellectual pursuit. Our classroom space was beginning to blur at the doorway and extend out the hall. It was beginning to look more like figure 14.7.

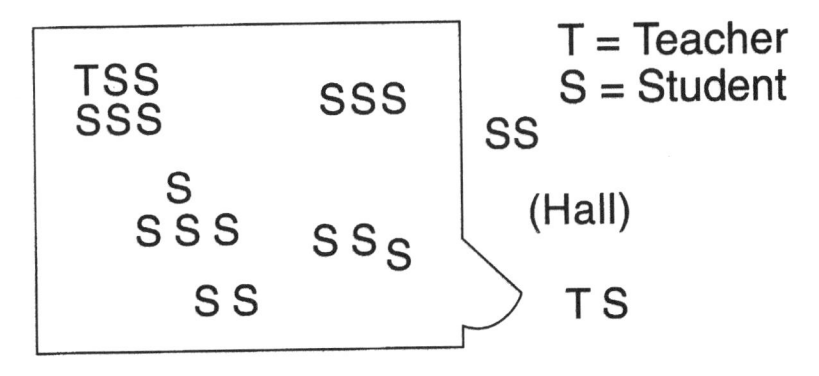

```
   TSS        SSS       T = Teacher
   SSS                  S = Student
                 SS
       S
     S S S    S S        (Hall)
               S
       S S              T S
```

Figure 14.7

Our weekly "Community Foray" assignment encouraged the students to leave the classroom altogether, completing (in pairs, in groups, or individually) a research assignment somewhere in the vicinity beyond the Ricker Center. We wanted to create in our curriculum a way for students to see the community as a rich field for research and a place for testing assumptions expressed in some of our readings. In releasing our students after a half day on Thursday, we gave up some of our authority and "space" in order to trust our students (and remember, these were developmental students) to pose original research questions, establish a methodology for answering the questions, and write coherently about their observations and experiences in the community. They visited the local Toys 'R Us and gathered data on so-called girls' versus boys' playthings. They drove through various neighborhoods and catalogued the kinds of lawn ornaments, attempting to see if they fit into Paul Fussell's categories for social-class distinction. They audio-taped couples discussing their marital relationships. They watched television ads, cartoons, and mini-series, and they wrote down and analyzed lyrics to popular songs. We believe that, for the most part, the expansion of our classroom milieu contributed significantly to most students' conscious awareness while in that classroom and beyond. Our classroom space, then, can be viewed as a model evolving into something more like figure 14.8.

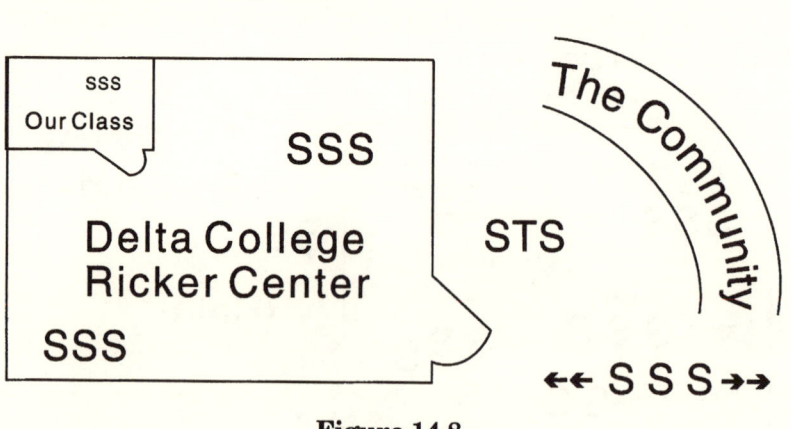

```
SSS
Our Class        SSS           The Community

Delta College    STS
Ricker Center
SSS
                              ←← S S S →→
```

Figure 14.8

During the course of the semester we read Gloria Steinem's "Men and Women Talking." We read Shirley Chisholm's "I'd Rather Be Black than Female." We read Paul Fussell's "Notes on Class" and a few students chose to read Shahrazed Ali's *A Black Man's Guide to Understanding Black Women* and differed violently with some of her conclusions. We read the sophisticated "Common Paternity: War and Violence Against Women" by Martha Burk, which had appeared in the *National N.O.W. Times*. In our very heterogeneous student group (black, white, men, women, young, old: a woman whose identity as a pastor's wife was key to the respect the community extended to her, a convict on an electronic tether, a young man brain-injured in a devastating car accident) the theme of "Race, Class, and Gender" naturally led to differences of opinion and occasional anger. We were especially pleased that women, so often marginalized or "chilled out" in the traditional classroom setting, held their ground in conversations where women students have so often been hushed into silence.

In one seminar, an exasperated young man heatedly spat, "I don't want to hear any more about rape." A formerly subdued young woman shot back, "Then you can just step out into the hall, because I'm not finished talking." Months later when one of us ran into her during another semester, she said, "I'm struggling in a math class, but I went right to the professor and got my questions answered. *I will never sit quietly by and flunk a class again."* As for the man, we have had continuous contact with him since he was a student in that course. He sat through the discussion on rape. And he went on to remark to a group of our colleagues in a workshop, "When I started that class, I was asleep. Now, I am awake." He and his wife have four sons and, most recently, a daughter. All will enjoy an atmosphere of feminist consciousness at home.

It is our perception that a different respect for the teacher pervaded the room: it was a respect for the teacher as learner. Students asked us how our thinking and writing about the course theme were going. They critiqued our work and asked us to substantiate statements we made, just as we asked them to do. Patrick Hill, whose "Multi-Culturalism: The Crucial Philosophical and Organizational Issues" had informed our thinking about the nature of democratic pluralism in the classroom, describes the desirable situation in which "conversations of respect" (42) characterize classroom exchange. Hill defines conversations of respect as those in which

> "intellectual reciprocity" allows participants to . . . learn from each other . . . [and] expect to change as a result of the encounter. . . . One participant does not presume that the relationship is one of teacher to student . . . parent to child, of developed to underdeveloped. The participants are co-learners. (43)

Our handouts and lesson materials from the course are revealing in their shift to a more communal student and teacher territory. They aren't voiceless, and they aren't impersonal. One difficult assignment asked each student (and the teachers, too) to actively do something that would take the learner out of a comfort zone involving race, class, or gender. Roz admits on the handout that she would have trouble, due to her notions of class appropriateness, attending a World Wrestling Federation event. Elaine admits that she couldn't bring herself to go to the designer salon of a local department store. It would violate the blue-collar notions planted firmly in her childhood. By participating so actively in our own assignments, we found we had virtually 100 percent response from students. A consequence of our immersion in the class was that students tried, if anything, to top our efforts.

Elaine's personal writings, June 1991: It is early afternoon of a long teaching day. Wired on coffee, I am aware of the hands of the clock moving on, wondering if the community is in sync with my one or two golden points in the lesson. I collect my array of colored pens, overhead transparencies, papers, and move to the back of the room to let Roz pick up the threads of the lesson and move on.

Our class meets in what used to be an elementary school classroom, and the cozy wide ledge across the back of the room used to be a child-size counter top. Right now that counter top is as accommodating as a 1950s sofa for this adult. I slump there, relieved that it's Roz's turn. Once propped and attentively listening, it dawns on me what a seamless transition in the flow has occurred. Roz picks up the train of thought with rich examples and moves into areas of film and popular culture, which are her own areas of specialized expertise. I find myself so relieved for all of us: the students, Roz, and me. It feels like all of us are learning here. I feel exactly right on the ledge, transferring the more active teaching moment to Roz. Students will step in throughout the lesson and probe, question, and have their own moments in the active role. The more I am on the ledge, the more I wonder how I ever did it all alone before, and how I can ever go back to that again.

Colleagues might rightfully wonder how we functioned as a teaching team (and *taught* things) in a space that often was not rigidly constructed or controlled by us. We found an apt analogy for this communal and noncompetitive teaching space in Gail Griffin's *Calling* as she describes distinctions in the modes in which men and women view work. Griffin, a professor of English and cofounder of the Women's Studies program at Kalamazoo College, began to rethink the work space when an anthropologist friend told her, "Men . . . define their jobs as they are defined. Their model is the football field where everyone has an assigned task. Women . . . have a different model—the kitchen, where your job is whatever needs doing" (10). While we certainly did not abandon instructional planning and preparation, our roles in the evolving classroom matrix of reading and writing often fit the kitchen model closely. We valued the notions of keeping some ingredients crisp and letting others simmer. We moved readily from student to student in patterns modeled on Tannen's notions of symmetry. Students told us our methods fit well with their needs as writers and readers. Course evaluations emphasized students' overall reaction that we were available, responsive, and accessible.

In a world where the natural order of things is to compete, we have chosen to cooperate and commiserate. Our office, which we believe was the space in which we began the experiment in defining space that has altered the way we view classroom and intellectual space, is less like the headquarters of an accounting firm (where everyone has an assigned task) and more like a kitchen, where burners must be turned off under scorching pots, soups must be tasted, and recipes and gossip must be shared. We are convinced that it is a model more in keeping with the way women, left to their own devices and documented by Tannen's work, construct their spaces. Even professional women. Academic women. And we believe the latter is not a contradiction in terms or a subtle oxymoron.

The year following the initial learning community, an extra office became available. Everyone assumed one of us would move. Virtually simultaneously, we opted to accept this second space, just down the hall, and to define it as our joint "Conference Room/Lounge." We called the appropriate department and had the sign for the door made before anyone checked on precedent or protocol. By adding a couch, some wallpaper, a circular table, and a tasteful Georgia O'Keefe print, we created a sedate space in which students can gather for study groups or discussions. Sometimes one of us slips away to this room for private time. There's a tape player and a selection of tapes (Patti LaBelle and the Bluebells, Bach, The Uppity Blues Women) and a selection of magazines. When our Dean did a double-take walking down the hall one day, we heard her say, "Karls/Weedman Conference Room/Lounge?" She moaned, "Oh, no! Now *everyone* will want one." Roz didn't hesitate: "They can have one. They just have to buddy up."

This year we were hired to tenure-stream positions and a few colleagues have asked if we have any plans to separate the two offices, but most sent greetings and joint gifts (some "Two Virgins" brand coffee, a big green plastic frog planter). The vision of our institution has played significantly into the scope of our own joint vision. Perhaps we've all taken too literally Virginia Woolf's notion of "A

Room of One's Own." Perhaps a woman occupying space that's still configured in a masculine way does not constitute ownership. Only by seeing the possibilities and value of reconfiguring that space as women and as feminists, by consciously interrupting hierarchy and opting for the value of symmetry, do we finally find not just a room of our own, but room.

REFERENCES

Bartholomae, David, and Anthony Petrosky. *Facts, Artifacts, and Counterfacts*. Upper Montclair, NJ: Boynton/Cook, 1986.

Griffin, Gail. *Calling: Essays on Teaching in the Mother Tongue*. Pasadena, CA: Trilogy, 1992.

Hill, Patrick. "Multi-Culturalism: The Crucial Philosophical and Organizational Issues." *Change* July/August 1991: 38–47.

Sarton, May. *The Small Room*. New York: Norton, 1961.

Tannen, Deborah. *You Just Don't Understand*. New York: Ballentine, 1990.

Jamie Barlowe and Ruth Hottell

15
Feminist Theory and Practice and the Pedantic I/Eye

This chapter deals not only with our collaboration as feminist scholars and teachers, but also with the concept of the classroom as a collaborative community. Our awareness of the differences between traditional pedagogy and our feminist classroom theories and practices has been heightened because twice in the past three years we have team taught an interdisciplinary course in feminist theories. Not only did this awareness spark dialogues between us about our academic, theoretical, political, and pedagogical backgrounds, but it also generated classroom discussions. Foregrounding such issues in the classroom allowed us to examine and explore several important ideas: feminism is not a single path, nor one belief; feminisms' so-called conflicts are instead dialogues between those who share some fundamental ideological principles, but who manifest them in radically different ways, depending on their unique trajectories—personal/private, professional, and theoretical (see Kenway and Modra). Each feminist carries her past experiences and her culture with her, often finding it necessary to examine each as it informs and is informed by feminisms. Individual and collective rereadings of ourselves as feminist scholars and teachers allow us to acknowledge these relationships. In our particular case, we reread ourselves in relationship to what we call "the pedantic I/eye": teacher as subject, student as object; text as subject, reader as object; academy as subject, feminist academic as object. The following feminist narrative of our academic and theoretical journeys argues for our version of collaborative feminist pedagogy as it refutes the pedantic I/eye of our profession.

Although everything about the academy discourages collaboration and prioritizes authoritarianism, hierarchies, and competition, we have found as scholars and teachers that some of our most provocative work has come about as a product of our collaboration. Concurrently, we have discovered that a form of extralinguistic communication has established itself as a by-product of our collaboration and continues to benefit us as colleagues on college and university committees. Or, perhaps, the extralinguistic communication predated our collaboration, caused in part by common ground. As Constance Penley says: "In the analytic situation, as we have seen, knowledge is not contained in the Other, but in the interplay of two partially unconscious speeches, each of which does not (alone) know what it is saying" (174).

We soon discovered that each of us was primarily trained to do *explication de texte*/close reading (based on the principles of French structuralism for Ruth, and on the principles fundamental to classical literary poetics and rhetorics for Jamie). Both kinds of analyses rest on a stable relationship between signified (meaning) and signifier (text), which assumes a reader implied by the text. Since these theories attempt to understand how the text achieves its ends—structural, rhetorical, and aesthetic—they do not generally lead to conclusions that can account for the subtle, unacknowledged power structures operating in the text, between the text and reader, between teacher and student as they examine texts, or between formal theorist and text. Our awareness of the inadequacy of these theories to explain such dynamics led each of us in graduate school to take the added step of articulating the ideological significance of the meaning of the text.

Yet neither the theoretical nor the textual gaps were addressed by this move; moreover, we now see this two-step model of theorizing as undermining the principles on which feminist analyses are based. In other words, complicating formal theoretical models—adding another layer of textual analysis or another voice in the dialogue between text and reader—does not destabilize the relationship between the text and its meaning, a move we see as fundamental to feminist theories.

These feminist theories—which for us also reenvision and revise psychoanalytic theories, film theories, rhetorical theories (including deconstruction), semiotics, and cultural analyses (including class and race)—stepped into this theoretical gap and provided the means with which to analyze textual gaps. Stated metaphorically, the formal theories we learned work like x-rays that reveal the skeletal structure, but the feminist theories examine and lay bare the masked, underlying problems. Put in yet other terms, feminist theories reveal the power relationships between text and marginalized Other that often exist outside textual language and textual analyses. Feminist theories are not submissive to hierarchies of power (textual, theoretical, professional, or pedagogical), nor can they be forced into the subject/object dyad (see Gore 46). Rather, they disrupt this bipolarity, creating a space between the subject and object.

Masculinist Lacanian theory argues that the unconscious is structured like a language and that included in the developmental stages is acceptance of the subject/object polarity and opposition. This fundamental misrecognition is termed the "mirror stage" and marks the passage from the imaginary to the symbolic. At the risk of oversimplifying, we see French feminists, in their reenvisioning of psychoanalytic and semiotic theories, as rejecting this dichotomy and seeking extralinguistic explanations. Feminist film theorists struggle to write women into the subject position. Feminist deconstructionists work to expose the opposition between subject and object, either multiplying the significations or questioning from the position allowed by radical, disruptive analysis. Cultural feminist theories maintain the subject/object split in order to examine the relationship between texts and the world, discussing, for example, the capital/consumer, master/slave, and colonizer/colonized complicities.

What we have each tried to accomplish as we have traversed this feminist territory is an integration of the theoretical with the personal, political, practical, and pedagogical (see hooks, *Teaching;* see also Gore). This integration allows us to question and subvert the pedantic/authoritarian subject position of teacher-mentor that participates in the traditional professional/pedagogical/mentoring model and obfuscates its objectification of the student. Furthermore, that model obscures our situatedness as women because it invites us to accept the subject/object polarity and its implicit oppositions. In other words, it asks us to pass through the mirror stage of the professional and pedagogical imaginary/symbolic.

Our reflective discussions about these issues led us to recognize other implications for us as feminist teachers and scholars; that is, we saw replications of the problematic subject/object dyad played out not only in classrooms and advisers' offices but also in the larger professional arena. For example, the authoritarian subjects of our profession—teachers, mentors/advisers, hiring and personnel committees, referees and readers for journals and conferences, to name a few—are set up as experts, whose unquestioned judgments and measurements determine the direction of careers and lives. In such a model, the student, teaching assistant, job applicant, untenured and/or marginalized faculty, and writer assume the object position, scrutinized according to predetermined but usually unarticulated standards—what Luce Irigaray calls "ready-made grids" (29; see also Morris); these standards more often than not misrecognize the object of their examination.

As many feminists have argued, this model is inadequate for the integration of feminists into the academy and into the classroom. Yet, despite almost twenty years of feminist demonstrations of this inadequacy and of arguments for change, the model generally remains intact. At best, an additive model is in place, one that simply and unproblematically adds some women/feminists to these classrooms, committees, and boards—what some feminists have called the "add women and stir" recipe—without examining the traditions and their measuring sticks (see, for example, Schweickart). We see a feminist examination as necessary to expose, destabilize, and disrupt traditionally stable power relationships between student and teacher, between text and student, between colleagues, and/or between the academy and its constituents, just as the destabilizing of the relationship between text and meaning is a necessary function of feminist literary and film theories (see Payne and Spender).

As the unexamined traditional academic model translates into classrooms, it inevitably props up a pedagogy that promulgates pedantry. The (usually unacknowledged) progression from graduate-student-working-with-teacher/mentor to becoming-teacher/mentor-working-with-students we call the "acquiring of the pedantic I/eye." This acquisition is the process of the former student-as-object becoming teacher-as-authoritarian-subject with his/her students now functioning in the object position as the receivers of knowledge who will be scrutinized and judged according to those "ready-made grids."

As in the academy-at-large model, the pedantic I/eye in the classroom hides the subject/object relationship with its pretense of objectivity, purporting further that its received beliefs (what it calls a "body of knowledge") are generally accepted, unquestionable truths; even feminist bodies of knowledge have presented themselves in such ways. The I/eye also obscures its own structural base of the inside/outside binary opposition and consistently discourages the kind of deep questioning that would expose its shaky foundations. Collaborative feminist pedagogy, we believe, depends on exactly that kind of questioning—generated initially by the recognition of the traces, spaces, holes, and gaps that the pedantic I/eye fails to see. The double dynamic at work here means that such questioning also exposes the possibility of a radical response—at the level of theory and of practice (see Gore).

A further distinction between collaborative feminist pedagogy and the pedantic I/eye is that, at best, the latter implies its own conclusions and at worst compels acceptance and adherence, while the former offers a space in which to question without determining the consequences of the questioning. What is possible in this space is a community of mutual inquirers rather than a mentor/scholar and his disciple/interlocutor; Jane Kenway and Helen Modra call such an idea of feminist pedagogy "a discourse of possibility" (139). Penley further explains the "incompatibility of feminist ways of teaching within the more typical pedagogical requirements of exclusiveness, authority, and hierarchy" (173; see also Treichler 69).

Our initial discussions led us to envision a course constructed around our collaborative feminist model, which, as we have shown, integrates feminist theories and personal, political, and pedagogical practices, and involves us as team teachers. We understand the concept of team teaching to be collaborative, as two teachers interacting with each other and with students rather than "splitting" responsibilities and taking turns disseminating knowledge. We were not thinking of a classroom in which collaboration and cooperation (between us as teachers and between our students and between them and us as teachers) existed only to oppose a competitive, pedantic, hierarchical, authoritarian classroom model, but as the means by which to question that model and the consequences of its practice. It allowed us to talk about ourselves as subjects not trapped in the subject/object dyad or that of authority vs. nonauthority or power vs. powerlessness (see Friedman; Culley and Portuges; Kenway and Modra; hooks; Edgerton; Orner). Even at the level of seating arrangements—our circling of the desks and our seating ourselves in the circle rather than at the head of the classroom behind a desk—acknowledged the problematic implications of the traditional classroom arrangement, without making the claim that merely circling the desks would change the institutional structure and its pedantic pedagogical practices. Rearranging the classroom at the beginning of every class became an act of resistance, based on a sense of agency, and the basis for further questioning and for examination of its implications for the eventual work places of our students (see Beckman). This was especially important because the students in our two classes were majoring in various disciplines, from English and French to Spanish, history, biology, education, business, psychology, environmental studies, political science, and physics. Thus, we envisioned our collaborative feminist classroom as similar to "a participatory, democratic process in which at least some power is shared" (Shrewsbury 7; see also hooks, Rutenberg, Schniedewind).

Although the relinquishing of pedantic authoritarianism is the first principle of our collaborative feminist teaching, and is in fact what brings us to the deeper levels of communication, it does not include our giving up our right to speak from our positions as feminist subjects. As hooks argues, "We must acknowledge that our role as teacher is a position of power over others. We can use that power in ways which diminish or in ways that enrich and it is this choice that should distinguish feminist pedagogy from ways of teaching that reinforce domination" (*Talking Back* 52; see also Ellsworth; Kenway and Modra). Carolyn Shrewsbury conceptualizes power—based on educators and theorists like Paulo Friere and Nancy Hartsock—as "focusing on empowerment, feminist pedagogy embodies a concept of power as energy, capacity, and potential rather than as domination" (8; see also Dunn).

Constance Penley, too, has addressed this issue when she says that "[i]deally, [the feminist teacher] carries out a very deliberate self-undermining of her own authority by refusing to be an 'authority' [authoritarian] at all . . . " (174). Penley's discussions are particularly pertinent for us, because Ruth had taken an interdisciplinary graduate class with her in which Penley's teaching served as a model—demonstrating the importance of inclusionary teaching methods as well as the teacher's sharing of her own written work with students.

As our collaborative course took shape in our minds, the College of Arts and Sciences at our university announced a Competition for teaching Fellowships. The course we proposed was one of two chosen to be funded for that year. Coincidentally, three significant collections of feminist essays and dialogues had just been published: Warhol and Herndl's *Feminisms*, Eagleton's *Feminist Literary Criticism*, and Hirsch and Keller's *Conflicts in Feminism*, which allowed us to explore the dialogues within feminism. That two of these new texts would articulate the conversations between feminists as conflicts was particularly interesting to us. Despite the fact that for us, the conflictual model—reinscribing the hierarchy of the subject/object dyad—does not adequately describe the space called "feminisms," we decided to use these texts and to name the class "Conflicts in Feminist Theory" (see Ede and Lunsford; see also Penley).

Because we believe that feminisms creates a space for dialogue among the many feminist perspectives and methods operating under its political rubric, the patriarchal notion of conflicts—and its adaptation to feminist studies—thus became another topic for discussion. In both classes, our dialogues began with the idea that conflicts and hierarchical competition between feminist perspectives occur when feminist studies mirrors the traditional academic model. Not all of the students, of course, agreed with us: some found the idea of conflicts to be energizing and potentially radical; others worried that even open dialogues in a marginalized space like feminism would give the impression that feminists are inept and/or that they are easily co-opted.

In the first class, we also witnessed the phenomenon of some students reducing all feminist dialogues to a continuing conflict between theory-as-monolithic and feminism, as we discussed earlier (see hooks). We had mistakenly assumed a prior knowledge of theory in that class—most of whom were graduate students in English and French and upper-division English, French, history, and psychology majors. We neglected to anticipate the resistance to theory, especially to deconstruction and psychoanalysis—and to their genesis in French structuralism, linguists, philosophy, anthropology, semiotics, and psychology. Some students voiced concerns about the improbability of feminist revisionings of deconstruction and psychoanalysis and about the extent of the exclusion they felt when reading the difficult essays.

In the second class—an undergraduate interdisciplinary honors seminar—we tried to avoid this pitfall by grounding the introductory readings in American academic feminist revisions of literary criticism and the literary canon. Consequently, all of the students, regardless of their major disciplines, could relate to the essays because they were familiar with traditional ways of reading and analyzing literary texts that feminists such as Showalter, Fetterley, Radway, Stimpson, and Robinson have called into question and resisted since the 1970s. Because of their high school and undergraduate required courses in English and American literature, the students knew what kind of texts were part of the old-guard's syllabi and which were excluded. Thus, when we moved to analytical applications of a highly theoretical nature, the students were already engaged in interaction with the readings and with the classroom community. Hence, they did not write off theory as irrelevant to their lives and disciplines; instead, they were able to weave their own narratives into the theoretical discussions—as were we as teachers, remembering bell hooks's words:

> When education is the practice of freedom, students are not the only ones asked to share, to confess. Engaged pedagogy does not seek simply to empower students. Any classroom that employs a holistic model of learning will also be a place where teachers grow, and are empowered by the process. That empowerment cannot happen if we refuse to be vulnerable while encouraging students to take risks. (*Teaching* 21)

To supplement our readings in the first class, we chose films which represent the gynophobia of mainstream film in its violent manifestation—films like *Peeping Tom,* the prototype of the camera as phallic weapon, and *The Big Sleep* in which women function as "bad girls" who must either be punished/erased from the text or brought back into the confines of the System. We wanted to show our students that exposing the underpinnings at work in hegemonic texts is a transformative, transgressive activity. As Flitterman-Lewis so aptly remarks about the cinema: "[Its] effective functioning ... as an apparatus is only possible on the basis of [the] concealment of its operations; through the invisible conversions from discourse to history a 'pseudo-viewer' is created which every spectator can appropriate at will" (15). We expected our collaborative atmosphere to enable us to articulate sexual difference in film and to trace the exclusion of the Other (in terms of class, ethnicity, race, gender, sexual orientation)—as well as examine the limiting stereotypes of men (significant since there were male students in the class)—but some of the students expressed resentment about viewing these films (although we explained that no one would be required to watch them). They said they were concerned that just by showing the films we were valorizing texts that portray violence against women and practice exclusion of the Other. Our discussions became mired in the class's binary opposition of radical transformative critique vs. valorization. bell hooks perhaps best answers this kind of problem when she explains that she must see and write about specific films in spite of (and/or because of) their gynophobia and their perpetuation of the stereotype of the African American male (*Black Looks* 102).

Although we still believe in reading and showing texts representative of the widespread repression of the System, we did take the students' criticism to heart—that, instead, we should be showing only examples of subversive texts. Since we see the need to articulate the exclusion—particularly when gynophobia is still rampant in mainstream film and texts—we read the comment as *also* rather than *instead* and set about to rectify our omission. The quarter following the first class, we sponsored a women's film festival, showing a variety of films, from narrative fiction by women (explicitly feminist or not) to experimental avant-garde feminist films. After the screenings, we met in informal settings and discussed the films. In the months and years since that class, we have watched as students synthesized experiences from both the class and film festival and put their findings to use in various forms, both academic and nonacademic; for example, honors theses, doctoral dissertations, applications to other graduate schools, film and music festivals, conferences, and performances.

In the second class, we showed films that, although ostensibly "women's films," actually promote the position of women as objects rather than as subjects, either showing their desire as merely a projection of man's desire, or containing their desire as perverse or maniacal. Mary Ann Doane's chapter, "*Female Spectatorship and the Machines of Projection; Caught* and *Rebecca*," proved particularly useful in highlighting the elements obscured by components of the cinematic apparatus in these two films. In class, we also showed examples of videos and feature films that subvert the systemic code of phallocentric texts, as well as examples of phallocentric texts, particularly music videos. This second time, our women's film festival ran concurrently with the class, in the evenings.

Following the sections on film and film theory, we read feminist texts that examine issues of race, class, and culture in the United States and the consequences of patriarchy and colonization in other nations and continents. For example, Mary Childers and bell hooks's dialogue, "A Conversation about Race and Class," compelled us to reexamine our privileged positioning in the United States. Evelyne Accad's sensitive (and theoretical) analysis in *Sexuality and War: Literary Masks of the Middle East*—and her willingness to express her pain in her personal narratives—alerted students (and us) in both classes to our privileged position as Americans, inviting them (and us) to reexamine our relationships to the personal and political. Chandra Mohanty argues that "the notion [of] 'the personal [as] political' must be rethought" as we consider issues of domination/resistance, identification, agency, and political action as these are "figured in the minute, day-to-day practices and struggles of third world women" (39).

Near the end of her essay, "Theory as Liberatory Practice," in *Teaching to Transgress*, bell hooks expresses her "gratitude to the many women and men who dare to create theory from the location of pain and struggle, who courageously expose wounds to give us their experience to teach and guide, as a means to chart new theoretical journeys" (74). As a classroom of collaborators, we could feel the passion, excitement, and pain of many of the theorists we read. To continue in the false vein of objectivity and to deny personal voices is to deny diversity and to contribute to the promulgation of the white, male, heterosexual, bourgeois paradigm of repressive cultures. Perhaps Evelyne Accad sums up the situation best in a passage in which she justifies inclusion of personal narratives and emphasizes the importance of vulnerability:

> This book is a result of my emotional and intellectual commitment and history of the last twenty years. It has grown out of my condition as an Arab woman, which made me leave my

country of birth, Lebanon, at the age of twenty-two, in order to free and assert myself as an autonomous human being. It has come out of my anguish and pain at seeing my beautiful country destroyed senselessly over the last fourteen years. . . . [A] change has already started taking place with personal and political actions aimed at solving the problems rooted in oppression, domination, and the victimization of women. Writing this book has been one of those actions. (165–66)

Throughout Accad's work, we marvel at her ability to include women across political, racial, and social boundaries in her personal/political narrative. We see feminist collaboration among scholars, teachers, and students as functioning similarly. The space of community created (both inside and outside the classroom) is not just a safe environment, nor is it entirely free of all pedantic authoritarianism, but it is a place where all groups and individuals can come to voice, to "critical consciousness" (hooks, *Talking Back* 50), and learn to use struggles to create other inclusive environments. As feminist collaborators, we must, as Adrienne Rich urged us to do twenty years ago, take "ourselves seriously" (240); in so doing we can take our students seriously, collaborating with them and with each other recursively, rereading ourselves as we reread our worlds.

──────────── REFERENCES ────────────

Accad, Evelyne. *Sexuality and War: Literary Masks of the Middle East.* New York: New York University Press, 1990.
Beckman, Mary. "Feminist Teaching Methods and the Team-Based Workplace: Do Results Match Intentions?" *Women's Studies Quarterly* 1 & 2 (1991): 165–77.
Childers, Mary, and bell hooks. "A Conversation about Race and Class." Hirsch and Keller. 60–81.
Culley, M., and C. Portuges, eds. *Gendered Subjects: The Dynamics of Feminist Teaching.* Boston and London: Routledge, 1985.
Doane, Mary Ann. "Female Spectatorship and the Machines of Projection: *Caught* and *Rebecca.*" *The Desire to Desire: The Woman's Film of the 1940s.* Bloomington: Indiana University Press, 1987. 155–75.

Dunn, Kathleen. "Feminist Teaching: Who Are Your Students?" *Women's Studies Quarterly* 15.3 & 4 (1987): 40–46.

Eagleton, Mary. *Feminist Literary Criticism*. London: Longman, 1991.

Ede, Lisa, and Lunsford, Andrea. *Singular Texts/Plural Authors: Perspectives on Collaborative Writing*. Carbondale: Southern Illinois University Press, 1990.

Edgerton, Susan Huddleston. "Love in the Margins: Notes toward a Curriculum of Marginality." *Understanding Curriculum as Racial Text*. Ed. Louis A. Casternell and William F. Pinar. Albany: State University of New York Press, 1993. 55–82.

Ellsworth, Elizabeth. "Why Doesn't This Feel Empowering?: Working Through the Repressive Myths of Critical Pedagogy." Luke and Gore. 90–119.

Flitterman-Lewis, Sandy. *To Desire Differently: Feminism and the French Cinema*. Urbana: University of Illinois Press, 1990.

Friedman, Susan Stanford. "Authority in the Feminist Classroom: A Contradiction in Terms." Culley and Portuges. 203–208.

Gore, Jennifer. *The Struggle for Pedagogies: Critical and Feminist Discourses as Regimes of Truth*. New York: Routledge, 1993.

Hartsock, Nancy. *Money, Sex, and Power: Toward a Feminist Historical Materialism*. New York: Longman, 1983.

Hirsch, Marianne, and Evelyn Fox Keller, eds. *Conflicts in Feminism*. New York: Routledge, 1991.

hooks, bell. *Black Looks: Race and Representation*. Boston: South End, 1992.

———. *Talking Back: Thinking Feminist, Thinking Black*. Boston: South End, 1989.

———. *Teaching to Transgress: Education as the Practice of Freedom*. New York: Routledge, 1994.

Irigaray, Luce. *This Sex Which Is Not One*. Ithaca, NY: Cornell University Press, 1986.

Kenway, Jane, and Helen Modra. "Feminist Pedagogy and Emancipatory Possibilities." Luke and Gore. 138–66.

Luke, Carmen, and Jennifer Gore, eds. *Feminisms and Critical Pedagogy*. New York: Routledge, 1992.

Mohanty, Chandra. *Cartographies of Struggle: Third World Women and the Politics of Feminism*. Bloomington: Indiana University Press, 1991.

Morris, Pam. *Literature and Feminism*. Oxford: Blackwell, 1993.

Orner, Mimi. "Interrupting the Calls for Student Voice in 'Liberatory' Education: A Feminist Poststructuralist Perspective." Luke and Gore. 74–89.

Payne, Irene, and Spender, Dale. "Feminist Practices in the Classroom." *Learning to Lose: Sexism and Education*. Ed. Dale Spender and Elizabeth Sarah. New York, 1980. 174–79.

Penley, Constance. *The Future of an Illusion: Film, Feminism, and Psychoanalysis*. Minneapolis: University of Minnesota Press, 1969.

Rich, Adrienne. "Claiming an Education." *Lies, Secrets, and Silence*. New York: Norton, 1979.

Rutenberg, Taly. "Learning Women's Studies." *Theories of Women's Studies*. Ed. Gloria Bowles and Renate Duelli-Klein. Berkeley: Women's Studies Department, University of California, 1980. 72–78.

Schniedewind, Nancy. "Teaching Feminist Process." *Women's Studies Quarterly* 15.3 & 4 (1987): 15–31.

Schweikart, Patrocinio. "Reading Ourselves: Toward a Feminist Theory of Reading." *Gender and Reading: Essays on Readers, Texts, and Contexts*. Ed. Elizabeth Flynn and Patrocinio Schweikart. Baltimore: Johns Hopkins University Press, 1986. 31–62.

Shrewsbury, Carolyn. "What Is Feminist Pedagogy?" *Women's Studies Quarterly* 15.3 & 4 (1987): 6–14.

Triechler, Paula. "Teaching Feminist Theory." *Theory in the Classroom*. Ed. Cary Nelson. Urbana: University of Illinois Press, 1986. 57–128.

Warhol, Robin, and Diane Price Herndl, eds. *Feminisms: An Anthology of Literary Theory and Criticism*. New Brunswick, NJ: Rutgers University Press, 1991.

Biographical Notes

EDITORS

JoAnna Stephens Mink is an associate professor of English at Mankato State University. She has presented many conference papers and published several articles. She is coeditor, with Janet Doubler Ward, of *Communication and Women's Friendships: Parallels and Intersections in Literature and Life* and *The Significance of Sibling Relationships in Literature* (both by Bowling Green State University Press, 1993) and *Joinings and Disjoinings: The Significance of Marital Status in Literature* (Bowling Green, 1991). Her current research project focuses on the relationship between Victorian working-class images in the popular media and literature.

Elizabeth G. Peck is an associate professor of English at the University of Nebraska at Kearney. Her articles have appeared in *Images of the Self as Female, ATQ, ChLA Quarterly,* and in *Critical Essays on* The Adventures of Tom Sawyer. She has presented papers at several conferences and various Women's Studies forums. Her current research interests include nineteenth-century American literary and cultural studies and feminist criticism.

CONTRIBUTORS

Mary Alm is an adjunct professor of composition and Assistant Director of the Writing Center at the University of North Carolina at Asheville. She has presented papers on a variety of topics concerning teaching writing and women's writing practices.

Melodie Andrews is associate professor of History at Mankato State University, specializing in Early America and U.S. women's history. She has written several articles on women and technology in the nineteenth and early twentieth centuries.

Jamie Barlowe is an associate professor of English and Women's Studies at the University of Toledo. She has published essays on feminist theory, on nineteenth- and twentieth-century American writers, and on women writers. Her book *Re-Reading Women: The Scarlet Mob of Scribblers* is forthcoming.

Anne C. Bell is a graduate student at the Faculty of Environmental Studies, York University, Toronto, and a director of the Wildlands League chapter of the Canadian Parks and Wilderness Society. Her research has been published in *Alternatives, The Trumpeter,* and *Pathways* and is financially supported by the Social Sciences and Humanities Research Council of Canada.

Helen Cafferty is William R. Kenan, Jr., Professor of German and the Humanities and chair of the German Department at Bowdoin College. In addition to her collaborative work with Jeanette Clausen in coediting the *Women in German Yearbook,* she has published in the areas of East German Literature, Women's Studies, German drama, and pedagogy.

Jeanette Clausen is an associate professor of German and Chair of the Modern Foreign Languages Department at Indiana University–Purdue University at Fort Wayne. In addition to coediting the *Women in German Yearbook,* she has published on German women authors and coedited the anthology *German Feminism: Readings in Politics and Literature* (State University of New York Press, 1984).

Sally Barr Ebest (formerly Reagan) is an associate professor of English and the Director of Composition at the University of Missouri–St. Louis. Her publications include *Writing With: New Directions in Collaborative Teaching, Learning, and Research* (State University of New York Press, 1994) and *Writing From A to Z* (Mayfield, 1994).

Angela M. Estes is an associate professor of English at California Polytechnic State University, San Luis Obispo. She has published articles on Louisa May Alcott and Margaret Wise Brown and is currently at work with Kathleen M. Lant on *Wild and Queer: Imagining the Lesbian in the Works of Louisa May Alcott*. Her collection of poems, *The Uses of Passion* (Gibbs Smith, 1995), was winner of the 1994 Peregrine Smith Poetry Competition.

Joel Haefner is the coordinator of microcomputer labs for the English Department at Illinois State University. He has published articles on Romanticism, the essay, and computers in teaching. He coedited, with Carol Shiner Wilson, *Re-Visioning Romanticism: British Women Writers, 1776–1837* (University of Pennsylvania Press, 1994).

Leslie J. Henson is a Ph.D. candidate in English at the University of Florida, where she teaches Women's Studies and English. Together with Mary Ann Leiby, she has presented several conference papers on feminist collaboration and pedagogy, and she has published essays and poetry that focus on issues of lesbian identity.

Ruth Hottell is an associate professor of French and Women's Studies at the University of Toledo. She has presented papers and published articles on nineteenth-century French literature, French Francophone film and filmmakers, and on feminist film theories, as well as published translations. She is currently completing a book on Agnes Varda.

Elaine Allen Karls is an assistant professor in English and education at Delta College. She has presented at many conferences and workshops on learning communities, oral history, and reading and writing pedagogy. She recently served as writing director of the Huron Shores International Writing Institute on Lake Huron, from which the multilingual anthology *Breakwall VII* evolved.

Kathleen Margaret Lant is a professor of English at California Polytechnic State University, San Luis Obispo, where she teaches American literature, women writers, and computer applications in the liberal arts. Her publications include work on many nineteenth- and twentieth-century authors. She is currently at work with Angela M. Estes on *Wild and Queer: Imagining the Lesbian in the Works of Louisa May Alcott*.

Mary Ann Leiby has a Ph.D. in English and is a lecturer in Humanities at the University of Florida's Communication Center.

For several years, she taught composition and Women's Studies courses collaboratively with Leslie J. Henson, and together they have presented conference papers on their collaborative feminist theory/practice.

Diane Lichtenstein is an associate professor of English at Beloit College; she also teaches in the Women's Studies program. She has published *Writing Their Nations: Nineteenth-Century American Jewish Women Writers* (1992) and is currently researching U.S. women novelists of the 1920s and 1930s. Other interests include collaborative classroom practices, post-colonial theory and U.S. literature, and the dynamics of canon formation/reformulation.

Nancy R. MacKenzie is professor of English at Mankato State University where she directs programs in technical communication. She has presented papers, directed workshops, and published articles on writing theory, collaborative critical thinking, and topics in technical communication. Her textbook is *Science and Technology Today: Readings for Writers* (St. Martin's, 1994).

Kimberly A. McCarthy is a psychologist and music composer at Columbia College Chicago. She has presented papers and published articles on creativity, feminist theory, and the arts, and is currently studying the role of theater in community development.

Paula D. Nesbitt is assistant professor of Sociology of Religion at Iliff School of Theology in Denver. She has published articles on gender issues related to the clergy, and on business ethics. She recently completed a monograph, *Feminization of the Clergy in America: Occupational and Organizational Perspectives* (Oxford University Press, 1996), and is working on *Corporate Social Responsibility for a Global Environment*.

Anne O'Meara is professor and chair of the English Department at Mankato State University where she teaches writing, writing pedagogy, feminist theory, and women's literature. She has presented papers, directed workshops, and published articles on writing pedagogy, collaborative critical thinking, and gender and writing.

Rachel Plotkin recently graduated with a Master's degree in Environmental Studies from York University, Toronto, where she investigated the role of a sense of wonder in environmental education. She is currently teaching with the Bronte Creek Project, an outdoor education secondary school. She has also worked in wildlife rehabilitations and protection.

Virginia Powell is a visiting associate professor of Sociology at The College of William and Mary. Her scholarly interests include links between gender and fertility, the possibilities of a feminist/multicultural pedagogy, and the dynamics of race, class, gender, work, and family among white women domestics.

Constance L. Russell, an environmental learner and educator, is a doctoral student at the Ontario Institute for Studies in Education, University of Toronto. Her research interests include the role of experiential learning in the social construction of nature and of animals, ecofeminism, and critical environmental education. She has published articles in the *Journal of Experiential Education, Society and Animals*, and *Trumpeter: Journal of Ecosophy*.

Carol J. Singley is an assistant professor of English at Rutgers University, Camden. She is the author of *Edith Wharton: Matters of the Mind and Spirit* (Cambridge University Press, 1995) and coeditor of *Anxious Power: Reading, Writing, and Ambivalence in Narrative by Women* (State University of New York Press, 1993) and *The Calvinist Roots of the Modern Era* (University Press of New England, forthcoming).

Sandra Steingraber is a biologist and a poet. *Post-Diagnosis*, her first book of poetry, was released by Firebrand Press in 1995. She is currently writing a book on women, cancer, and the environment for Addison-Wesley Press.

Susan Elizabeth Sweeney is associate professor of English at Holy Cross College. In addition to her work on postmodernist fiction, detective fiction, and feminist narratology, she has coedited *Anxious Power: Reading, Writing, and Ambivalence in Narrative by Women* (State University of New York Press, 1993). Her current project is a book manuscript, "Bluebeard's Daughters: Gothic Narratives as Feminist Pretexts," about contemporary feminist revisions of the Gothic romance.

Linda E. Thomas is assistant professor of Anthropology and Religion at Iliff School of Theology in Denver, CO. She has presented papers on religion and politics in the Republic of South Africa and on womanist perspectives in the United States. She is currently writing a book about healing rituals in African initiated churches in South Africa.

Roslyn Z. Weedman is an assistant professor of English at Delta College. She has presented papers and given workshops on learning communities, gender issues in communications, images of women in popular culture, and other teaching-related matters.

Carol Shiner Wilson teaches literature and Women's Studies at Muhlenberg College and coordinates the Women's Studies Coalition, Lehigh Valley Association of Independent Colleges. She coedited *Re-Visioning Romanticism: British Women Writers, 1776–1837* (University of Pennsylvania Press, 1994) and is currently editing *The Galesia Trilogy and Manuscript Poems by Jane Barker* for Oxford University Press.

Index

Aaron, Jane, 53
abolition, 21, 26
academic collaboration: active resistance by females, 229–35, 244; analysis of, 217; and the "believing game," 244; and business writing, 210; characteristics of effective collaboration, 210; collaborative "resonance," 221; dealing with female resistance, 244–45; descriptive terminology, 218–19; and "division of labor," 215; and "the doubting game," 243; drafting, 211–12, 219–20, 224; and "dual authorship," 218; and the equitable classroom, 180–81; factors for success, 210; and gender studies, 210; and hostile environments, 179; and the humanities, 210, 222–23; and male-centeredness, 180; and multiple perspectives, 216–17; the need for outside readers, 221; passive resistance by females, 235–43, 244; peer revision, 233–35; and personal voice, 237; and physical sciences, 210; processes, 222–24; rates and styles, 210; and Reader Response Theory, 238–40; scholarly vs. business, 222–23; and "single authorship," 218; strictures against, 178–79; writing context, 222–24
Accad, Evelyne, 278–79
access to professions. *See* women's political rights
Adams, Pauline, and Emma Thornton, 129
"add women and stir" recipe, 272
Advocate of Moral Reform, 25
"affirming community," 178
African-American male stereotypes, 277
Aisenberg, Nadya, and Mona Harrington, 137
Alcott, Louisa May, 56
Alexander, Sally, 13
"alternative politics," 24
"ambivalent interdependence," 26
American Academy of Religion, 41
"Anita Hill/Clarence Thomas syndrome," 43
Anthony, Susan B., 26, 63
anthropocentrism. *See* feminist collaboration
anthropomorphism. *See* feminist collaboration

anti-Contagious Diseases Acts campaign, 23–24
anti-lynching crusade, 26
anxious power, 65–67
Apple, Michael, 228
Aptheker, Bettina, 26
Arnot, Madeleine, 180
Ashton-Jones, Evelyn, 126, 130
Astell, Mary, 12, 15, 16
Atwood, Margaret, 66
Austin, Ann E., and Roger G. Baldwin, 193, 210
authentic transformation, 48

Bakhtin, Mikhail, 68
Baldwin, Roger G., 193, 210. *See also* Ann E. Austin
Barbauld, Anna, 52, 58
Barker, Jane, 56
Bartholomae, David, and Anthony Petrosky, 257
Bate, Barbara, 126–27, 132
Battersby, Christine, 56
Bedford College, 20
Beecher, Catharine, 20
"beginnings of sisterhood," 19–20
Behn, Aphra, 12, 16
Behrendt, Steve, 54
Belenky, Mary et al., 68, 126, 130, 137, 210–11, 220, 227–28, 237, 240
Benjamin, Jessica, 70
"beyond feminism," 35
biculturalism, 44
binarism, 57
"binary logic," 57
Birkeland, Janis, 146
"Bluestocking Circle," 16–17, 56, 58, 61
Bodichon, Barbara, 23–25. *See also* Smith
The Boston *Liberator*, 21

Brady, Laura, 72
"breaking the sentence," 161
Brodkey, Linda, 56, 68
Brown, Julie, 182
Bruffee, Kenneth, 68, 123, 127, 132, 178
Buechler, Steven, 18–19, 21
Burk, Martha, 264
Burnett, Rebecca, and Helen Ewald, 136
Burroughs, Catherine, 53
Butler, Josephine, 23–24

Campbell, Betty, 188
Caplan, Paula, 143–44, 151–52
Carter, Elizabeth, 16
Cavendish, Margaret, 15
Chait, Richard, 143
Chase, Geoff, 229
child abuse, 184–85
Chidley, Katherine, 15
Childers, Mary, 278
Chiseri-Strater, Elizabeth, 137. *See also* Donna Qualley
Chisholm, Shirley, 264
Chodorow, Nancy, 69, 100
Christ, Carol, and Judith Plaskow, 65
Cisneros, Sandra, 66
Cixous, Helene, 69, 163–64
classical literary poetics, 270
class oppression, 183–86
Clinchy, Blithe, 68, 126, 130, 137, 210–11, 220, 227–28, 237, 240. *See also* Mary Belenky
close reading, 270
collaboration: barriers to, 210–11; definition of, 63–64; and "diffusion of self," 100; and "disciplinary chauvinism," 100; and "enforced selflessness," 100, 177; long distance, 71, 85;

methods, 127–29, 131; and "obliteration of ego," 100; seminars, 124; surveys and studies, 124. *See also* academic collaboration, feminist collaboration, lesbian collaboration
collaborative friendship, 129–30
collaborative learning: and seating arrangement, 274
collaborative research: criteria for quality, 42; definition of, 32; from a womanist perspective, 38; models, 47; and pluralism, 40; practicality of, 41; problems of, 33–34; risks in, 33; and student evaluations, 41–42
collaborative talk, 212–15
"collaborative voice," 134–35
collaborative writing: dialogic forms of, 59–60, 209, 218, 222; forms of, 59–60; hierarchical forms of, 59–60, 209, 222; purpose of lesbian, 160–62; questions of validity, 162–63
"common voice." *See* "shared voice"
conflictual model. *See* dialogues within feminism
conscious perception, 113
consciousness-raising sessions, 63
constructed knowledge. *See* stages of women's acquisition of knowledge
Contagious Diseases Acts of 1864 and 1866, 23–25
"conversational" discourse, 72
"conversation of mankind," 123, 127, 131–32
Cooper, Anna Julia Haywood, 47
Corinne, 59
Cott, Nancy, 11, 14
Crawford, Patricia, 14–15
creative power: definition of, 100

Crick, Francis, and James Watson, 101
Cristall, Anna Batten, 52
"critical consciousness," 279
cross-sex collaboration, 117
Crumpacker, Laurie, and Eleanor Vander Haegen, 186
"cult of true womanhood," 19
cultural feminists, 271
Curran, Stuart, 51–52, 54, 58

"default" mode of office space protocol. *See* masculine territorial mode
Dahl, Karin, 134. *See also* Jill Dillard
DeJean, Joan, 51, 58–59
de Lauretis, Teresa, 158, 167–69, 176–77
de Pizan, Christine, 12, 66
De Staël, Madame, 59
dialogic collaborative discourse, 72, 94–96, 125–26, 211
dialogues within feminism: conflictual model, 275
Dillard, Jill, and Karen Dahl, 134
Dippo, Don, 178
"a discourse of possibility," 273
divorce. *See* women's political rights
Doane, Mary Ann, 277
"domestic ideology," 19
dominance and marginality, 31
Dorris, Michael, and Louise Erdrich, 72
Doty, Alexander, 158, 168
double standard of learning, 20
"duologues." *See* feminist collaboration
Durkheim, Emile, 133

early women's publications, 15

ecriture feminine, 69
Ede, Lisa, and Andrea Lunsford, 51, 60, 71–72, 82, 91, 94, 96, 123–25, 127, 130, 132–33, 209–11, 214–15, 222, 227, 245, 275
Egerton, Sarah, 15–16
Elbow, Peter, 243–44
Elbrecht, Joyce, and Lydia Fakundiny, 70, 75
elitism, 45, 48
Ellison, Julie, 54
Ellsworth, Elizabeth, 181–82
"emergent ideas," 137
English Woman's Journal, 25
epistemic modal forms, 71
equality: definition of, 13
equal pay. *See* women's political rights
Erdrich, Louise, 72. *See also* Michael Dorris
Ervin, Elizabeth, and Dana Fox, 136
Escher, M. C., 108
"ethics of care," 69, 175
"ethics of justice," 69
Evernden, Neil, 150
Ewald, Helen, 136. *See also* Rebecca Burnett
executive talk, 86–87, 224. *See also* writing talk
"explication de texte." *See* close reading
extended collaboration, 88
extralinguistic communication, 270

Faithfull, Emily, 25
Fakundiny, Lydia, 70, 75. *See also* Joyce Elbrecht
"faulty generalization," 39
Faver, Catherine A., 193. *See also* Mary Frank Fox

"female/male dichotomy," 57
female passivity, 64
female theology, 65
female vs. male prose: the alienated sensibility, 54
female vs. male prose: concepts of vision, 54
feminism: definitions of, 11–13, 38–39, 198–99, 269; ethics of, 44; and institutional forces, 19–20; and language, 65–66; manifestations of, 12, 13; militancy, 26
feminist collaboration: and anthropocentrism, 144, 150; and anthropomorphism, 144, 150; and authorship, 114, 132, 147; and balance, 58–59; characteristics of, 81–83; and coauthorship, 94, and common style, 134; and communications research, 126; and compatible partners, 75; composition, 67; and compulsory heterosexuality, 183–85; concerning other minorities, 117–18; concerns, 142–43; and conflict, 174; conflicts in, 73–75; and "connected autonomy," 105; and content, 102–103; contradictions in, 81, 89–96; and "conversation," 70–72, 85–86; definition of, 60, 82, 193; and dialogue, 70–71; and "duologues," 103, 105–109, 114; and education, 141; effects on institutions, 206; and environmental studies, 141, 150; and feminist pedagogy, 175–76; and feminist theory, 175–76; and individual authorship, 94; and individual empowerment, 135; and interdisciplinarity,

199–200; and linearity vs. non-linearity, 102; and literary studies, 199; and maintaining the self, 146; measurement and evaluation, 142–43; and methodology,102; and multiple voices, 66–67; and music composition, 101, 103, 109–17; and "mutual recognition," 70; and narrative theory, 65, 67; and pedagogy, 175–77; and pedagogy for difference, 177–80, 186–88; and pedagogy of difference, 177–80, 186–88; and personal ownership, 94; and poetry, 104–105, 109–17; and the politics of transformation, 96; and post-structuralist theory, 67; and rhetoric, 67; risks, 135; and science, 100–101; and self-disclosure, 182–83; and self-other relationship, 103; and self-reflexive articles, 215–16; and sociology, 199; and "star" theory system, 92; and stylistic differences, 57; and subjectivity vs. objectivity in interpretation, 103; suspicions about, 100; and theater, 106; vs. cross-sex collaboration, 117; vs. non-feminist collaboration, 95–96
feminist classroom theories vs. traditional pedagogy, 269
feminist *coincidentia oppositorum*, 93–94
feminist consciousness: class interests, 18–19; development of, 18–19; and racial identification, 18–19; stages of, 14, 15–16
feminist deconstructionists, 271
feminist film theorists, 271
feminist leadership, 203–207
feminist leadership: and co-leadership, 205–207
feminist mentoring, 89
feminist periodicals: first of the nineteenth century, 25
Feminist Research Group, 56
feminist solidarity, 92–93
Feminist vs. Formal theories, 270–71
feminized space. *See* marginalized space
Fifteenth Amendment, 24, 26
Flynn, Elizabeth, 227, 245
Ford, Susan Allen, 54
Foucault, Michael, 17, 228
Fox, Dana, 136. *See also* Elizabeth Ervin
Fox, Mary Frank, and Catherine A. Faver, 193
Frank, Joseph, 56
Franklin, Rosalind, 101
Freedman, Estelle, 27
Freire, Paulo, 70, 180, 274
French feminists, 271
French structuralism, 270
Fuller, Margaret, 23
fundamental literary poetics, 270
Fussell, Paul, 263

Garnett, Constance Grace, 52, 59
Garrison, William Lloyd, 21
Gere, Anne, 227
Gilbert, Sandra M., and Susan Gubar, 16, 72–73
Gillam, Alice, 71. *See also* William Van Pelt
Gilligan, Carol, 69, 175, 227–28
Gilman, Charlotte Perkins, 66
Giovanni, Nikki, 31, 32, 45
Giroux, Henry A., 175, 177, 180–82, 227, 229

Giroux's learning responses: accommodation, 229; opposition, 229; resistance, 229
Goldberger, Nancy, 68, 126, 130, 137, 210–11, 220, 227–28, 237, 240. *See also* Mary Belenky
Griffin, Gail, 250, 266
group talk, 86–87. *See also* social talk
Gubar, Susan, 16, 72–73. *See also* Sandra M. Gilbert
gynophobia: in mainstream film, 276–77

Hall, Catherine, 19
Harding, Sandra, 124, 145
Harrington, Mona, 137. *See also* Nadya Aisenberg
Hartsock, Nancy, 274
Hazlittian "familiar style," 57
Heilbrun, Carolyn, 100–101
Hemans, Felicia, 52–53, 58
"heteroglossia," 68
heterosexism, 45, 183–84
heterosexist patriarchal discourse, 163–64
heterosexual privilege, 183–84
hierarchical discourse, 72, 89–92, 94–96, 125, 211
hierarchically defined relationships, 253
Hill, Patrick, 265
Hoehner, David, 186
holistic research, 40
Homer, 59
homophobia, 177–78
Hood, Jane, 130
hooks, bell, 101, 181, 186, 188, 271, 273, 275–79
horizontal violence, 43
Howe, Florence, 74
Hubbard, Louisa, 25–26

Hutcheon, Michael, 72

"intellectual friendship," 138
internalized racism, 42–43
intimate collaboration, 126, 127. *See also* dialogic mode
intradisciplinary courses, 256–57
"invisibility" of gender, 55
Irigaray, Luce, 69, 162, 169

Johnson, Mary Lynn, 54
Johnson, Samuel, 56
Johnston, Marilyn, 148
Jones, JoAnne, 182–83

Kaplan, Carey, 51, 57, 74–75, 81, 83, 93, 126, 129, 130, 132–33, 135, 143, 152, 193. *See also* Ellen Cronan Rose
Karach, Angela, and Denise Roach, 82
Keller, Evelyn Fox, 56
Kelley, Abbey, 22
Kensington Society, 24
Kenway, Jane, and Helen Modra, 273
Kingston, Maxine Hong, 66
Kolodny, Annette, 167, 245
Kraditor, Aileen, 12
Kutz, Eleanor, 134

Lacanian theory, 271
Landon, Letitia (L. E. L.), 52, 58–59
Langham Place Circle, 23–24
Lather, Patti, 148, 151
"laugh of the Medusa," 164
learning communities, 255–57
LeFevre, Karen Burke, 221
Leonardi, Susan, and Rebecca Pope, 70, 75, 82, 93, 96
Lerner, Gerda, 12, 13–14, 26

"lesbian" as metaphor, 126
lesbian collaboration: as choreography, 160–61; and "coming out" to readers, 155–56; and "euphoria of sisterhood," 155; and *posteuphoria*, 155–56; tactics, 161–62; tasks of, 161
lesbianism: place and process, 159
lesbian laughter, 164–65
"The Lone Author Myth," 130
"Los Angeles Poverty Department," 106
Lucas, George, 136
Lunsford, Andrea, 51, 60, 71–72, 82, 91, 94, 96, 123–25, 127, 130, 132–33, 209–11, 214–15, 222, 227, 245, 275. *See also* Lisa Ede
Lyon, Mary, 20

MacKinnon, Catherine, 255
Maher, Frances, 180, 227
Malpede, John, 106
marginality. *See* dominance and marginality
marginalized space, 251
married woman's property law, 23. *See also* Women's political rights
masculine territorial mode of office space protocol, 249, 258–59
masculinist theory. *See* Lacanian theory
Masque, Maria, 188
May, Mariam, and Jamie Shepherd, 94
McClintock, Barbara, 51, 56
McGann, Jerome J., 54
McLaren, Peter, 180
McNenny, Geraldine, and Duane H. Roen, 212–13
Meese, Elizabeth, 160–61, 164

Meigs, Mary, 155–56, 164–65
Melder, Keith, 19–23
Mellor, Anne K., 51
Mercer, Kobena, 181
Metropolitan Magazine, 24
Michie, Helena, 74
Midgley, Mary, 145
Midwest/Modern Language Association, 211, 223
Mill, John Stuart, 24
Miller, Jean Baker, 69
Miltonian/Wordsworthian vision of the writer, 58–59
Miner, Valerie, 161, 164
Minnich, Elizabeth, 39,
Mitford, Mary, 52
Modern Language Association (MLA), 210–11, 223
Modra, Helen, 273. *See also* Jane Kenway
Mohanty, Chandra, 278
Momaday, N. Scott, 186
"monovocal synthesis," 72
Montagu, Elizabeth, 16
moral superiority of women, 13, 20
More, Hannah, 52, 58
Morrison, Tony, 66
Moschkovich, Judit, 185
Moses, Yolanda, 36
Mott, Lucretia, 22–23
Mount Holyoke, 20
Murphy, Patrick, 150

nascent feminism, 14, 21
nascent feminism: petitioning campaigns, 14
national Prohibition Convention (1897, Newcastle, England), 11
"natural truths," 45
Nelson, Marie Wilson, 128, 132
New England Great Awakening, 19

"new women," 27
Nineteenth Amendment, the, 26
non-traditional learners, 262

Opie, Amelia, 52
opposition. *See* Giroux's learning responses
Ostriker, Alicia, 100
Owenson, Sydney, 52

Palmegiana, Eugenia, 24
Pankurst, Emmeline, 17
"partial knowledge," 39
Pascoe, Judith, 54
patriarchal codes, 164
"peak experiences," 104
Penley, Constance, 270, 273, 274–75
Perry, William, 228
Petrosky, Anthony, 257. *See also* David Bartholomae
phallocentric texts, 278
phallocentric traditions, 163
Phelan, Shane, 157, 168–69
Pheterson, Gail, 177–78
Plaskow, Judith, 65. *See also* Carol Christ
Plowman, Lydia, 82, 86, 93, 132
pluralism. *See* collaborative research
"polyphonic" collaboration, 72
Poovey, Mary, 57
Pope, Rebecca, 70, 75, 82, 93, 96. *See also* Susan Leonardi
private speech, 253
procedural knowledge. *See* stages of acquisition of knowledge
procedural talk, 71, 86–87, 212–13, 224
property rights. *See* women's political rights
public speech, 253

Qualley, Donna, and Elizabeth Chiseri-Strater, 137
Queen's College, 20
Queen Victoria, 58

"rapport talk in public," 253
Ray, Ruth, 245
"real" talk, 130, 131, 135
received knowledge. *See* stages of women's acquisition of knowledge
Reid, Elizabeth, 20
Rendall, Jane, 12, 18, 19, 23, 24
resistance. *See* Giroux's learning responses
"reverse discourse," 17
Revolution, 25
Rhodes, Keith, 134
Rich, Adrienne, 69, 73–74, 119, 157, 166, 183, 279
Roach, Denise, 82. *See also* Angela Karach
Robinson, Lillian, 57
Robinson, Mary, 52–53, 59
Rockford Seminary, 20
Roen, Duane H., 212–13. *See also* Geraldine McNenny.
Rogers, Katherine, 15–17, 54
Romantic Aesthetics: revisioning of, 55–56
Romantic poetesses, 58
Ronald, Kate, 126–27, 134
Rose, Ellen Cronan, and Carey Kaplan, 51, 57, 74–75, 81, 83, 93, 126, 129, 130, 132–33, 135, 143, 152, 193
Roskelly, Hephzibah, 127, 134
Ross, Marlon, 54

Sapphic vision of the writer, 58–59
Sappho, 58–59
Sappho/Corinne Myth, the, 58–59

Sarton, May, 258
Schlueter, June, 54
Schon, Donald, 244
Scott, Ann, 20
"second evangelical awakening," 19
Seneca Falls Declaration (1848), 63
"separate knower." *See* stages of women's acquisition of knowledge: constructed knowledge
Seward, Anna, 52
sexual identities as socially constructed, 157
shared voice, 134
Shepherd, Jamie, 94. *See also* Mariam May
Shield, The, 25
Shinman, Lillian Lewis, 11, 19, 23–25
Showalter, Elaine, 245, 276
Shrewsbury, Carolyn, 274
Sidney, Mary, 66
"silence." *See* stages of women's acquisition of knowledge
"singular" tradition of the writer, 59
Smith, Barbara, 23–25. *See also* Bodichon
Smith, Barbara, 184
Smith, Barbara Leigh, 21
Smith, Charlotte, 52–53
Smith, Hilda L., 12, 15–16, 17
Smith-Rosenberg, Carroll, 19, 69
Smythe, Mary Jeannette, 126–27
Snowden, Ethel, 26
social construction of knowledge, 132
social homogeneity, 25
social talk, 71, 86–87, 213–15, 224. *See also* group talk
Society for Technical Communications, 209
"solitary genius," 56
Somerset, Lady Henry, 11

"sororophobia," 74
Spender, Dale, 127
stages of women's acquisition of knowledge (Belenky et al.): constructed knowledge, 240; procedural knowledge, 240; received knowledge, 240; silence, 240; subjective knowledge, 240
Stanton, Elizabeth Cady, 21, 22–23, 26, 63
Steinem, Gloria, 264
Stember, Marilyn, 193
Stone, Lucy, 21
"strategies of expediency," 26
subjective knowledge. *See* stages of women's acquisition of knowledge
substantive talk, 71, 86–87, 213–14, 224
suffrage, 12–13, 15, 18, 24, 25, 27
Sullivan, Patricia, 68
symbiotic partnership. *See* synergistic
symmetrically defining relationships, 253
symmetry, 267
synergistic partnership, 249
synergy, 131–32, 164

Talbot, Catherine, 16–17
Tannen, Deborah, 253
Tarule, Jill, 68, 126, 130, 137, 210–11, 220, 227–28, 237, 240. *See also* Mary Belenky
Taylor, Anita, 127
team teaching, 41, 178-81, 273–79
"third voice." *See* "shared voice"
Thornton, Emma, 129. *See also* Pauline Adams
"tokens," 118
"token" syndrome, the, 36

transformation: definition of, 40
Truth, Sojourner, 47

Vander Haegen, Eleanor, 186. *See also* Laurie Crumpacker
Van Pelt, William, and Alice Gilliam, 71
Vesey, Elizabeth, 17
Vicinus, Martha, 18
Victoria Press, the, 25
Violanti, Michelle, 136–37

Walker, Alice, 56
Watson, James, 101. *See also* Francis Crick
"ways of knowing," 69
Wells, Ida B., 47
Welter, Barbara, 19
Wharton, Edith, 65
White, Cynthia, 188
Wilkins, Maurice, 101
Williams, Helen Maria, 52
Wolfson, Susan, 54
womanism: and African-Americans, 40
"womanist:" definition of, 35

"woman question," the, 11, 22–23
Woman's Journal, 25
Women and Work, 25–26
Women in German (WIG), 83–85, 87, 89, 91–94
women's film festivals, 277–78
women's movement, 84
women's movement: and authorial credit order, 85; and democratic inclusiveness, 88; early, 166–67; modern, 18; nineteenth century (factors), 19
women's political rights: access to professions, 27; divorce, 18, 27; equal pay, 20, 27; married women's property law, 23; property rights, 18
Women's Temperance Association: *Journal*, 25
Women's Trade Union League, 26
women's writing: denigration of, 54
Woolley, Hannah, 15
World Antislavery Convention, 22
Work and Leisure, 25
writing talk, 71, 86–87, 214, 224. *See also* executive talk